AI FOR YOU

AI FOR YOU

The New Game Changer

Shalini Kapoor and Sameep Mehta

Foreword by Shankar Maruwada

BLOOMSBURY
NEW DELHI • LONDON • OXFORD • NEW YORK • SYDNEY

BLOOMSBURY INDIA
Bloomsbury Publishing India Pvt. Ltd
Second Floor, LSC Building No. 4, DDA Complex, Pocket C – 6 & 7,
Vasant Kunj, New Delhi, 110070

BLOOMSBURY, BLOOMSBURY INDIA and the Diana logo
are trademarks of Bloomsbury Publishing Plc

First published in India 2022
This updated edition published 2025

Copyright © Shalini Kapoor and Sameep Mehta, 2022, 2025

Shalini Kapoor and Sameep Mehta have asserted their right under the
Indian Copyright Act to be identified as the Authors of this work

Bloomsbury Publishing Plc does not have any control over, or
responsibility for, any third-party websites referred to or in this book.
All internet addresses given in this book were correct at the time of going
to press. The author and publisher regret any inconvenience caused if
addresses have changed or sites have ceased to exist, but can accept no
responsibility for any such changes

All rights reserved. No part of this publication may be: i) reproduced
or transmitted in any form, electronic or mechanical, including
photocopying, recording or by means of any information storage or
retrieval system without prior permission in writing from the publishers;
or ii) used or reproduced in any way for the training, development or
operation of artificial intelligence (AI) technologies, including generative
AI technologies. The rights holders expressly reserve this publication from
the text and data mining exception as per Article 4(3) of the Digital Single
Market Directive (EU) 2019/790

ISBN: PB: 978-93-69523-73-3; eBook: 978-93-54352-32-4
2 4 6 8 10 9 7 5 3 1

Typeset in Manipal Technologies Limited
Printed and bound in India by Gopsons Papers Pvt. Ltd., Noida

To find out more about our authors and books visit www.bloomsbury.com
and sign up for our newsletters

Advance Praise for the Book

'AI is the way forward for every organization that's eyeing digital transformation today. A game changer, AI can free humans from mundane tasks and open up a whole new set of possibilities to make life more productive. As business leaders take a step forward to familiarize themselves with the wonders of AI, *AI for You: The New Game Changer* will come in handy; it is a great contribution to the AI literature. The AI mindset framework backed by real-world examples makes it a worthy read.' *C.P. Gurnani, Managing Director and CEO, Tech Mahindra*

'This book explains key aspects related to AI adoption and has several stories on how organizations have achieved transformational improvements through successful deployment of AI. Traditional organizations can marry new-age technologies by embarking on an AI journey, adopting the necessary mindset as outlined in the book.' *Girish Wagh, President, Commercial Vehicles, Tata Motors*

'Investing in AI and driving usage across multiple engines are critical to businesses. This book provides an extensive methodology for that and hence is an invaluable resource.' *Shanti Ekambaram, Group President, Consumer Banking, Kotak Mahindra Bank*

'It is evident that the book builds on decades of experience of Sameep and Shalini. The framework is elegant, complete, and actionable. The validations from industry icons through their personal experiences should encourage others to follow and adopt an AI mindset. A must-read for not just AI but also product and business leaders.' *Hitesh Oberoi, Managing Director and CEO, Info Edge*

'This is the book I have been waiting for. It is a must-read for all business leaders on the mission to embrace the AI revolution!' *Ritu Arora, CEO and Chief Investment Officer, Asia Pacific, Allianz Investment*

'India has the inherent strength to be the next superpower, and this book is a torchbearer in that journey.' *Abhishek Singh, CEO, National eGovernance Division, Digital India Corporation and MyGov*

'This book brings to fore the fact that AI is not so much about technology as is commonly understood but more about a culture of servant leadership and growth mindset, which in turn create a culture of business transformation, leveraging AI and other exponential technologies.' *Pankaj Rai, Group Chief Data and Analytics Officer, Aditya Birla Group*

'Coursera co-founder Andrew Ng firmly believes that "AI is the new electricity". To power ahead in today's digital economy, AI has become a critical skill for all professionals—be it engineers or non-technical and domain experts. It is evident that this book builds on decades of experience of Shalini and Sameep. The framework is elegant, complete, and actionable. The validations from industry icons through their personal experiences should encourage others to follow and adopt an AI mindset.' *Raghav Gupta, Managing Director, India and APAC, Coursera*

'Getting the strategy right in an AI journey is key for an organization to be successful in its digital transformation. This book is a must-read for students and digital transformation leaders to understand the AI journey.' *Professor Rajendra Srivastava, Novartis Professor for Strategy, Marketing and Innovation, Indian School of Business*

'While there are numerous books on deep algorithmic aspects of AI, it was refreshing to see a new dimension—how to transform an organization with AI—being address[ed] by Shalini and Sameep, which is critical to the enterprises. The industry very much needed AI mindset framework to understand what it takes to be an AI-transformed organization. This book should be on the reading list of every business and technical person who is thinking of spearheading AI-driven transformation in their organization.' *Dr Ruchir Puri, IBM Fellow and Chief Scientist, IBM Research*

'This book presents a framework for business leaders to help them successfully adopt AI for their organizations. It covers different aspects of leveraging AI in an organization, like strategy, innovation, technology, user orientation, talent, etc., while avoiding getting into the AI jargon. Organizations will find it useful in their AI journey.' *Dr Pankaj Jalote, Distinguished Professor (Founding Director 2008–2018), Indraprastha Institute of Information Technology Delhi*

'AI has begun to touch our lives but still isn't clearly understood by decision makers. Hence they approach it with either enthusiasm or caution. Shalini and Sameep have done an excellent job of simplifying AI and helping leaders make informed choices. The book is a must-read for every leader in today's world.' *T.N. Hari, Co-founder, Artha School of Entrepreneurship*

'This is one of the finest books on AI. It is a one-stop shop for people looking for learning AI, formulating ideas, building solutions, and identifying the right methodologies with examples of amazing case studies.' *Dr Shivani Rai Gupta, Head of Data Science, Jio*

'A must-read for every business leader trying to harness the power of AI, rich with examples, stories, and real-life lessons from the India market. Shalini and Sameep are outstanding technologists and have synthesized their years of experience into a practical and prescriptive framework to set up organizations for success in leveraging AI.' *Sriram Raghavan, Vice President, IBM Research AI*

'This is a handbook for all kinds of businesses meaning to leverage the transformational benefits of AI. Shalini and Sameep have decluttered, demystified, and prescribed ways of successful AI implementation. The case studies and interviews you are about to explore will prepare you for the future.' *Atul Jalan, entrepreneur, author, and futurist*

'AI books are written by AI experts for aspirants, by researchers for implementers, or by philosophers for normal people. *AI for You* is the book written by experts for businesspeople who value results and evidence as much as innovation.' *Himanshu Nautiyal, Chief Product Officer, Fractal Analytics*

'This is going to be a great asset in the AI world for generations to come. While there are many books addressing the technology execution of AI, it is a fact that many organizations fail in succeeding as there is a problem with the AI mindset and culture to build this right from formulation to design to adoption/evangelisation. [The authors] were spot on to pick AI mindset as the theme for the book. It is also interesting to see the mix of real-world examples blended well with the concepts.' *Muthumari S., Head of Data Science, Brillio, Global 40 under 40 Data Leaders, 2022*

'This book addresses the gap that lies between the promise of AI and the impact of AI for businesses. The authors have used their vast experience and captured the different facets of an organization that need to align to make this technology a game changer for their business.' *Nitendra Rajput, Vice President, AI Garage, Mastercard*

'I really enjoyed the AI mindset framework proposed by Sameep and Shalini. The framework is complete and flexible to fit diverse enterprises. The book provides a unique and much-needed take on AI adoption.' *Pranshu Patni, Co-founder, Hello English, and Vice President, BYJU'S*

'Innovators who deploy AI should do so wisely. The authors provide a succinct view of what can go wrong at the intersection of AI and innovation, and propose concrete steps to minimize the possibility of unintended consequences.' *Varun Nagaraj, Dean, S.P. Jain Institute of Management and Research*

To my parents, Yash and Veena Malik, who gave me wings, and to Rajeev, Rohan and Keshav, who provided the air for me to fly.
—Shalini Kapoor

To my parents, Pradeep and Madhu Mehta, for their blessings, and to Ankita and Parth, for always being supportive and encouraging.
—Sameep Mehta

CONTENTS

Foreword	xiii
Preface	xv
Introduction	1
Reimagining Organizations in the Age of AI	1
The AI Mindset Framework	15
The AI Journey	25

1 AI Strategy — 37
Type of Organization — 38
The AI Strategy Flywheel — 49
Kotak Mahindra Bank: Setting the AI Strategy Wheel in Motion — 75

2 AI and Innovation — 80
Facets of Innovation — 84
Technology Trends — 96
Viome: Pushing the Boundaries of Science via Technology — 109

3 AI and Technology — 112
Journey to AI: From PoC to Transformation — 113
Data and AI Life Cycle — 119
Niramai Health Analytix: AI Transformed Healthcare — 163

4 AI and Talent — 167
How to Make Your People Learn AI — 167
Talent Map for an Organization — 175
Envestnet Yodlee: Reskilling for Tomorrow — 193

5 AI and Culture — 197
- Partnership with AI — 199
- How to Address the Fear of AI — 201
- Max Life Insurance: Partnering with AI — 209

6 AI and Users — 216
- Outcome versus Process — 220
- User Journey for AI — 222
- HealthifyMe: Transforming Lives — 226

7 Onwards, to an AI-Powered Future — 230
- INDIAai: India's AI Foundation — 236

8 AI Is Here to Stay — 240
- The AI Mindset — 242
- AI and Strategy — 243
- AI and Innovation — 244
- AI and Talent — 247
- AI and Users — 248
- Towards an AI-Powered Future — 249

9 Towards GenAI — 255
- Common Use Cases for GenAI — 259
- Generalized LLMs vs Focused SLMs — 267
- Mapping GenAI to the Proposed AI Mindset Framework — 268

Notes — 275
Acknowledgements — 286
Index — 289
About the Authors — 301

FOREWORD

When Shalini Kapoor and Sameep Mehta first wrote *AI for You*, the world was just beginning to grasp the scale of change that artificial intelligence (AI) would bring. In the years since, that change has accelerated beyond anyone's expectations. What remains constant is the need for understanding—not only of what AI can do, but of what it should do.

This book was written for that purpose. It helps readers see AI not as a distant science, but as a practical force shaping the world around us. It simplifies the complex ideas that often intimidate people, and it brings together the disciplines of technology, design, and ethics in use cases which enterprises find value in. *AI for You* offers clarity and confidence in equal measure, whether you build products, lead teams, or simply want to understand how AI is changing work and life.

In India, the promise of AI is larger than productivity. For more than a decade, India has shown what scale and purpose can achieve together. From Aadhaar to UPI, from DigiLocker to Bhashini, we built digital systems that millions could trust and use daily. These were not isolated innovations. They were layers of a national architecture designed to empower people, businesses, and institutions to grow.

AI now gives us the chance to take that idea forward. We can build use cases that are not only smarter but also fairer, more adaptable, and more capable of solving complex problems. This book shows how AI can create value across domains, from healthcare and education to enterprise, finance, and everyday life. It also reminds us that technology only delivers impact when people understand

and guide it. The path from lab to field, from concept to value, depends on how we design, test, and deploy AI responsibly.

The challenge ahead is not to invent faster, but to build wisely. We need AI that explains itself, that earns trust, and that improves with human oversight. We also need the humility to see AI not as the answer to everything, but as a tool for better decisions and better systems. Use case adoption would be central for AI to learn and better itself.

India can lead this movement. Not because we have the largest population, but because we have shown how digital systems can scale with safety and purpose and now can do with AI use cases. Our experience with digital public infrastructure has taught us that progress is not about size, but about intent.

This new edition of *AI for You* arrives at a time when optimism and caution must coexist. It reminds us that progress depends less on what AI can do, and more on how we choose to use it. India has the experience, the talent, and the conviction to show that technology can scale without losing its humanity.

If the first digital revolution connected us, this one must empower us. And that begins with understanding—the kind that this book makes possible.

Shankar Maruwada
Co-founder and CEO, EkStep Foundation

PREFACE

'Any sufficiently advanced technology is indistinguishable from magic.'
—Arthur C. Clarke

An idea whose time has come is unstoppable. The concept of this book was germinated by our curiosity about the journeys of organizations into artificial intelligence (AI). We had an innate desire to bring to the forefront success stories in the changing landscape of AI adoption in organizations. This curiosity compelled us to peep into the minds of leaders across industries who are infusing and adopting AI. We found common threads and generalized them as the right AI mindset for a business. We observed that organizations were struggling to realize the true potential of AI and often mistakenly assumed that it is all hype. Our quest taught us that the gap between the promise and the actual impact of AI is due to the absence of a framework, methodology and, most importantly, the right mindset for AI adoption.

Another precipitative agent for this book was the market readiness for AI. People's trust in science and technology has recently been bolstered by the production of COVID-19 vaccines in record time. The confidence and optimism about AI's capability to solve larger societal challenges related to health, sustainability and the environment are at an all-time high.

The global race for AI leadership is on, and countries and organizations are investing big to stay ahead. AI is set to become a national priority for countries, and, to illustrate this, deep investments are being seen across start-ups, academia, and large enterprises. There is an urgency in the industry to build AI skills and transform business processes. Each nation has a chance to lead with the power of AI. There is a tremendous opportunity for it to be the catalyst in building technology that will improve billions of lives.

While there is a plethora of books to guide readers on the technical aspects of AI, we did not find many books on the AI mindset and the processes an enterprise needs to follow to be AI-ready. Therefore, we have geared the book towards educating and enabling business leaders to scale AI for enterprises. We intend to lay out the building blocks that will decode buzzwords and help CXOs get through the challenges when they scale AI from prototype to scale. Specifically, the book provides a prescriptive approach to taking AI from lab to field while satisfying different stakeholders' concerns. Readers will learn AI patterns, methodologies for AI infusion in processes, design for AI, components for building an AI solution and trust in AI.

In this book, we have endeavoured to provide world-class AI methodologies, practices and innovations validated by us in interviews with dozens of diverse organizations. We reached out and had extensive conversations with industry stalwarts in AI, including start-ups and venture capitalists. We had a challenging task to identify and highlight AI experiences that combined technology with game-changing impact while providing diverse viewpoints. Our research on interviewing the right people was as important as choosing the correct AI methodology or technology. Before writing this book, we did not know most of the people we interviewed professionally. We chanced upon them through our networks primarily because of their exemplary work in AI; they had the right AI mindset and were trendsetters in their respective industries. All our interviews with these leaders have been collated to provide insights into their AI journeys, best practices, and the hurdles they overcame. We believe readers can customize these examples and case studies for their use. Finally, the book touches upon the most critical but overlooked aspects of skills, processes, and mindset changes for this transformation.

We hope this book will become a must-have for all CXOs embarking on their AI journey, technology professionals wishing to learn the right building blocks of an AI application, and students embarking on a career in AI. As a foundation, the book is technology agnostic as we want to stress that AI is about a mindset.

It is our attempt to be a beacon of light amongst the clutter of information all around.

Happy discovering!

Introduction

Reimagining Organizations in the Age of AI

We want predictability in our lives: Will it rain tomorrow? What are the chances of a flood in August? Will a fraudster be able to unlock my phone despite the face recognition lock I have set up? Will this new drug work for my father? Will this vaccine guard against all future mutations of the virus? What are the chances of this airplane's engine failing? Will these computations find me a new material to replace plastic? What are the chances of someone finding a cure for Stage-3 cancer over the next three months?

We invited artificial intelligence into our lives. We demanded AI in businesses. We created new businesses powered by AI. We asked science to discover new frontiers for us. We pushed the boundaries of technology to make AI more predictable, more trusted, more confident. We, the humans, created AI. Artificial intelligence is here to stay. It will define our lives; rather, it will *be* our lives.

In prehistoric times, Neanderthals had the cognitive capabilities to understand rationality and social ties. Research has proven an overlap of cognition between Homo sapiens and Neanderthals. A defining characteristic of Homo sapiens is understanding the need for smarter and more effective ways of working. Humans have rationalized that working on mundane tasks is not particularly valuable and that is where machines come in. This is, for instance, the thought behind the Egyptians inventing ramps and levers to aid construction processes, circa 3000 BCE, pushing boundaries to make work easier so that they could focus on building obelisks and new irrigation systems. To this day, humans continue to come up with inventions to solve complex problems and devise methodologies so that these inventions are faster and safer. For centuries, urbanization, industrialization, communications, and computations posed complex problems which humans learnt to navigate. Today's complex problems relate to health, wellness, climate change, and poverty. All these issues affect billions around the world and require newer innovations which are faster, cheaper, and safer.

The reason the Bronze Age and Stone Age were called so was due to the materials that governed the development and behaviour of humans during that time. Stone, concrete, steel, and, more recently, silicon have opened new frontiers for building civilizations. There was tremendous excitement when a new material like graphene was invented in 2004. It changed the world. The discovery of new materials and drug compositions will continue to define humans even in the future. But do we know how long it takes to discover a material? According to a report on ScienceDirect, discovering a new material with specific properties takes approximately ten years and costs $10 million–$100 million (₹75 crore–₹750 crore) on average. For a new drug to reach the market, it can take twenty years and up to $2.6 billion (₹20,000 crore).

Drug discovery is an exceptionally long process which starts by understanding a disease and its underlying conditions. Existing research on how to treat diseases and probable ways of targeting symptoms or underlying causes helps researchers understand biological targets for a potential medicine. They then create potential 'drug targets' which could be based on the DNA, RNA, a protein, or some other molecule related to the disease causing pathogen. Researchers must conduct several experiments and studies on animals and human cells to explore if the target can be influenced by a medicine. This may direct them to a lead compound—a potential molecule which could become a medicine. This is just the first step of drug discovery as after this many clinical trials need to be conducted before the medicine hits the market. Less than 12 per cent of the candidate medicines that make it into Phase 1 clinical trials will be approved by the USA's Food and Drug Association (FDA).

COVID-19 has shown us that what used to take decades can now be done in a year. Never had any vaccine been created in less than a decade, but the pandemic created an urgent need for one. For this to happen, new molecular combinations, chemical processes and atom bindings needed to be modelled, predicted and tested in shorter times, and that was where AI came in. AI algorithms reduced time cycles and the need to spend millions of dollars.

Why would Homo sapiens not refine and further science by using AI when they have used tools for efficiency since prehistoric times?

A multi-institutional team including researchers from the National Institute of Standards and Technology (NIST)[1] developed an AI algorithm called Closed-Loop Autonomous System for Materials Exploration and Optimization (CAMEO)[2] that discovered a potentially useful new material without requiring additional training from scientists. NIST claims on its website that this helps reduce the amount of trial-and-error time scientists spend in the lab while maximizing productivity and efficiency in their research. If a researcher is interested in how a material's properties vary with different temperatures, then they may need to run ten experiments at ten different temperatures. But temperature is just one parameter. If there are five parameters, each with ten values, then that researcher must run the experiment 10 x 10 x 10 x 10 x 10 times—a total of 1,00,000 experiments. It is impossible for anyone to run that many experiments due to the years or decades it may take, according to NIST researcher Aaron Gilad Kusne. CAMEO can ensure that each experiment maximizes the scientist's knowledge and understanding, skipping over experiments that would give redundant information. It is a self-learning AI that uses prediction and uncertainty to determine which experiment to try next. In the words of Kusne, 'Think of this process as trying to make the perfect cake. You're mixing different types of ingredients, flour, eggs, or butter, using a variety of recipes to make the best cake.' Different recipes or experiments are being sifted through to determine the best composition for the material.

AI algorithms, tools, and processes can potentially solve complex problems across industries. These algorithms have been improvised and applied in several domains and many potential benefits have emerged. Today, the research-lab-to-product cycle time has decreased, and newer AI models are impacting industry much faster. If AI can help advance science and bring in efficiency by reducing decades of work into hours, then it is imperative that businesses harness its power for their own growth.

So why can't AI help businesses and consumers? Why do businesses still struggle to benefit from AI? Why is there so much fear and confusion about AI? Why do organizations have failed AI projects? Why are there such few skills in the market and why are data scientists so hard to find and hire?

As technology veterans, my co-author and I have witnessed the evolution of AI over the past twenty-five years in individual capacities. Between us, we have worked with hundreds of institutions and organizations and interviewed several of them in depth during writing this book. Our experiences form the basis of this book as we are genuinely interested in helping industry leaders in their AI investments while pushing the frontiers of innovation. We are super excited when we see AI solving some tough problems, and sharing how these breakthroughs can apply to industry domains brings even greater excitement. We want to bring methodology to a chaotic environment, provide direction to unbridled innovation, and revitalize business domains with the power of AI.

First, we need to tackle the elephant in the room and understand the promise, the fear, and the confusion that AI inevitably causes.

The Promise

Enterprises are reimagining the way they work. The enigma of predictions and forecasts is luring several of them to re-engineer processes so that AI can be used to reduce costs, increase efficiency, and enhance customer experience. These are no doubt lofty promises that can be fulfilled, but the first question that comes to one's mind is: how did the promises come about? AI is not new; it has taken years to develop but there have been some momentous events and breakthroughs which have improved its perception in the market to a vast extent. These are not necessarily all research-related breakthroughs, as that will surely be a different list. We are focusing on the potential of AI and how it is becoming more believable and tangible for enterprises and consumers.

One of the earliest pioneers in AI was the English mathematician Alan Turing, who developed the Turing Test[5] in 1950—to test a machine's ability to exhibit intelligent behaviour. He proposed machines which could 'think' and learn. Today, all computers would fall in this category.

The next big moment came in 1997, when IBM's computer 'Deep Blue' defeated world champion Garry Kasparov in chess and proved to the world how machines could think, plan, strategize, and take faster decisions than humans. Another conquest was won when IBM's computer Watson won at a game of *Jeopardy!* in 2011,[4] establishing that AI could reason and make inferences and connections at a greater speed than a human being. Watson eventually progressed from being as big as a room to the size of a phone or tablet.

In 2016 came another momentous event: DeepMind Technologies' AlphaGo[5] became the first AI system to defeat professional GO player Lee Sedol in four consecutive games. GO is the most challenging strategic game for AI because of its complexity, which is greater than that of chess. AlphaGo had no prior knowledge of the game except for the basic rules. Within three days, the programme learnt so much that it could surpass a champion, and within twenty-one days it beat a master of the game. It did this entirely from self-play, with no human intervention or historical data, based on reinforcement learning in which AlphaGo became its own teacher. In each iteration, the game's algorithm improved itself and became more reliable and better. It was essentially a neural network working along with a robust search algorithm to create a smarter version of itself over time.

In June 2018, AI achieved yet another milestone. IBM's Project Debater[6] became the first AI system that could debate humans on complex topics. In a world of misinformation and doctored narratives, it is a boon that a system can provide us with informed viewpoints. AI has pushed the boundaries of its function by understanding language more deeply, interpreting idioms and advancing sentiment analysis. Project Debater can distinguish between anger, frustration, and joy through spoken language as well as pick up cues to respond accordingly. The capability of constructing a well-structured speech, building arguments, and performing rebuttals show that AI can reason and limit the influence of emotion and bias. It can help us make decisions, period.

Smaller, pocket-sized versions of AI are now rampant across the globe. The breakthroughs have led to significant advancements in science and have favourably altered the perception of the masses. These advancements, in turn, have led to a boost in frameworks, tools and technologies around AI. The promises of AI are revolutionizing the modes in which organizations aim to operate, think, and mould themselves for the future. AI can help them reduce the cost of operations and bring in efficiencies, increase revenues, and improve their customers' experiences.

AI in the Real World

During the COVID-19 pandemic, BigBasket's walk-through, touch-free, self-checkout automated retail vending machines became popular in apartment complexes in most of the big cities in India. In such machines, there is an understanding of consumer behaviour through data that is collected daily. Computer vision, sensor data, and deep-learning models help detect fraud and register each item picked up by the user.

Retailers can harness the power of AI to predict fashion trends and suggest merchandise to customers. For instance, Airbus has an AI-powered assistant[7] for the International Space Station (ISS) crew, helping improve productivity and reducing stress. Netflix is another business that curates personalized content for each user. Twitter uses AI to recommend relevant tweets for an individual and remove abusive messages. Online retailer Flipkart is able to perform an image analysis of millions of products by vendors and check them for quality and safety. That's not all! Even insurance companies are benefitting from AI: Max Life Insurance (covered as a case study in Chapter 5) is fast becoming an admired digital insurance company that uses AI to provide a better customer experience and reduce the cost of operations.

A spate of digital and AI healthcare companies are transforming the health landscape in India. HealthifyMe[8] offers nutrition and diet plans through an AI system called Ria. Wysa,[9] a mental health start-up, offers AI-guided bots blended with professional advice from counsellors. Niramai.ai[10] uses AI to detect breast cancer using a methodology that is non-invasive, radiation-free, low-cost, no-touch, and safe. In the fintech space, Envestnet Yodlee[11] can use data to provide recommendations to clients.

Blue Sky Analytics,[12] an environmental start-up, has developed a geospatial AI platform called Zuri[13] which uses satellite data and on-ground IoT (Internet of Things) sensors for solving the stubble-burning issue in Punjab that causes massive air pollution in Delhi and the national capital region. Zuri uses historical data to understand the history of farm fires, predicts high-risk zones and the expected volume and calorific value of crop waste, and then enables farmers to sell their stubble instead of burning it by providing information on the marketplace.

Increasingly, AI is transforming technological innovation, leading to more accessible technology for everyone. Across sectors and industries, AI is being infused and interweaved in use cases, making it easy to use and more importantly relevant in our daily lives. Hence, the promise of AI is far-reaching.

The Fear

While the promise of AI is gigantic, the fear of it is equally sizeable. Change has always been a harbinger of fear and uncertainty, and AI is no different. As with anything else, there are enough reasons which have warranted this fear, so it is not entirely baseless. There are many stories we hear or read about, primarily related to security, privacy, and the supposedly controlling power of AI. But why are these fears there? Who or what nurtures these fears? And what triggers them?

The fear of AI stems from a perception of superintelligence beyond reasonable limits. There are scientists corroborating it, like Nick Bostrom from Oxford University, who argues that machine brains will surpass human brains in general intelligence. Then this superintelligence will replace humans as the dominant life form on Earth. Bostrom's book *Paths, Dangers, Strategies*[14] is a bestseller and has personalities like Elon Musk and Bill Gates agreeing to his theories.

When Elon Musk, who is considered an innovator par excellence, made headlines by saying that AI could be more dangerous than nuclear weapons, the entire world took notice. Several theories exist about the time frame in which AI will achieve this superintelligence. Michael Nielson,[15] the pioneer of the Open Science movement, has estimated that the probability of intelligence explosion is between 0.2 per cent and 70 per cent by 2100. Well, isn't that a varied probability spectrum!

There were more exciting estimates by Bostrom and Muller in 2012– 2013, which gave a median forecast of 2050 for a 50 per cent probability of human-level machine intelligence and a median estimate of 2105 for a 90 per cent probability.[16] In another such experiment, 41 per cent of participants in the AI@50 conference (2006)[17] stated that machine intelligence would *never* reach the level of human intelligence. This conference commemorated the fiftieth anniversary of the erstwhile Dartmouth AI conference workshop which is considered the founding event of AI as a field.[18]

So, is the fear of superintelligence the only reason people fear AI? Here, we explain this fear through one particular example: the well-known 'trolley problem'.[19] Imagine a trolley full of big boulders coming down a hill. On its path down, there is a pram that has a small baby in it. You are standing some distance off the downward path and have access to a mechanism that can jump and divert the trolley away from the baby. However, doing so would mean setting it towards five old men who are having tea. Do you save the baby or the five old men? It is a moral dilemma.

Now, let us look at a similar situation through an AI lens. Suppose you are in your expensive self-driving car, worth lakhs of rupees, relaxing in the rear seat and reading a newspaper. Suddenly, a baby's pram comes in front of your vehicle. Your car decides it has two options: to save the baby and crash into the divider, which can lead to the car overturning and possibly your death, *or* to crash into the baby, which would mean certain death for the baby, but not you. What would your car do in such a scenario? Save its owner who paid a premium and bought it for its intelligence? Or be humanitarian and protect a living being who happens to be in the car's way due to human error and in violation of road safety guidelines? This is not just an anecdotal use case. In fact, Germany has already constituted and implemented an ethics rule framework[20] to address issues like this. One guideline is that human life has priority over property and animals. But when the choice is between human lives, it gets more complex.

This is not just an ethical problem, but one that conveys the underlying unease when it comes to letting AI systems make decisions based on what they have learnt. We are talking about the decision capability of algorithms, but the point to ponder is: Have humans been able to discover how they will react if a man with a dagger tries to stab them? What will be the reaction if that man is a White or a Black or a Muslim? Are human biases accentuated during moments of danger? With what decisions do we train the models? Biased ones? If so, whose biases?

We have talked to experts and business leaders across industries on the subject. The fear of AI is based on not just its superintelligence and power to control but also the notion that it will take a lot of jobs off the market. However, this fear is unfounded, as proved by an International Data Corporation report,[21] which found that 53 per cent of people said that AI helped employees do their jobs better and made them more productive.

While we will delve deeper into the fear of AI later in the book, we would like to leave you with a thought. Did the invention of Deep Blue replace human chess players? No, millions of schoolchildren can today play online chess, analyse their moves, and improve strategies with algorithms that use AI.

The Confusion

Why is there so much confusion surrounding AI?

Many organizations are struggling as they can't find a single time-tested approach on how to start using AI and, more fundamentally, they find it hard to understand *what* AI means for their organization. Could it be directed towards curing cancer, or could it help them formulate a better customer experience? Where should they start? There is enough confusion on the terms, technologies, success rates, and dangers. Is intelligent automation also AI? We discovered that the confusion around AI and its terminologies, components, dangers, methodologies, technologies, and frameworks are slowing down its adoption by companies more than any other factor.

To start with, the word AI itself has so many interpretations—Augmented intelligence? Autonomous intelligence? Assisted intelligence? Some enterprises believe any form of an analytics system means that they have an artificial intelligence system in place without having collected a shred of data. Some people believe that a system that identifies cancer is AI, while the chatbot they have developed to manage customer queries is not an example of AI. Organizations that can benefit a lot from the intelligent automation of processes are clueless today as they believe that AI is an esoteric term referring to something that will help only a few. More confused are CXOs who understand the need for it but do not know where to start. Will it be expensive for them to implement AI? Which business process should they begin with for the best return on investment? These executives end up hiring expensive consultants to guide them only to get disillusioned with the fact that the money they have put in is leading to intangible outcomes.

Some organizations which do commence their AI projects get confused about the performance of their deployed AI models as they do not get the promised results. They get worried about biases which have crept into their models, leading to undesired outcomes. Some businesses do not trust AI outputs despite using the best technologies to develop the models.

People do not realize that AI has been around for more than fifty years, and, in fact, most machine learning (ML) models were around even thirty years ago. What has changed in the last decade which has resulted in everyone wanting to get on the AI bandwagon? Let us discuss a few changes which have increased the need for and hence adoption of AI.

1. Democratization of AI

AI is no longer a tool which only a few sophisticated and deeply technical people can build, use, and sell. In recent times, we have observed a huge rush in the developer community to build tools that enable everyone to build AI.

Practitioners can now train AI models for tasks like image search, text mining, and speech recognition in a mode which requires low or no coding. There are visual development tools which allow users to drag and drop components to build AI models. Open-source ML libraries like TensorFlow[22] hide all the complex mathematics and statistics behind easy-to-use functions. Cloud infrastructure allows users to deploy, monitor, and monetize their AI systems in a point-and-click mode. One does not need to invest in expensive hardware to host the models and software to manage them. One can now get the best managed services for a few dollars a month.

We talked to an organization which spends only 1 per cent of its annual revenue on infrastructure. Sounds unimaginable? This is true: just 1 per cent. This company's sole business is monetizing AI models at scale, and it can generate over $30 million revenue by spending $300,000 on AI model hosting and management. What this means is that the barrier for entry is low, and those enterprises which are not agile enough to adopt AI will get left behind. A word of caution—while it is getting easier to build and deploy AI, let us not forget that AI remains a highly technical area which is evolving amazingly fast. So, unless an enterprise invests in the right talent and skills, it will be tough to stay ahead of the curve.

2. AI as an Academic Subject

AI is now taught not just at the graduate level[23] but also at the school level.[24] This is a signal that everyone is betting big on AI, and it will continue to generate impact for the next fifty years. An important leg of our research focused on high-schoolers and college students and their skilling needs—they are interested in the concept of AI for all. Interacting with students made our belief stronger that AI need not be taught only to those who know science and maths. It needs to be understood by biology students, economics students, commerce students, and even history students. The doctors of tomorrow should know AI as the equipment used by them will use AI. Students of economics need to understand that social experiments can get better with AI as it becomes the tool to predict behaviours based on past happenings and incidents. We will talk more about this in the later chapters.

3. AI Beyond Labs

An important shift in the rise of any technology occurs when businesses get convinced that they can make money out of it. Unless there is a pot of gold at the end of the rainbow, there will not be proliferation of a technology. Yes, academia will continue to make progress, but the progress will not be at the scale or speed as we are seeing in AI. The opportunity for businesses to make money is an important motivator (perhaps the most powerful one) for any technology. Look at the case of image recognition. One of the reasons for its newfound prominence is applicability of the technology in self-driving cars, healthcare, security, and other such areas. AI is at a point of inflection. It is now outside the labs, being field tested, and a part of many applications that impact us every day. As per a rough estimate, AI will unlock a $14 trillion economy.[25] That number is too big for enterprises to ignore!

4. AI as Combinatorial Invention

AI is a result of diversified and multidisciplinary innovations which point to a better way of doing things. Combinatorial invention happens when something new is created using resources that are already available. Google's Eric Schmidt says in his book *How Google Works*[26] that combinatorial invention happens when 'there is a great availability of different component parts that can be combined or recombined to create new inventions'.

Of course, for him, the components are technology, behavioural data, tools, and computing. Schmidt's quote is related to how Google has used this concept as its search tool evolved. During the initial days of Google search, most of the queries were related to adult-oriented content. Google tried bringing in pornography filters, but that did not help. US Supreme Court Justice Potter Stewart defined porn as 'I know it when I see it',[27] and Google asked a small team of engineers to use algorithms to solve the problem using this philosophy.

The engineers combined several insights together to create the 'safe search' mode, which would effectively block inappropriate images. This technology was skilled in understanding the content of an image, like a visual of skin, and would understand the context by seeing how users were interacting with it. When someone searched for a body part with porn in mind, only for an anatomy-related medical image to turn up, he or she would not click on it or browse the site for long. This gave them the most effective filter as the result was a combination of context, insight, interaction, and algorithm.

This invention improved over the years and Google applied the same concept to several other problems. Today, users can search on Google through an image rather than text—you can input a picture of a gigantic garden and Google will identify it as the Vrindavan gardens in Mysore. Thanks to the technology which was developed to filter out porn!

AI is about combinatorial innovation, and several multidisciplinary teams need to get together to make an AI system succeed. Simply figuring out the credit score of an individual requires a combination of finance experts, ML technologists, mathematicians, and behavioural scientists. No one person can build such a system alone and claim ownership.

For such a simple model to be devised, each person needs to understand why the model needs to be built with AI, how it can fail and why it can be the best tool. This needs an AI mindset and skilling on AI across roles, and not just by data scientists. We have worked extensively with school students, especially those in grade 11 and 12, and built an AI curriculum[28] for them. At the end of our sessions, we normally provide several capstone project problems to them and request them to solve them using AI. Every time, without fail, the best AI models are created when students from mathematics, biology, and humanities backgrounds get together rather than only the computer science students.

AI is ready to make an enormous impact over the next few decades. Enterprises that will catch this trend early on will be the market leaders. The pertinent question that needs answering is that if everything is so good, why are organizations not already on their AI journey? The short answer is that it is a tough and prolonged process which requires a mindset shift.

Demystifying AI and making executives understand it for better adoption in their enterprises is one of this book's main objectives. AI is not black magic which will solve umpteen problems without stakeholder involvement, a defined methodology, and a mindset to bring in change.

The AI Mindset Framework

As businesses and enterprises adopt AI technologies and use tools to implement them, they often overlook a critical ingredient: a sense of preparedness for AI. A lot has been written about data preparedness. But we often forget that humans are at the centre of implementing and adopting AI. It's humans who are building, training, accepting outcomes or rejecting them, and introducing their own biases into algorithms. The mental construct needed for implementing AI in an organization is the most overlooked part and it needs a lot more focus than what it is getting today. No one is talking about the culture of AI which needs to be brought into all functions in an enterprise. What is needed is the AI mindset!

The AI mindset is needed in leadership, sales, products, engineering, marketing and HR, financial analysis, and for front-line workers, agents and even users. How prepared each person in a role is to understand that their job and the way they go about doing it will change (for the better), how their inputs will define the success or failure of AI, and how they are an important cog in the wheel of AI innovations. AI is not a data scientist's job. It's not a programmer's job. It's not a technical skill like Java or Kubernetes which can be acquired by enrolling in a course. We have to internalize it, weave it into our organizational structures, imbibe it in our values, and adopt it as a discipline. Our mental model is the one which needs to adapt to AI and make it further, business outcomes.

This AI mindset will not settle in automatically. Organizations need to prepare themselves by understanding their people and then developing plans. AI impacts each role in an organization differently, which implies that different roles/personas will have different perspectives on AI. The different perspective will necessitate different and personalized communication and have varied expectations. Some questions organizations need to ask while preparing for an AI mindset are:

- How does AI innovation happen in an enterprise? Who is responsible for it?
- What are the best practices for preparing for AI and what are the major roadblocks?
- What are the guardrails and checks to make sure that an organization is moving in the right path for AI adoption?
- How essential is AI to the core competency of the business? How will the usefulness of AI be quantified?
- Is AI different from digital transformation journeys? How?
- What is the responsibility of each role building or using AI? How will that role change after the introduction of AI?

- How will failures be handled?
- Is there a persona-based journey map for AI learning in each role? How will learnings be shared across organizations?
- Is the organization committed to investing in an AI roadmap?
- Who are/can be the role models or exemplary employees to lead this transformation?

So, if an AI mindset is needed for the success of AI in business, then why don't we just embrace it? Are there any prescribed steps which will make an organization AI-ready? How do we infuse this mindset across all layers of an organization so that true transformation happens? What are the impediments to such a mindset?

In this book, we have attempted to answer these questions. Let us see what it needs to prepare minds for AI across different functions in an organization. When we say minds, we mean YOU! You might be a builder of AI, consumer of AI, sponsor of AI, or seller of AI. Irrespective of the industry or organization, you will fall into one of the above categories. Let's try mapping roles in an organization to these four areas. You are bound to find yourself here.

- AI builders: chief information officers (CIOs), chief technology officers (CTOs), data scientists, developers, testers, engineers, domain experts, product managers, technical specialists, support staff.
- AI consumers: These are both internal and external. Internal ones include department heads, functional leaders, product managers. External ones are users, end clients.
- AI sellers: CEOs, sellers, technical sellers, customer support staff, agents, domain experts.
- AI sponsors: CFOs, LoB owners, AI offering managers.

You will find some roles overlap, and that's natural as you may be an AI builder for some time and then begin selling your innovation to others.

We talked to scores of people across these roles to understand what they want to achieve from AI, where it fails, why it has become a success in some organizations, and what it takes to build the technology in such a way that it eases adoption. We studied organizations from varied industry sectors and spoke to people from different backgrounds.

Infusing the AI Mindset

Let's go back to the question of how we can infuse the AI mindset across all layers of an organization. We will talk about the different stages of an AI journey from proof of concept (PoC) to AI infusion to transformation and touch upon the need for change, people's role, data strategy, and technology roadmaps. But first let us look at each ingredient of the AI mindset step by step. We are here introducing an AI mindset framework which includes the broad areas that enterprises need to focus on when they move on the AI journey to transform their businesses. In the upcoming chapters, we will break down the individual components of this AI mindset framework. Let's first understand what these components are and why they are needed.

FIGURE 0.1: AI Mindset Framework

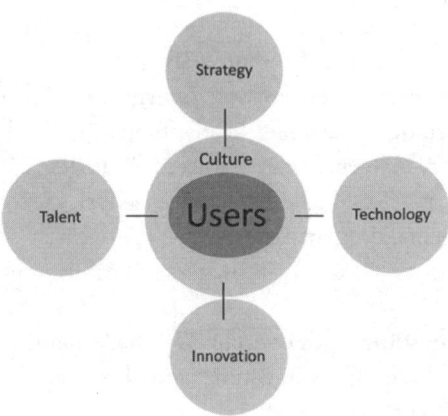

The AI mindset framework necessitates an AI strategy while embracing innovation and a culture of change, commitment to investing in AI talent and technology with an unrelenting focus on users.

Strategy

If AI is so important that it changes businesses and gives birth to new ones, then why would organizations not make it part of their core strategy? AI is not just a technology, it's a way of running a business efficiently and effectively. If it's to be an equal partner in a business, then it must be treated as aligned to the core strategy. There needs to be a special emphasis on laying down an AI strategy for the organization.

During our engagement with clients, we have discovered that when we are included as partners in defining the core strategy, we tend to see faster results of our AI projects. Why limit it to enterprises? Several nations across the globe have been working on a national AI strategy to help set the pace and drive investments in the right direction. They are laying down policies, frameworks, and principles of an AI strategy. In fact, the right AI strategy will help in getting the maximum benefit out of AI. While we have been working directly with enterprises and governments, advising them on investing in the right sectors, nurturing the right skills, following time-tested frameworks, and setting AI governance metrics, we have collated all our examples and experiences into an AI strategy flywheel which will be introduced in Chapter 1. The flywheel sets the AI initiatives into motion. Then we introduce an AI maturity model which helps us measure how good our AI is.

How does an organization choose the right use cases? Is your organization ready to embark on the AI journey? How can CEOs and business unit leaders be convinced of the benefits of AI? Should there be a wait and watch approach or should the AI investment be done right away? If huge investments have been put into AI proof-of-concepts, when will it scale? Chapter 1 will be a revelation on what fails and what leads to success while working with AI.

Innovation

Innovation in the field of AI is twofold: one in the core AI technology space and the other in the adoption space. In core technology, it's about how new algorithms are breaking barriers and pushing the frontiers of science. Some of the latest advancements in AI have been:
- Generative adversarial networks (GANs)[29] which have the potential for transforming facial images to video sequences.
- Generative pre-training (GPT) and GPT-2[30] to generate synthetic text automatically.
- Reinforcement learning[31] coupled with temporal value transport (TVT) to make better decisions about the present and send messages to the future. Understanding decisions and applying the learnings to the future can be a game changer.
- Upside-down reinforcement learning to expedite the training process by giving reward as an input, decreasing a lot of the time required in AI workflows.
- A neuromorphic chip which will revolutionize computing, like IBM's TrueNorth chip[32] which is helping build a brain-inspired computer.
- Other advancements like genetic algorithms (GA), neural networks with continuous layer models leading to infinite layers, deep neuroevolution, AutoML using NASnet; the list goes on.

While the above are science-centric innovations, they lead to thousands of applied innovations for industry and specific-use cases. The above algorithms can be fed into products and solutions and used in businesses and day-to-day life. For instance, L'Oréal's AI-powered virtual reality tool for personalized beauty care,[33] Kuri's mobile robot for family interactions, and AI wearables like AlterEgo[34] which can detect what you say.

There are a lot of avenues like scientific journals, trade shows, academic conferences, etc., where enterprises can learn about new innovations. However, it is essential that enterprises distinguish between innovation that matters and fads like shiny pieces of technology. It is amazingly easy to get carried away on the innovation charter and start doing things which will succeed technically but fail when it comes to RoI (return on investment). Therefore, it is important that organizations set up proper mechanisms and structure to evaluate AI infusion and transformation via innovation and an RoI lens.

A significant cornerstone of the innovation charter is that it requires a visionary technologist with an eye for business. This is definitely not an easy combination to find—someone who understands the technology and marries it with business, so that the organization will be able to innovate smartly for a business and not for superficial appearances.

Should enterprises wait and watch as innovations occur or take the plunge as soon as a new one comes up? Should they be the guinea pigs of new scientific advancements that would give them access to newer markets? Are there examples of organizations which are AI facing and resulting in great AI innovation? Is there a methodology to adopt deep innovations in AI and derive use from them in a viable way? We will discuss these in detail in Chapter 2 which is dedicated to how innovation is important for the AI mindset.

Technology

While users drive requirements, technology is responsible for delivering on those requirements. Scaling and monetizing AI is all about choosing the right technology stack. Think about a recommendation algorithm which suggests the people you can be friends with (a standard feature on any social networking portal), or what you think is the most efficient data store for such use cases. If you answered 'graph' or 'RDF stores',[35] then you are correct! Any other data store can be made to work but eventually the efforts on workarounds will overtake the real work. The same thought process can be extended to all layers—the right programming language and model, the correct deployment pipeline, effective monitoring, etc.

Now, due to easy access to AI development tools (open source and integrated development environments or IDEs) coupled with cheap cloud services, many organizations tend to overlook the technology and take it as being either too easy or too widely available. The truth cannot be farther from this. Yes, the tools and technologies are available, but it will need decades of experience and an experienced team to make the right architectural choices. We will discuss this in detail later, but enterprises should not get blindsided by the fact that all tools are available as OSS (open-source software) or are unbelievably cheap. Swapping a piece of technology stack is not easy and will have a significant impact on quality of service (QoS) and cost. In Chapter 3, we not only discuss several technological choices but also explain buzzwords and technical terms in detail.

Talent

During the AI journey, organizations grapple a lot with AI skills and people. AI jobs are the highest paid and many organizations baulk at the idea of picking AI projects because of the fear of cost of AI talent. Well, innovations and growth do come at a cost. But the question of whether companies should hire, buy skills, or retrain employees looms large in the minds of CEOs and CIOs.

Reskilling and making an organization future-skill-ready and re-engineering the entire workforce towards change and AI readiness is no small undertaking. It is not only time-consuming but needs vision, clarity, and grit to make it happen. During our research for this book, we met a head of marketing who had just given a public interview declaring his organization to be an 'AI-powered organization' with 'AI experts' to lead them in the journey. But, during our discussion with the same organization's chief analytics officer, we were told how the head of marketing had rejected an AI skilling plan for marketing folks, forcing the analytics team to just focus on the AI project deliverables! Looking for short-term gains and shifting the onus of AI only onto data scientists can never make for a successful AI journey.

How will people learn? Which roles in the organization should learn about AI? How are traditional roles changing and what should be done to keep themselves relevant in the AI world? Prices of hiring or buying AI skills are hitting the roof. How should organizations optimize? Which skills should they buy, which should they hire and which should they re-engineer? These questions will be dealt with in detail in Chapter 4, where we bring in perspectives of several industry leaders on how they carried out AI skilling in their organizations.

Culture

All major transformations in an organization are driven by significant and sometimes painful cultural change. Culture is driven by the leadership but is embraced by the entire organization. AI is most successful when it is a part of the culture change and driven by the top-most leadership in an organization. This encompasses allaying fears of AI, changing organization structures for better empowerment, which will produce higher business results, and communicating a strong message about partnership with AI.

We have worked with organizations where AI failed even though there was a mandate from the CEO. It happened because the business unit leaders were unprepared and not ready to address their AI fears. An organization-wide mindset changes and a readiness to adopt AI is what is needed as a foundation for AI to succeed. A growing organization which wants to innovate, break age-old shackles, and have a leadership which removes obstacles to change would face the issue of AI resistance. The fabric of the enterprise should be geared towards change, transformations, and progressive growth. Only then can AI concepts, technology, and projects be accepted and have room for expansion.

A culture of positivity is a must-have for the AI mindset to set in, and it is a key differentiator between organizations which become AI-ready faster and those which keep fearing AI.

Why do organizations resist AI? What are the best examples of bringing about positive cultural changes? What are the fears of AI and how can we remove them? Is AI really going to rule us and destroy humans? We will answer all these questions and discuss relevant examples in Chapter 5.

Users

Users are the end recipients and use the product created by AI. Many times, they do not know that AI is being used in it. Does a storekeeper know that AI is being used when he looks at his phone and logs in? Most users have neither any technical understanding of a product nor do they intend or need to know about it. Users can be rash, jerky, impatient, and always demand more as they want the system to think like their own minds. All that a busy pizza delivery boy is concerned about is navigating traffic and Google Maps giving him the fastest route to his destination. He demands better routes, reroutes, alerts when there are road closures, and real-time decisions to be taken for him.

But in enterprises, users have business roles like storekeeper, warehouse manager, maintenance engineers, office space planner, doctors, health workers, etc. None of them have technological experience or the knowledge of AI systems. But these are the people whose usage and adoption defines the success of a prototype and its journey towards AI infusion and transformation in the enterprise. Hence, users are central to establishing an AI mindset in an enterprise. We need to design systems for them, we need to create AI models keeping in mind the impact on them and we need to educate them about the process, so they become partners in the AI journey. Any AI system which is designed to prove a technology but omits users is bound to fail. As a warehouse manager, will you care about the AI model which best optimizes inventory levels and route plans for spare parts movement across warehouses if you are unable to use it? For an AI mindset to set in, we must keep users at the centre of our plans. We will discuss this in detail in Chapter 6, along with how AI can be designed for better adoption and a shift towards an AI mindset.

The AI Journey

An enterprise's AI journey is not an overnight one. It will take months (and years) for an organization to be fully transformed and imbued with AI. Like any momentous change and transformation, this will require careful planning, investments, risk appetite, and a culture overhaul. We are here articulating the key phases of the AI journey and what an enterprise should expect and undertake to do in each phase. Please note that this is not a prescription, rather, it is a blueprint which needs to be customized to each instantiation. Based on decades of experience in advising customers and driving these changes first-hand, we propose to segment the AI journey into three phases: PoC, infusion, and transformation. Each of the phases has unique characteristics in terms of investments, value generation, and lessons for planning the next stage. In the subsequent chapters, we will describe the HOW to operationalize this journey but, for now, let us focus on WHAT these phases entail.

FIGURE 0.2: AI Journey

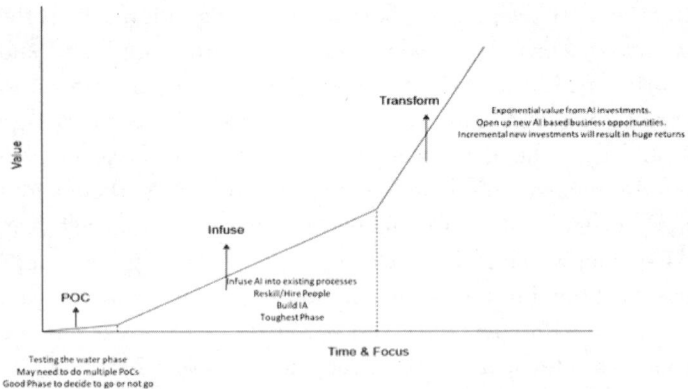

Phase I: Proof of Concept

Just like taking a test drive before buying a car, PoC is a test drive of AI for an enterprise. This is the first small step of an organization to observe first-hand the value which AI can deliver. The PoC is usually a low-investment and low-value-generation activity. The scope of PoC is very focused, small, and non-adventurous (cautious). It could be difficult to differentiate between AI and automation. Owing to its specific nature, the realized value of the PoC is very small.

Many times, a company's value statement is only projections. For example, a PoC might involve showing how a company can understand customer demands and hence increase customer acquisition from its social media feed. The PoC will require complex NLP (natural language processing) models to understand the informal text frequently used on social media. It may be built on a sample (a few thousands) of locally available social feeds and show how the NLP model can correctly identify tasks and sentiments. The results will then be extrapolated to millions of feeds from hundreds of online sources to project the expected benefits of the final system. This is a great first step towards understanding the power of AI/NLP models and almost serves the point of a good technical PoC.

There should be a concentrated effort to complete the loop of linking the technical PoC with business KPIs (key performance indicators) even if it is on an extremely small scale. In the example above, identified customer leads should be shared with the sales team and the percentage of leads that are converted to actual customers should be recorded. This conversion rate will provide a realistic expectation of RoI. Overlooking linking the technical or functional PoC with a business's KPIs is a pitfall which should be avoided by careful planning.

The other mistake is underestimating the complexity of scalability, performance, security, or other non-functional requirements. Continuing our customer acquisition scenario, we need to evaluate the feasibility of handling millions of feeds from hundreds of sources. This poses a chicken-and-egg scenario; one cannot test scalability without provisioning hardware, software, and data licences. However, procuring all this will defeat the purpose of a PoC exercise. This dilemma is usually solved by looking at prior art, industry standards, blueprints, architectures, etc. to get confidence on the feasibility, should the enterprise go to the next step. This is akin to a leap of faith but with due diligence. It will help in understanding what the PoC to deployment journey entails in terms of investments, complexity, etc. The importance of this phase should not be undermined by low investments and the low value it generates. If done right, the PoC will convince all stakeholders of the value of AI, shine a light on challenges and bootstrap the execution plan. Let's not forget that there will and should be multiple PoCs before a decision is taken about the next step.

Let's also look at how the various components of the AI mindset framework behave during the PoC phase. Figure 0.2 captures the phase of AI journey and how much the enterprise should focus on each aspect of the framework.

An AI *strategy* need not be in place for a PoC to start; in fact, the PoC might not even be aligned to the AI strategy at the outset. However, the organization should have started thinking about which areas they need to focus on for AI adoption, what could be the broad use cases for early investment and what the competition and industry are doing in AI. The need of a comprehensive AI strategy should be felt, analysed, and seeded during this phase.

Technology focus during this stage could be from medium to high as this is the stage where the technology is being evaluated and tested. We have consulted several clients who, in fact, spend months on vendor selection during this stage and analyse tools and technologies at an in-depth level. This is encouraged; clients must understand the data tools for creating the right data sets, then compute the availability and shortage, if any, in their organization, the skill demands of each tool, and the runtimes needed to run their AI projects. This stage can be daunting, and the caution is to avoid this becoming the nemesis of an AI project.

Let us look at the role of *innovation* at this stage. Innovation focus on this stage should be from medium to high as innovation starts early and must be the reason the PoC may have been identified. Organizations wanting an early-mover advantage can gain miles if their PoC has an innovation focus and they can leave the competition far behind. Imagine Uber not experimenting with user data to derive insights out of it!

Most new-age organizations start innovating and conducting several PoCs before AI paves the way for them to scale up. That takes us to the last component, *talent*, which at this stage is less of a priority. PoCs can be done using a lower level of skill within the organization, and most of the talent can be outsourced. There could be several PoCs, with different vendors, and employees within an organization could start their learning journey by identifying simple courses that they need to undergo to understand the journey they are about to begin.

Culture might not be a prime factor for success at this stage as PoCs are done within boundaries and their impact is quite local in nature. A PoC could be within a division or a department to prove a simple hypothesis or even a technology.

During the PoC stage, *user* involvement is low to medium. The PoC objective must have users in mind, but their engagement level can be low. Do not forget that users are at the centre of an AI mindset so they can *never* be forgotten.

Going back to our initial example, while one may buy a car after a test drive, the drive will never be so detailed as to capture all possible scenarios like driving in congested traffic, crossing a flyover, etc. That experience will only come once we get into the driver's seat to head to a destination.

Phase II: AI Infusion

Now we have taken the test drive and decided to buy the car. We need fuel, driving skills, a map to keep us on course and, of course, some excitement which motivates us to move forward on the road ahead.

AI infusion is the most critical step for any organization, in which it goes all in for AI adoption. Typically, this phase includes looking at existing processes and evaluating how AI can help in making them better or optimized. The definition of 'better' will change based on context. It could refer to making a process faster, cheaper, accurate, scalable and so on, depending on the metrics. This is easier said than done!

During this phase, it is not just one or a couple of processes which get infused with AI; instead, AI becomes pervasive across the organization. Every department or business unit discusses improvements through AI and making their processes AI-enabled. For a banking organization, this does not mean just setting up a successful virtual chatbot, but also using ML in customer analytics, recommendation engines and applying RPA (robotic process automation) across customer-facing and back-end processes.

This phase comes with a need for investments in technology, talent, and culture. As we saw in our customer acquisition example, scalability is a mandatory aspect. To scale up, a company needs to invest in the compute infrastructure which includes hardware, software stack, network connectivity, and maintenance to build, run, and manage AI-infused applications. The cost for these could be very high if done at once and in-house. Fortunately, with the cloud technology, SaaS (software as a service), platform as a service (PaaS), open source and pay-as-you-use model, the cost is now manageable. For example, Viome, a biotechnology start-up based in New York, was able to bring down its costs by 90 per cent by moving the in-house stack to a major cloud vendor.

The next important aspect is *talent*. AI skills are in short supply and are likely to remain so. An organization needs a combination of a hiring and reskilling strategy for this. It may be worthwhile to start thinking of a chief analytics office division to oversee the AI roadmap for the whole enterprise.

Now that we have the fuel (in terms of investment for infrastructure) and the drivers (in terms of talent), let's look at the importance of the map or strategy of the enterprise. The AI infusion will most likely be a multi-year process with intermediate and continuous RoIs. To make sure the process is smooth, it needs to be continuously and always aligned to strategy. This alignment ensures that, while the long-term AI roadmap is under execution, there are continuous benefits. It is important for short-term activities to be aligned with long-term strategy so that one does not have to wait till the end of Phase II to generate value.

Enterprises need to ensure that all three components (technology, talent, and strategy) are in sync to maximize the probability of success and to keep getting RoI during this phase.

The *strategy* for AI should be of a low to medium focus, which means it needs to be in place with the identification of AI adoption areas, pattern identification, and the need of skills. There should also be a broad roadmap. The strategy need not be executed at full horsepower as this is just the beginning of change within the organization. The strategy itself might have a course correction based on the learnings within the organization. We discovered a manufacturing organization which wanted to focus on human resource (HR) use cases more than pure shop floor use cases just because they discovered that more efficiency could be achieved through the model created for their HR functions, and the manufacturing process had noisy data issues which were taking longer to resolve.

Technology focus continues to stay high at this stage as this is the time where an organization prepares itself to not just infuse AI but to lead with AI. No shortcuts should be taken at this stage. Enterprises should hire good talent, study industry-standard architectures, keep in mind not just present needs but future scaling, security and performance requirements while developing the technology stack. Any suboptimal decision will have an exponential impact (in undesirable fashion) in the future. While the technology components can be cheaply provisioned using cloud services, the magic lies in which components to choose and integrate.

Innovation focus continues to stay between medium and high as one cannot remove the focus from innovation. New paradigms, new markets, new AI applications, and new AI adoption models must be considered. Focus on innovation in core AI science and adoption for creating products and use cases is an essential step.

Focus on *talent* at this stage is also high as the organization must reskill itself, launch AI for all skilling programmes, and have AI learning paths identified for each role within the organization.

The focus on *culture* should be somewhere between medium and high. This stage could need interdepartmental collaboration and trust within each department. The organization should be ready for change and employees' growth mindset is the key to success—there is a need for open-mindedness. If a culture change is not embarked upon at this stage, AI infusion will not be successful, and the AI project will languish at the PoC stage. If a creditworthiness model is being launched in a bank, then the credit risk officer must trust the model and work hand in hand with data scientists to launch it. Business units and data scientists have to collaborate for this to be possible.

During this stage, the focus on *users* is between medium and high. Users start using the AI system and provide valuable feedback which needs to be incorporated back into the training stage. Users are not voluminous at this stage as the AI project is not at scale, but their involvement nevertheless is needed to check if the AI system is working and having an impact. Going back to the previous example of creditworthiness in a bank, the credit risk officers need to use the model with different customer segments to believe in it, provide feedback, and validate if it behaves consistently and is being fair to everyone.

What is next? The last phase of the AI journey which is when the organization enters the transformation stage.

Phase III: AI Transformation

Till this point, we have reimagined existing processes with AI and sorted out talent and technology with a focus on strategy. Now is the time to reap its benefits. This is the time where we start to not just get a high RoI but also open up new business revenue streams. One of the key aspects of AI infusion is that all processes start to follow the standard architectural principles. For example, instead of having siloed data sources, the enterprise would have designed a common data lake to fuel all the processes. Similarly, there will be a common governance and policy management layer to safeguard and audit the processes. While this unification and integration results in less maintenance costs and decreases repeated efforts, in the long run this has an amplification impact. Now that all enterprise artefacts, including data, models, policies, etc., are integrated, it opens up unlimited opportunities to roll out new offerings at a fraction of the cost. As an example, the AI team can focus on building newer and better models to support the offerings and not spend time on getting data access. Studies have shown that, without a common access layer, it takes around four to six weeks to get data access approval!

The reimagined AI enterprise is now ready for transformation. So what should be the focus? At this nirvana stage, should the investments and focus be similar, or can we achieve some economies of scale? The AI journey is now powered by the AI mindset.

Let us look at all the aspects one by one:

TABLE 0.1: Focus vs AI Journey Progress

	Users	Culture	Strategy	Technology	Innovation	Talent
PoC	Medium	Low	Low	Medium	Medium	Low
Infuse	High	High	High	High	Medium	High
Transform	High	High	High	Medium	High	Medium

Strategy focus continues to be high at this stage. The AI strategy is working at this stage, and we cannot afford to remove this focus as it governs investment plans and is the anchor for the transformation. As we will discover in Chapter 1, the strategy gets powered up even more and several PoCs and AI infusion across enterprise-wide processes have a transformational effect in the organization. The organization gets talked about in the industry as the gold standard for AI-powered transformation and its strategy starts getting noticed by all.

Technology is not really in focus. Investments have already been made during the AI infusion stage, and most AI vendors have tools and products which provide lower usage rates when volumes are high. The initial investments start paying out at this stage and organizations also discover lower rates and optimized methods of deploying technologies. Even though volumes are high at this stage, the actual investments and running costs per user is much lower. For example, the online grocery retailer BigBasket attributes lesser focus on and investment in technology than what they started with.

The focus on *innovation* continues to be high as the organization cannot afford to do away with its competitive advantage.

The focus on *talent* is not high as the heavy lifting would have happened at the AI infusion stage. Employees for all the required roles would have been hired or outsourced and, though continuous investment and focus would be needed to learn newer aspects, the manic focus on reskilling and explaining AI would have been done and dusted.

There is an extremely heavy focus on company *culture* at this stage. Cultural transformation and AI transformation goes hand in hand. The entire organization should be aware of why changes are being instituted and how employees need to continue to transform themselves. The organization is a new one now.

User focus is at an all-time high. The entire AI mindset is geared towards improving user experience, and interestingly they will not even realize that it is AI which is helping them make decisions. We now know that our current viewing choices on Netflix govern what we are recommended next. User inputs and scale make enterprises reach scale, and the reverse is true too. Users are highly engaged, their inputs govern AI models, and they need to be available across age, sex, race, and location. It's important to acknowledge that this journey is applicable at different levels of granularity. For example, instead of enterprise-wide change, one may follow the same methodology for a single process. Needless to add, RoI in the last phase is dependent on the extent of AI infusion. Table 0.2 captures investment versus RoI for each step. The rubber hits the road in the last phase but, just like everything good in life, to reach that state, an enterprise needs to go through the PoC and infusion stage. As long as these steps are aligned with strategy, it should be a smooth (and possibly long) process.

TABLE O.2: Value and Investment during an AI Journey

	Value	Investment
PoC	Low	Low
Infuse	High	High
Transform	Very High	Low–Medium

What to Expect Next

In this chapter, we detailed the need to adopt an AI mindset with the eventual goal of transforming an organization. This is an exciting but not a simple journey and different pieces need to come together to reap the benefits of AI.

In the coming chapters, we will delve deeper into the components of strategy, innovation, technology, talent, culture, and users as these together power the AI mindset. We answer questions like: How does an organization embark on the AI journey and keep the momentum going? How do we innovate and foster a culture of innovation at an organization? How should leaders think and take decisions about data, algorithms, and the technology stack? How do we learn AI and how can we build an AI organization? CXOs would find answers to questions like: How can I remove the fear of AI and make my organization adopt AI? Finally, we will discuss why users are the most important stakeholders in the AI journey and why they need to be the central focus of an AI mission.

Each chapter has multiple examples of organizations which are doing it right as well as caveats from industry leaders on how to avoid common mistakes. We have also covered case studies of industry-leading organizations at the end of each chapter. These organizations are not just trendsetters but are investing deeply in furthering AI with focus and attention from their boards and CEOs. Our decades of experience and two years of interviews and discussions have found their way into the following chapters.

In this ever-changing gizmo world of reduced attention spans, we have attempted to talk about core principles and illustrated them with exciting examples. For a leader who has the right vision for AI in place but does not know how to execute it, the chapter on technology will decode all the buzzwords and help them understand the language data scientists are speaking. For a business leader who is focussed on maximum RoI and wants to kickstart new initiatives in this mind-boggling new field of AI, the strategy chapter is a good place to start, followed by the chapters on talent and culture. The chapter on innovation is a must-read for all as we cannot discover new opportunities mindlessly. There needs to be a method to the madness. For AI builders and product managers, the chapter on users will provide examples of how organizations are understanding users and their needs to rake in millions of dollars.

For understanding the AI mindset completely, reading all the chapters together will set you on the right path.

Over to new learnings!

I

AI Strategy

Artificial intelligence is at a juncture where the promise to impact billions is yet to be realized, but it has turned around so many organizations that no one can ignore its benefits. As organizations embark on their AI journey, they would need a blueprint for an AI strategy before taking it on. Without a crisp strategy in place, they would be directing their efforts in multiple directions and hence losing the momentum to gain speed and distance in any one direction. Organizations need to understand their current mindset, what drives them, which AI use cases will fuel growth, and what would be the right steps to implement their strategy. While it is fine for organizations to perform initial prototypes and wet their feet, sooner than later, they would need an AI strategy to drive coherent plans. Without a well-thought-out AI strategy, the organization would be like a rudderless boat going nowhere. A sound AI strategy should be driven by leadership—probably the CEO—and should be communicated to all. Having a strategy is not enough; there also needs to be direction on how it should be implemented and an understanding of reasons for failure which can be used to drive better results.

But before we start on what your strategy should be, it's important that we first do some soul-searching. The same AI strategy will not be applicable for all kinds of organizations; hence, we need to first understand the type of organization with respect to an AI mindset. When should an organization take the AI plunge?

Type of Organization

When to adopt AI is a paradox which baffles organizations across the globe. They are worried about how to adopt it and where to start the journey. There are essentially three kinds of organizations when it comes to AI adoption:

AI-Enabled

These are organizations which want to invest in AI because they fear that the competition will outstrip them if they don't do so. These might be traditional organizations which have seen new-age AI enterprises disrupt markets and realized the need to embark on this journey lest they miss out. These organizations are ready to work on an AI mindset as they are progressive and have a mindset towards the growth of their enterprise. However, they do not know how to begin or what to do. They need a sound AI strategy, and this section is crafted especially to be of help to them.

An example of a successful AI-enabled company is Axis Bank, which is the third-largest private bank in India with over 4,500 branches and more than 11,300 ATMs. As per a case study by INDIAai,[1] Axis Bank embarked on an AI strategy by launching an innovation lab called Thought Factory. The executives of Axis Bank knew that, if they did not adopt AI, their organization would be outrun by new companies and banks like PayTM or the relatively new Airtel Payments Bank. Moreover, convenience to customers was the main business driver which prompted them to adopt AI. The case study outlines how the bank has so far implemented AI across more than 125 processes and cognitive automation across ninety processes to reduce turnaround times. This led to an over 700 per cent reduction in data entry time—fifteen minutes of a data entry exercise by an employee was reduced to a mere two minutes. This not only reduced human error by 85 per cent but also increased compliance and operational efficiency.

Locus,[2] a start-up based in Bengaluru, providing logistical and optimization AI solutions for supply chains, was approached by BigBasket to help in their route optimization and tracking of their last-mile delivery. Locus's solution enabled BigBasket to get AI-enabled. Locus delivered 10 million+ orders for BigBasket with 99.5 per cent on ground SLA adherence, while helping BigBasket deliver 12 per cent more orders with the same resources.

We use Locus for automatically planning our delivery routes and tracking our last-mile delivery. They have worked closely with our Product team to keep enhancing the product.

The new feature which they deployed recently with real-time alerts and planned vs actual comparison in an extremely simple UI has really helped our Ops teams to manage the last-mile deliveries effectively. We are happy with the commitment they have to the client's needs and the focus on constant improvement.
—V.S. Sudhakar, co-founder and executive director, BigBasket, a TATA Enterprise

AI-Led

These are organizations that are bold and want to adopt AI regardless of what the competition is doing. They feel the need to adopt AI because that is the best way forward for them to grow and re-engineer. They consider it the best decision for them to move ahead as they want higher market shares and are looking to create new markets to be ahead of the game. They are in prime position to become industry leaders and pathbreakers as their decisions are based on bold moves. These organizations need an AI strategy flywheel which will help them gain momentum faster. This chapter will introduce you to that flywheel later. Examples of some AI-led companies are Flipkart, BigBasket and Envestnet Yodlee.

We interviewed Dr Swati Jain, vice president, analytics, at EXL. She was not aware of the research we had been doing for the book, but we were surprised to observe that her ingredients for an AI-led organization matched ours! It's no wonder that Swati is amongst the fifty most influential leaders in AI and in the 2021 top twenty-one women in AI as per INDIAai.[3] She shared with us some of the best practices of AI-led organizations where she had led several AI initiatives.

- Moving away from HIPPO (highest paid person's opinion) culture and remaining focused on data and facts.
- Involving customers from the start, educating and providing them technology support for quick adoption.
- Setting realistic expectations with respect to AI and model effectiveness.
- Becoming future-ready to ensure preparedness one year on (enhancing capabilities, hiring the right skill set, etc.).
- Focusing on empowering employees to accelerate a mindset change by doing the following:
  - Robust capability development: Organizing technical aspects (Python, Pyspark, TensorFlow, Scala, cloud, ML methodologies, etc.) as well as participating in digital leadership trainings.
  - Creating diverse teams and ensuring that an AI team comprises not only engineers but also folks from other disciplines, including economics and management to ensure robustness and diverse opinions which are critical for success.
  - Ensuring interaction of data engineering, dashboarding, and modelling/ML teams (such as by placing them on the same floors next to each other), promoting visibility

and better understanding of the entire spectrum to help achieve the AI vision in a smooth fashion.
- Creating an innovation culture: Organizing knowledge-sharing and guru-speak sessions, hackathons, idea generation contests, digital fairs, and creating digital experience centres. Regularly discussing AI and emerging technology trends and organizing focused group discussions.
- Including proactive AI interventions as part of employee goals and scorecards, making bandwidth available to facilitate folks in imbibing AI.
- Celebrating failure along with success and publicizing best practices.
- Keeping a focus on values and soft attributes like trust, empathy, collaboration, communication, agility, and flexibility required in the new environment (such as the ability to work with scarce data, being open about test and learn approaches, etc.).
- Emphasizing brand positioning to embed transformation into employees' minds (such as by leveraging screensavers, stationery items, and other things to create awareness, even aligning corporate social responsibility activities to align to that cause).
- Focusing on outcome metrics (customer satisfaction scores, efficiency, revenue enhancement) versus SLA-based metrics.
- Considering AI as a discipline and not technology alone, focusing on decoding and demystifying it to ensure that every person in the process understands their role in the AI transformation.

AI-Born

Such organizations exist because of AI; for them there is no concept of AI adoption as 'data first' is their primary strategy.

AI is not an enabler for such organizations as it is the very basis of their existence. These organizations create not just new markets but new spaces which did not exist before. They are true innovators and pioneers in the industry.

An example of an AI-born organization is Wysa,[4] a mental health start-up. Its AI algorithm focuses on the ability to respond to free-text appropriately and with empathy, allowing it to function as a mental health support service. Wysa understands the user's input along with the context and is able to provide an appropriate empathy-driven response. Its conversational AI utilizes CBT-based psychological interventions and allows for a free-flowing anonymous conversation between a user and the conversational agent.

This enables it to offer support any time and anywhere. Wysa uses this capability to provide low-friction, low-cost support for mental health problems at scale. It is the responsive, empathetic '4 a.m. friend' which is available 24x7. Wysa has had over 4 million people reach out to its conversational agent. While it has human mental health professionals extending therapy sessions and journaling advice to Wysa's users, this empathetic and always available AI model is one of its key offerings.

Creating empathy is a combination of science and art. The science is focused on building strong AI models using our 100 million-odd conversations to understand user inputs (we have more than 100 of these), to recognise a gamut of emotions like anger, grief, sadness or anxiety. The art in this is about writing content in a way that is robust, is based on evidence-based techniques, and driven clinical input and review. Yet, it should feel accessible and friendly, and use colloquial language that is easy to understand.

—Jo Aggarwal, founder and CEO, Wysa

There is also a fourth type of organization: *AI-scared*. They are always questioning the need for AI and its benefits. But let us leave them to their challenges and focus on the first three.

So, what kind of organization should you be? Let us delve deeper into this topic and understand what is happening around us.

About two decades back, information technology (IT) was an enabler. Marketing and finance folks were the main heroes and heroines. They ended up being CEOs. Organizations were run on brand strategies and fiscal disciplines, and IT was an enabler. Technical folks were seen as those in softer roles which got them well-paying jobs. IT was an enabler, maybe a disruptor, but not a leader. Today, IT is the leader, a new market creator. The birth and rise of Google, Uber, Amazon, and Netflix prove that companies can exist and grow on the strength of technology alone and leave the brick-and-mortar models behind. Tech-born and tech-led companies have the largest market capitalization, and their stocks are sky high. Seven out of the top ten richest people on the *Forbes* list are those who have founded these tech-born or tech-led organizations. Several decades ago, no one would have thought that Mark Zuckerberg would be able to topple oil and steel czars. Technology has moved from just being an enabler to being the reason organizations exist.

AI is at the initial stage which IT used to be at—it's perceived as being an enabler and not as a leader. Industry pundits feel that it can be added as just another use case to traditional organizations; anybody and everybody can do it. What they do not realize is that AI-born and AI-led companies will rise and challenge the existence of all AI-enabled organizations. AI-born and AI-led organizations are already mushrooming. It is difficult to imagine that a company can be run by just AI bots or AI-powered recommendation engines. Venture capitalists are hedging bets on tech and SaaS companies now as they are uncertain whether to go all-in. But we certainly know that the organizations of the future are going to look vastly different because AI has forced us to reimagine them.

The Paradox of AI Adoption

It is easy to understand AI-born organizations, but the real struggle is between AI-led and AI-enabled organizations. How is the strategy of one different from the other? Let us discuss a simple game theory[5] example to understand the behaviour and choices of these two types.

Here is an intriguing problem that illustrates the scenario of enterprises today. It's called Newcomb's Paradox.[6] There are four entities: a player, two boxes (A and B), and a super-intelligent predictor called Oscar. The player knows the following:

a. Box A is transparent and has $1,000 in it.
b. Box B is opaque, and it can contain a million dollars or nothing at all.

The player can choose to pick only Box B or both A and B. Oscar predicts the player's choice with near certainty, whether the player will pick Box A or Box A+B. Now:
- If Oscar predicts that the player will pick both Boxes A and B, then Box B will contain nothing.
- If Oscar predicts that the player will pick only Box B, then the box will have $1,000,000 in it.

The player does not know what Oscar has predicted or what is inside Box B while making a choice. So, if the player chooses both boxes and Oscar's prediction is also the same, the player will always get $1,000. If the player chooses only Box B and Oscar also predicts the same, then the player gets $1 million. Easy? Is choosing Box B always the answer? No.

If you were given a choice, what would you choose? Think for five minutes as to *why* you would make that choice and then read what is written below.

Now, let us look at the options available.

Player's Choice	Oscar's Prediction	You Win
A + B	A + B	$1000
A + B	B	$1,001,000
B	A + B	$0
B	B	$1,00,0000

The boxes are already on the table so some people might think to pick both boxes as that outcome is better than nothing. At least you get $1,000 dollars—you do not want to leave any money on the table! The other way to look at it is of maximizing returns. As everyone will think of taking both boxes to get at least $1,000, why not play the high-risk game as the probability of ending up with $1 million is at least 50 per cent.

These are two distinct kinds of decision theories and rational behaviours.

Let us go more in-depth and analyse the choices and why people choose any one of the above options. As this problem has been around for quite some time, game theory offers two different strategies to solve the problem.

The first strategy relies on the 'expected utility' hypothesis.[7] The usage of this concept happens when an individual must decide under uncertain conditions—in other words, the decision must be taken without knowing the outcomes that may result from the decision. In such a situation, the individual will choose a decision which, according to them, would result in the highest expected utility, which is the sum of products and utility over all possible outcomes. The concept of expected utility is the reason people buy insurance policies to cover them from adverse consequences. For an insurance policy, the actual result is unknown; hence, they consider making a decision that has maximum utility in case of an adverse outcome.

So, as per this hypothesis, the player in the case outlined above will choose Box B. He will believe that the probability of Oscar being right is almost always inevitable. It is just like the probability of an adverse outcome in the insurance example will bring maximum benefit to the insured, so the individual will buy the insurance policy as it protects him during the most adverse outcome. This concept governs the player of our game and so his choice of Box B maximizes winning and sets him at $1,00,000 per game.

The second strategy relies on the 'dominant strategy' principle[8] of game theory. This strategy means that a player will make a better decision than all the alternatives, regardless of which move the opponent can make. This strategy is used a lot in corporate warfare when companies are fighting for market share. As per this principle, our player will choose a strategy that is always better—so choosing both A + B will always give him $1,000 more than choosing only Box B.

So, why are we discussing this here? What does this have to do with AI adoption by enterprises? Several parallels can be drawn between the Newcomb's Paradox methodologies and enterprises' response to the adoption of AI.

There are enterprises that have transformed themselves completely by adopting AI and have launched new business units or enhanced their business models entirely. On the other hand, there are organizations that are playing a wait-and-watch game. Delaying the decision to adopt AI is harming these organizations more and making them lose competitive advantage. Some of these organizations are making half-hearted attempts in adopting AI, investing in small, unimportant processes that do not affect their bottom line at all. When we consider all the enterprises that want to adopt AI, we see that almost all of them are vacillating between the 'expected utility' hypothesis and the 'dominant strategy' principle. The enterprises following the former are AI-enabled and those following the latter are AI-led.

AI-enabled organizations think that they should decide to invest in AI as this will protect them from any severe, lousy outcome. What if their traditional model fails? What if their competitors, the so-called new-age disruptors, launch a business model that will make the whole organization redundant? The amount of data owned by an e-commerce company about a shopper far exceeds any physical stores, and this can help them leverage their sales in far greater ways. Traditional organizations want to invest in AI as they want to avoid any future shocks, so investment in AI is like an insurance policy. Refer to the example of the 'expected utility' principle we talked about, and it will become clear.

AI-enabled organizations are struggling to decide upon which business process to start with that will give them the maximum RoI. They are grappling with questions related to how an AI team should be structured, built or bought/hired, and what AI technologies are being used by the market leaders in their industry. These organizations also need to address the mindset issue as several old-time leaders resist AI and talking about AI in an acceptable way is a challenge for them. We will provide prescriptive methods and answers to these questions for AI-enabled enterprises.

AI-led organizations want to invest in AI as they genuinely believe in the technology and feel that this strategy is better than *not believing* or investing in AI. They follow the 'dominant strategy' principle and know that investing and believing in AI is better than all other approaches. Investing in AI is a better alternative for them than to deliberate and wait for the competition to catch up. Such organizations do have some failures (though early failures are good) because they are moving fast and experimenting with technologies.

AI-led organizations are keen to invest in AI as they have realized its potential, but their issues are related to scaling AI from prototype to actual deployment, AI governance, and the guard rails of fairness, robustness, accuracy, privacy, and security. In the subsequent chapters, we will cater to these AI-led organizations and bring forth several examples garnered from years of experience as authors on this subject.

Throughout the book, you will find examples of B2C and B2B organizations that have adopted AI. These examples are derived from interviews conducted by us with leaders in AI and/or data scientists from AI-born, AI-enabled, and AI-led organizations. Our interactions with AI leaders, coupled with our experience of creating AI technologies for clients, have been structured in this book to create more value from AI for AI-born, AI-led, and AI-enabled organizations.

One point we need to note is that, whether an enterprise follows the 'expected utility' hypothesis or the 'dominant strategy' principle, they all want to win. All these organizations have just one objective in mind, and that is how to maximize returns and deliver more shareholder value. They all want to embark on the AI mindset journey. It's just that their styles, behaviours, entry timing, and boldness might differ. An AI mindset across an organization will only be instituted if there is a well-defined AI strategy in place which everyone understands.

Enterprises looking to embark on their AI journey need to have an AI strategy in place which will cushion them from failures and ensure they are deriving the maximum benefits from AI. AI strategy should not be confused with a regular technical or digital transformation strategy. So, the key questions are: Who in an organization will lead the strategy? What should it contain? Is it really needed, or should the benefits of AI be evaluated first?

An interesting point to note is that it's not just enterprises, but even countries across the globe that are spending enormous amount of time on building AI strategies to serve as a guide for all institutions and departments in the government. We have specifically worked with the governments of India and Singapore, and both have created a strategy roadmap for AI within the country. Recognizing the potential of AI and the need for India to strategize its approach, the NITI Aayog led the way in India and came out with a discussion paper on a national AI strategy. The paper outlines the prototypes which the Government of India should undertake, a national strategy of building a vibrant AI ecosystem in India and collaborations with experts and stakeholders.

Singapore's national AI strategy[9] was a nationwide effort encompassing researchers, citizens, businesses, and the government working together to bring out a plan. They identified five large projects and outlined the key enablers for a sustainable AI ecosystem. Such large-scale strategy efforts helped in setting the agenda and national-level confidence in AI. Not just countries, but even medium to large enterprises should focus on AI strategy. This gives a clear message to all employees on the focus areas.

Let's get into the details of AI strategy.

The AI Strategy Flywheel

There are several factors to consider while building your AI strategy. Here, we present the AI strategy flywheel which aims to create a rock-solid AI organization.

What Is a Flywheel?

A flywheel is a heavy piece of machinery which takes gigantic effort to move even an inch. You have to keep pushing it with consistent and persistent effort for hours together. Once it takes even a single turn, it starts moving forward, and if you continue to push with great effort it takes more turns and eventually picks up momentum. This makes it go faster on its own without the same initial effort. Its own heavy weight works in its favour; it starts turning by itself and becomes self-reinforced to a large extent.

This concept was first developed by Jim Collins in his book *Good to Great*,[10] where he talks about how people can put a great deal of effort into their business without much noticeable effect until the day when the flywheel starts to turn. This becomes the breakthrough moment—once the flywheel is in motion it will gain momentum and turn faster, with increasing returns to the business. The flywheel model gives exponential growth and becomes a force multiplier as each item in the flywheel is working at its best capacity and providing momentum to the other activities.[11]

The same concept applies to business strategy and AI strategy. Driving AI strategy is like getting a huge flywheel into motion. Initially, there is no movement and people think the strategy is a non-starter—it is impossible to imagine the flywheel at speed. With a lot of determination and perseverance by leadership, there are some initial satisfactory results in AI, and that gets the flywheel moving. These results are initially trivial yet promising enough to spur them to move towards more ambitious targets. As more results start coming in, people start rallying behind these targets and reliable results; the tribe grows, the culture starts changing, and the momentum of the flywheel builds and increases. Thousands of small results aligned in the same direction yield transformative results. The small efforts are all prototypes, leading to the AI infusion stage where the organization starts moving and rallying behind it, leading to the transformation stage when the flywheel has gained full momentum and the organization reaches the AI transformation stage.

Jim Collins explains[12] that there is no single push which can be attributed to the great momentum achieved by a flywheel. In similar fashion, in AI strategy, there are several reasons why the momentum becomes unstoppable. Let us discuss the components of the AI strategy flywheel and the relation between them to get the flywheel in motion.

The AI strategy flywheel has five important components: Why? Where? How? Who? And how good is your AI?

FIGURE 1.1: AI Strategy Flywheel

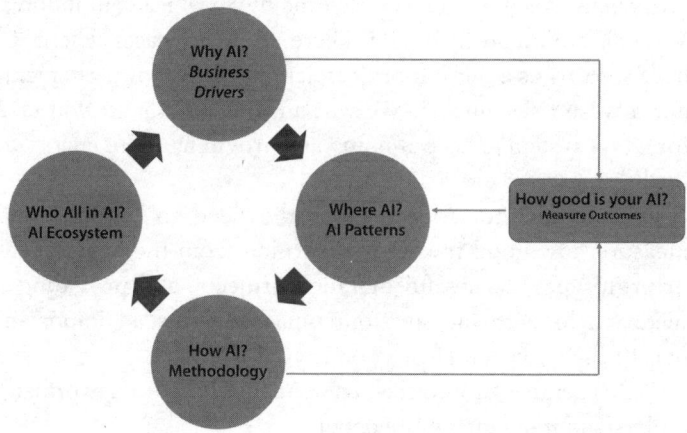

The first question an organization needs to answer is why it wants to adopt or invest in AI. For this, it needs to revisit its primary goals and objectives and discover where it wants the maximum impact—the bottom line or the top line. AI should help the business drivers or fundamentally change the way business is conducted. This is the first component of the AI strategy flywheel which needs to be fully aligned, or all attempts at adopting AI would fail.

The next component of the flywheel is identifying the actual use cases. Where do you apply AI? AI patterns help in identifying areas where AI would be the most effective. The patterns are a group of actual use cases compiled through our study of several organizations.

Once the use cases are identified, the methodology of infusing AI should be followed to ensure the project does not fail. How to apply AI? Many times, organizations just jump into an AI project and lose steam as they get either too absorbed by the technology or forget whom the project is meant for. We will detail an AI Infusion methodology to help avoid these pitfalls.

The last cog in the strategy flywheel is establishing an AI ecosystem which will ensure that the flywheel is set in motion. Who all are involved in AI? There are many cases where we have seen AI as a one-off project; it created a lot of excitement, but it wasn't sustainable. We will understand what it will take for an AI system to keep running and providing more energy to the business.

One should not forget about the need to monitor and measure how good the AI is. Learning from the experiences of prototypes, successful or failed projects, and providing a feedback loop to measure outcomes becomes an important part of the flywheel. How good is your AI?

Let us get deeper into each component of the framework and understand it in much more detail.

Components of the AI Strategy Flywheel

Why? (Business Drivers)

The most important question which an organization should ask is 'Why AI?'

Whether the company is AI-born or has adopted AI over a course of time, it needs to find out why AI should be infused and adopted at the first instance itself. This means figuring out the main reason to invest in AI and realizing how it will help the company eventually. It has to be a pressing need tied to the organization's core business objectives and key result areas. If it is not so, the introduction of AI would start with a big bang and end in a whimper. Business drivers are the key inputs that drive the operational and financial results of an organization. For these business drivers, each organization creates goals and objectives for itself, and AI results should be tightly tied to achieving these. Based on our research for this book, we talked to a range of organizations to discover business drivers which made them answer this question.

For Flipkart, it was about reducing cost of operations; for Max Life and Tata Steel, it was about improving efficiencies in their processes. Niramai.ai and Viome talked about pushing the envelope of what science can achieve, and BigBasket told us stories about gaining competitive advantage through AI. Envestnet Yodlee was proud to have opened new market segments, and Flipkart was delighted at the premium customer experience benefits through AI. Another big player in the business, HealthifyMe, felt that innovation in nutrition through AI was the main motivator.

Locus,[13] which we discussed in the earlier section as an AI-enabled example, is solving the 'Why AI' dilemma for the traditional and new-age organizations like Unilever, Mondelez, Nestle, BigBasket, Myntra, and Licious. These organizations have a pressing need to provide better customer experience, better efficiency, and reduced costs for their customers. Route optimization and planning in these organizations are critical but are primarily driven today by manual efforts on spreadsheets. Locus provides a technology platform that uses ML and proprietary algorithms to automate complex supply-chain decisions. Its website claims to have brought about reductions of more than 17 million kilogrammes in greenhouse gas emissions and more than 70 million kilometres in distance travelled, along with an increase of $150 million in serviceability ratios. Enough reasons to use AI!

Locus has done this by providing the following:
- Last-mile routing: Locus's routing engine considers more than 175 constraints while planning to enable the best delivery experience to customers.
- Field service dispatch planning: Helps field service executives in satisfying customer-preferred time slots while managing last-minute changes and cancellations and also considering service technician skill sets and availability.

- Dynamic route planning and optimization: Accommodates real-time orders into already complex operating models like multi-pickup, multi-drop; single-pickup, multi-drop, etc.
- Territory-based route planning: Reduces rider clashes in areas with a high density of orders by drawing territories and assigning the right delivery executive.
- Reverse/returns logistics: Locus's planning engine combines delivery and returns in the same plan to ensure a seamless customer experience while also reducing costs.

Where? (Patterns)

The next question to answer is: *Where* should AI be applied? As enterprises discover its benefits, they also realize that their road to AI is long and bumpy. Many CIOs understand the need for AI and want to transform quickly, without doing due diligence on the processes. Well, in an Agile (a methodology to build software) world, it is not a bad idea to pick a process, infuse it with AI, and then learn the pros and cons during the journey. The best way to learn is during the project rather than by researching several theoretical case studies. But there needs to be some method to the madness. Can we generalize some patterns and make it easy for business owners to apply AI? Let us first discuss what the common AI patterns are that we can apply to business processes. These patterns are based on our work with umpteen clients and their AI journeys.

For AI Infusion, it's important to identify use cases which align with business drivers and target them as areas of the first AI prototypes. In this section, we will discuss how we identify these AI infusion patterns. These patterns were first introduced by Shalini in an article titled 'How to Choose the Right Pattern to Infuse AI in Your Business' in *The Hindu Business Line*.[14]

FIGURE 1.2: AI Infusion Patterns

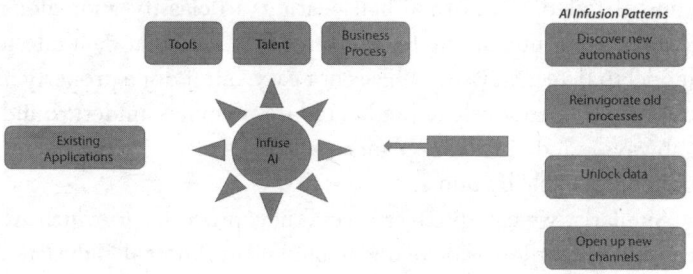

Pattern 1: Discover New Processes and Automations

This pattern is about finding new processes which were non-existent until now but were made possible through AI.

Let us consider an example of a machine which is becoming more defective with time because of degradation. An experienced mechanical engineer can evaluate from the sound generated by a machine whether it's in good condition or not. Today, there is no existing process wherein a mechanical engineer documents what he 'hears' from a machine. Well, there might be some scribbled notes during a maintenance check, but that's it. This is where we can discover new processes with AI. An acoustic model can be created which can analyse sound samples of a machine to predict failures.

Who thought of the fact that noise from a machine is important data and can be put to value? Isn't this common sense for an engineer, that a noisy machine is the first sign of a mechanical failure? Imagine driving in a car with a noisy engine down a highway and an alert popping up on the dashboard flashing the message, 'Please check lubricant'. It is certainly helpful and confirms the gut feeling of the driver that there's something wrong with the car.

Acoustic algorithms need to call out anomalies which are not trivial. Most models today use humans to classify data which is fed into the model, and over time the model learns to classify data on its own. For example, you need to gather at least sound clips of failed and normal ball bearings to classify anomalous sounds using human intelligence and then feed that data into a model to detect an issue. This is not easy, but if done properly it can help tremendously to predict failures in mines, underground subways, and nuclear plants—all extremely critical sites unapproachable by humans.

Similarly, we can discover several new processes to which AI can add a new dimension of understanding in almost all industries.

Pattern 2: Reinvigorate Old Processes

This is a great example of AI infusion wherein existing processes can be improvised by introducing AI.

Let us consider a simple day-to-day process in every organization: logging the data of when employees enter the office premises. This is an existing process and helps to check the occupancy and access control of each floor, and the movement of employees. Now, this process can be reinvigorated by introducing a slight change and then adding AI to derive deeper insights. Along with logging systems, we can install occupancy sensors on each chair to measure how many people are occupying any given floor.

This data can then be fed into an AI model to predict the usage of a floor or the entire building on certain days. This will be especially useful for captive IT organizations whose cost is associated with each desk provided, having a direct impact on profitability. Many people-intensive organizations are struggling to figure out how much office space they should lease and what floors they can let go of based on occupancy which can be optimized.

AI can help breathe new life into existing processes and give insights which were not possible to get earlier. Using AI models to predict events like client churn, machine failure, and energy usage in a household are all examples of how old processes can be reinvigorated with new AI models.

Pattern 3: Unlock Data

Organizations have oceans of data, and a lot of value can be derived from data which already exists within the systems.

This is useful when it comes to, for instance, detecting fraud in a system where all transactions are already logged and available. ML algorithms can spot discrepancies which would otherwise go unnoticed by humans. Another useful example is the manual of an asset in a factory or even readings of a machine's temperature, which are logged periodically. When a machine has a defect, very few service engineers would go back to the manual to read about the possible failure or look at all the 24x7 logs of temperature data.

ML models can be fed with this time-series data to discover anomalous patterns in temperature which would have caused a defect in the machine. Another model can be fed with asset manuals to quickly find contextual readings of the fault and solutions which can be applied. Handling unstructured data—which could be in the form of texts, videos, tweets, or handwritten notes—is one of the widely used examples of AI applications in businesses.

Several organizations have benefited from this pattern, including telecommunication companies which have millions of call records, banks with loan documents, manufacturing units with tons of work orders, retailers with records of client shopping behaviour, etc.

Pattern 4: Open up New Channels

This pattern has been adopted by several businesses successfully. It essentially entails starting a new channel of interaction with customers or employees using AI-based virtual assistants with NLP technologies.

With the emergence of the IVRS (interactive voice response system) several decades back, this new channel is helping organizations reach their clients and serve them in unique ways.

Pick any AI process, and it's sure to fall into one of the four patterns mentioned above. What is needed is the right understanding of which process to choose and then applying the right AI methodologies to solve a business problem. Once the process is chosen, apart from the mechanics of choosing the right algorithm and having the right data quality, one also needs to check for biases in the model.

How? (Methodology)

A CIO once mentioned to us how he was directed by his business to start an AI project because all the competitors were doing so! He did not prioritize the use case based on the benefit it would bring but ended up introducing AI for a use case which was tough for AI to resolve.

Many CIOs tell us that they start several AI PoCs simultaneously to evaluate which one will benefit their business the most. They take this decision as a lot of blogs suggest that 80 per cent of all AI projects fail. They are just experimenting. In this book, we do not want to debate the percentage of failures or successes, as it really does not matter. Any innovative technology hitting the market will have a degree of experimentation, and there is a learning after each experiment which can improve the ensuing efforts. We want to focus on protecting AI investment and increasing the strike ratio of the success of AI projects.

Locus, which we discussed earlier, looked at the problems of last-mile routing, where its routing engine considered more than 175 constraints while planning to enable the best delivery experience for customers. It gradually added a use case on field service dispatch planning which helped field service executives in satisfying customer-preferred time slots while managing last-minute changes and cancellations, and also considering service technician skill sets and availability. Then, Locus went bolder and realized that AI offered a great solution for dynamic route planning and optimization. This helped in accommodating real-time orders into already complex operating models like multi-pickup, multi-drop; single-pickup, multi-drop, etc. It found great value in territory-based route planning which reduced rider clashes in areas with a high density of orders by drawing territories and assigning the right delivery executive. Finally, it also solved the issue of reverse and returns logistics by building a new planning engine.

So, the pertinent question is: How do you pick the right project or use case which brings out the value of AI and provides RoI to the business? This can be figured out if we follow the methodology given below.

This methodology is based on our interactions with multiple organizations and a study of their AI journeys.

Step 1: Identify the First Problem
This is about identifying the right AI pattern based on the business drivers of the organization. It answers the 'why AI' and 'where AI' questions we talked about.

Step 2: Brainstorm on Why AI Is Needed
This step ensures that the real value of AI is realized in the use case and there are tangible benefits to the business. This would need some experts with knowledge of AI systems and experience in applying AI. If the AI pattern is about discovering a totally new AI-driven process, then knowledge of solving the same problem in a different domain is helpful. This step should focus on innovative ideas marrying implementable actions.

Steps 1 and 2 can be done as part of a design thinking workshop which is a standard methodology followed by many organizations these days. The workshop should be attended by all stakeholders who are keen to explore the usage of AI in the identified use case.

Step 3: Find the Right Skills and Resources

Once you are clear the problem can be solved through AI, you need to start the project. But who will implement it? Should it be people within the organization who know the domain, or data scientists from outside? The build versus buy question looms large in the mind of the business head. There is enough evidence to prove that projects done by in-house experts are always more successful than outsourced AI projects. However, having these skills in-house is not possible for all organizations. Data scientists are expensive and keeping them busy with meaningful work throughout the year is not feasible for all organizations. Some organizations invest and maintain an analytics department to churn out the right analytics as needed by several cross-functions. But data scientists are not the only specialists required; you would also need conversation specialists, data engineers, and NLP experts to deliver the AI-enabled process. Hence, in many cases, it makes sense to outsource an AI project and look for experts in that area. We delve deeper into this aspect in our chapter on AI talent.

Step 4: Standardize Tools and Technologies
After finding the right skills and processes, it is important that you standardize the tools and technologies. Most business heads ask that once they have decided to outsource the work, why should *they* worry about this step? Isn't it the responsibility of the hired experts to choose the right technology and tools?

Well, if you want to be dependent on external experts throughout the life cycle of the new application, you can certainly rely on them. But if you want to control your own destiny, then it is important that you take control and become an active member at this stage to evaluate all their decisions and lay down some guiding principles of choosing the technology and tools based on your organization's principles.

Your organization might have existing relationships with vendors which might bring down the cost of the entire project. Or it might have experience of a standard technology and hence would prefer the vendor to choose that, or there could be an organization policy to include open-source technology which you need to discuss in detail with the vendor. The tricky part is choosing the right technology from the many options available, especially for a person new to AI.

We discuss this step in detail in our chapter on AI and technology.

Step 5: Prototyping the Solution with Design Inputs
We recommend completing this step in the previously mentioned design workshop with all stakeholders to arrive at the right prototype. During the workshop, the participation of business and process owners and data architects is essential. The business process owners ensure that the right use case with clear benefits is chosen. They should also guarantee whether they can provide the data needed by the data architects. We consulted in a project where a model for an air compressor had to be refactored for turbines. The data scientist team kept waiting for turbine data from the business users and, after three weeks, realized that it was available only with the original manufacturer of turbines and could not be shared as per the contract's terms. This led to a frustrating scenario for everyone as without the data the project could not even begin.

A design workshop should help determine the minimum viable prototype which will prove that AI is workable for that use case. Sometimes data scientists work with synthetic data (artificially created data that is not generated by actual events) for prototypes but, later, businesses do not fund the scale of the project. How can we expect a vice president of a manufacturing unit to fund the full-scale development of an AI project when the PoC is an academic exercise? It must be as practical as it gets.

Marrying AI theory to practical uses is what makes AI interesting to business users. An important check at this stage is to answer these two questions after the end of the design workshop: Would the business users sign off with satisfaction on the achievement of the AI project's goals after the prototype is over? And do the data architects and data scientists have enough data to proceed to build, run, and test their models?

One needs to check on the progress with stakeholders and sometimes course-correct rather than wait for the end of the project. In one particular AI project, we could not propose any cost reductions as the AI model predicted no anomalies. We later realized that the entire data set belonged to a period in which there was no anomalous behaviour. We then advised the data scientist to pick up data from some other months, and that was when the anomalies show up. It validated the reason for which the business owner had funded the project.

Step 6: Playback to Stakeholders

Playback means explaining the prototype and its results to all those interested in the AI exercise. The most important questions on the minds of stakeholders are if the RoI of a project is worth spending money on, and if it will benefit the business. There are two principles of a successful playback. The first is storytelling and the second is truth-telling.

Storytelling: The results of AI projects should be conveyed in story form. Let us take another example. A data scientist conveys that based on the data of the door-opening times of a refrigerator and the resultant changes in temperature, the model she has created can predict whether the food inside the refrigerator will decay or not, and whether the temperature needs to be reduced even further. Another way to say this is that there is an 83 per cent chance that food will decay in the fridge as the door opens more than the stipulated times and the retailer needs to control the temperature. Which sounds better to the ears?

Sometimes, data scientists cannot be good storytellers and we may need to have architects who can understand the AI model and explain it with a story. The stakeholders should not feel that they are talking to a bunch of 'techies' who do not understand their business well. The architect should have industry domain expertise but, most importantly, have empathy towards the client's needs.

AI is a journey, and we all know that results cannot be achieved immediately. Whatever model or solution we build will only improve over a period. As a best practice, the AI journey and results should be conveyed through a persona. A persona is a fictional character based on the actual user of a system. This character feels, thinks, expects, and desires the same as the actual user. Persona-based storytelling and aligning the outcome of a project to what the persona wants as the output sets the scope and boundaries of the project and makes it credible. For example, Maya can be the persona of a space planner who wants to optimize occupants and plan seating arrangements on a building floor.

Truth-telling: An AI project can promise the moon but deliver only a small percentage of those outcomes. It is important to anchor the discussions on what *has* been achieved rather than what *can* be achieved. Of course, towards the end of the playback, the stakeholders would want to know what more needs to be done and how the AI model can be improved, but what is possible should not overshadow the work which has already been achieved. The moment we deviate from the truth, stakeholders invariably catch on and lose confidence in the project, which is the worst thing that can happen.

Another fact is that data speaks the truth. One should not tamper with the data to suit the outcome. It is important to convey the progress made in the project and the constraints and pitfalls encountered during it. Once, during a playback, where we were building predictions for pest attacks in the tomato crop, we had to tell stakeholders that we did not have the requisite data as all the sensors in the farm fields had been tampered by rats!

Step 7: Complement the Rules-Based Engine. Do NOT Replace It

Software systems in enterprises have rules built within them. Rules are if-then statements which help a system in making decisions.

For example, if a loan applicant is over sixty years of age, then the software will have a rule to check all their sources of income. AI models are learning systems that are predictive and probabilistic in nature while rule-based systems are deterministic in nature. Rule-based systems are needed for faster output and should not be replaced by ML blindly. Several organizations which are keen on automating processes through AI tend to replace the rules which are already built in. That should be avoided. A simple mechanism of segregating a lot of data based on income brackets just needs simple rules and not a new AI engine.

Step 8: Embed Human Experience
Artificial intelligence becomes augmented intelligence when it is created by humans and for humans. AI cannot be just models and algorithms; it must include what humans feel and see in the real world. Moreover, AI must work along with us and be our partner in recommendations rather than the overarching boss who commands us to do things. Embedding human experience also implies including empathy and routine human decisions into our algorithms. This does not necessarily always make machines behave like humans, which is a fear that most people have. But it makes AI more acceptable and inclusive in our work environments. This is also about embedding ethics and values in AI, which we will discuss in detail in a subsequent chapter.

Step 9: Reuse and Repeat for More Processes
Once we have done steps 1 to 8 and implemented our use case and seen early successes, we should repeat the exercise for more processes and make AI more widespread. Early failures will teach us how to fine-tune each step and see whether to do more or less of some things.

For example, HealthifyMe started with Ria, their conversation chatbot providing nutrition advice, but the organization soon realized that they could apply AI to creating entire diet plans for their users. Once you have learnt the methodology of applying

AI, the subsequent applications become easier, faster, and the results better.

Who All Should Be a Part of AI? (Ecosystem)

When AI needs to be scaled, each organization needs to set up an ecosystem so that the AI system becomes self-sustaining. AI needs to become a way of work where everyone in the organization is discovering use cases, learning technology, and understanding its benefits. It cannot be the bastion of a few from the IT department; it has to be pervasive within an organization.

An AI ecosystem includes various stakeholders involved in exchange of ideas and collaborations. The ecosystem uplifts you, motivates you, and makes those collaborations possible which fuel innovation. Working in silos would make you redo a lot of work which would have happened already. The maturity of an organization grows considerably if it has taken efforts to establish an AI ecosystem.

The Indian Ecosystem

At the macro level, let us look at an example from India, where an AI ecosystem had to be established to fuel innovation.

NITI Aayog, the Indian government's think tank, realized that India has an exceptionally large stake in the AI revolution. While establishing a national programme on AI, they understood that, to realize the maximum impact of AI, they needed to democratize access to it by establishing a robust ecosystem. In their 'National AI Strategy' discussion paper,[15] they suggested establishing an AI ecosystem. Here is a summary of the recommendations for public and private and policy makers, mentioned in their seminal strategy paper.
- Setting up of a centre of research excellence for pushing frontiers of research. An international centre for transformational AI for furthering application-based research

- Creating a national AI marketplace for enterprises keen on implementing AI, which would focus on data collection, aggregation, data annotation, and deployable models
- Setting up of infrastructure and compute power at academic institutions for deploying scalable models
- Setting up of ethics councils
- Starting an intellectual property (IP) framework and centres for innovation
- Furthering academia via private partnerships. Forming large national teams with large private players to undertake fundamental and applied research
- Development of AI technology parks
- Building talent for AI and skilling the workforce on AI through focused courses by top institutions and setting up open platforms for learning. NASSCOM Future Skills platform and SamShiksha are examples of such open platforms
- Working on a data ecosystem

NITI Aayog's suggestion of setting up a model AI marketplace is a perfect example of an AI ecosystem. It has government providing the grand challenges, anonymized data sets, and setting up goals in AI. It has private enterprises and PSUs which provide identified problem statements from their domain as well as industry data. It has academia engaged in core research and providing talent for AI. The ecosystem also has AI solution providers which would provide the solution components, technology, and work to solve problems. The AI ecosystem for the Indian government is about nurturing start-ups, investment funds, colleges offering AI/ML education, collaboration with countries, and collaboration between experts.

To bring up the need for an AI ecosystem as a national agenda, and to bring all the stakeholders together, the Ministry of Electronics and IT organized RAISE India Summit 2020.[16] The keynote in this summit was delivered by Prime Minister

Narendra Modi, who said, 'We need to make artificial intelligence in India and make artificial intelligence work for India.'

The RAISE India summit, as mentioned on their website, was a global meeting of minds to exchange ideas and charter a course to use AI for social empowerment, inclusion, and transformation in key areas like healthcare, agriculture, education, and smart mobility, among other sectors.

In similar fashion, several national governments have established AI ecosystems by setting up R&D centres, starting investment funds for AI start-ups, investing in network and infrastructure, and fuelling AI-related public procurements. China, USA, Japan, Singapore, and France are examples of countries which have committed huge investments to fuel their national AI ecosystems.

Nature.com featured an article titled 'The Race to the Top among the World's Leaders in Artificial Intelligence' in December 2020.[17] There is competition amongst several countries for research papers on AI, with the US and China leading the race. The article mentions that, in 2019, China published 102,161 AI-related papers and the US published 74,386. India, which came in third, published 23,398 papers. The article also outlines the AI plans of the US National Science Foundation, which established five new AI institutions at premier academic institutions. These institutions are focusing on improving climate forecasting accuracy, next-generation ML algorithms, discovery, and synthesis of new materials and drugs using AI, applying AI to teaching and learning, and improving research in fundamental physics. Each institute, as quoted by Nature.com, has a funding of $20 million over five years. Moreover, the paper states, the overall funding by governments in the US in unclassified AI research was $5 billion.

Ecosystem for Enterprises

At the micro level, what does the AI ecosystem mean for organizations? It means expanding beyond an organization's boundaries and reaching out to all those who are implementing AI, learning from AI, investing in AI, and expanding the horizons of AI. While working on this book, we talked to several organizations which were at different stages of the AI life cycle, and a few general best practices emerged during our discussions.

Well-established organizations have been organizing meetups with start-up companies to understand trends and fuel innovations in their own organizations. Some large organizations establish an investment unit which then funds several start-ups in the ecosystem. Qualcomm Ventures,[18] as stated on their official website, has more than a billion dollars' worth of investments in over fifty organizations across 5G, AI, IoT, cloud, automotive, and consumer sectors. They have also invested in Ziener—an organization which uses AI to provide field service automation solutions.

The industry–academia partnership can be a hotbed of innovations that fuels the ecosystem for all engaged stakeholders. We saw examples of organizations approaching the Indian Institute of Science (IISc), Bengaluru, Indian Institutes of Technology and Indian Institutes of Information Technology for partnerships and establishment of AI centres. NVIDIA technologies and IIT Hyderabad announced on 19 July 2020 the establishment of a new AI technology centre to focus on AI and its commercial adoption. According to their joint press release,[19] they agreed to focus on increasing crop yield through AI and creating better traffic intelligent systems for smarter cities.

Applied Singularity[20] is a group which organizes meetups, hackathons, workshops, and talks amongst students, researchers, entrepreneurs, investors, experts, and professionals on AI. Its main organizer, Nihal Kashinath, started this initiative as a small group which had grown into more than 16,000 members by 2021.

Corporate hackathons create awareness both internally in the organization and externally within the industry. Some organizations conduct focused workshops on successful use cases with independent consultants which helps the internal businesses get an outside perspective. Inviting experts for talks and panel discussions on focused topics is another way to build curiosity in teams and kick-start a cross-pollination of ideas. Some organizations even get into technological partnerships or acquire AI organizations to get quick access to technologies and/or skilled workers.

The establishment of a robust AI ecosystem can be a game-changer move for any organization that wants to build a complete, transformative AI mindset.

How Good Is Your AI? (Measuring Outcomes)

Once organizations are on their AI journey, they tend to ask themselves how they are doing and if there are any measurable outcomes which can define success or failure for them. There are several lessons learnt during AI implementation which may span across use cases, behaviours, change of culture, technologies used, and it is a promising idea to measure outcomes across various dimensions. Organizations should measure their maturity on AI from time to time to check how they are faring.

The co-author of this book, Shalini Kapoor, authored a paper with Rishi Vaish, Ashish Agarwal, and Robert Parkin on the 'AI Maturity Framework'[21] which highlights the essential dimensions to measure AI maturity of applications. The paper states:

> What constitutes 'good' AI is a challenging question to answer. The field of AI is rapidly expanding and there are always better models and techniques available to improvise our usage of AI. To be able to answer the question of goodness effectively, we studied various parameters. These range from how it impacts the business users; the direct value clients derive from AI; how sophisticated the chosen tools and frameworks are; the inclusion of bias detection and removal algorithms; the quality of data and

cleansing mechanisms; and how explainable the AI is to end-users.

So, how can organizations adopt and score themselves in an AI maturity framework which measures the outcomes of AI efforts across several business and technical dimensions? The AI maturity framework essentially provides an assessment of readiness of AI efforts across these dimensions. The authors of the above-mentioned paper created an AI maturity framework which we have modified here for this book to apply to organizations rather than for AI applications which the paper originally intended.

AI Maturity Framework for Organizations

This framework comprises seven dimensions which are a combination of business and technical capabilities that determine the success of AI in an organization. This framework can be used by AI-led, AI-born, or AI-enabled organizations. In Figure 1.1, we explain the seven dimensions and what question each one answers with respect to the questions 'Why AI?', 'Where AI?', 'How AI?', and 'Who all in AI?'. For each dimension, we have taken a scale of low, medium, and high, but the scale can be made more granular from 1–5 or even 1–10.

TABLE 1.1: AI Maturity Framework

	Dimension	Criteria	Maturity Level
Why?	Business impact	Business drivers relevant to organization	Low Medium High 1 2 3
Where?	Value to enterprise	Strategic use cases, differentiators	Low Medium High 1 2 3

	Dimension	Criteria	Maturity Level
How?	Data management	Data connect, collection, organization, and governance	Low Medium High 1　　2　　3
How?	Technology sophistication	Appropriateness of technology, learning techniques, possibility of reuse of models	Low Medium High 1　　2　　3
How?	Trustworthiness	Bias, explainability	Low Medium High 1　　2　　3
How?	AI infrastructure	Optimization, scale, monitoring	Low Medium High 1　　2　　3
Who?	AI skills	Sophistication of talent	Low Medium High 1　　2　　3
Who?	Ecosystem	Partnerships, connect with experts, industry, giveback	Low Medium High 1　　2　　3

We are not recommending adding up scores in each dimension to arrive at an aggregated score. We feel it is appropriate to have a single score in each dimension which defines where an organization is in the maturity curve. Different organizations are at a different level in each dimension, and an aggregate scoring scale is not a measure of success.

The dimensions provide a mechanism for organizations to measure themselves during their AI journey and improve in an incremental fashion. Further, the score of each dimension is plotted on a grid and organizations can measure themselves every six months on how they are improving on each marker. Interestingly, it is not mandated that each dimension needs to move from low to high. Organizations need to assess the cost and benefit of investing in the dimension based on business outcomes, benefits to users, and the cost of graduating from one level to the next.

For example, Figure 1.3 is the score of a sample organization plotted on the AI maturity framework. It is an AI-enabled organization which has successfully implemented an AI chatbot to handle its customers. The chosen AI use case of developing a chatbot improves business drivers as it reduces the cost of servicing customers which in turn reduces customer churn. Value to enterprise was rated as medium as the use case was relevant but not strategic. The organization did a fantastic job of collecting, organizing, and curating data for the chatbot and further chose advanced NLP techniques to make the chatbot effective. It also thought about scaling this chatbot and used sophisticated infrastructure to manage that. Hence, the score on data management and technology sophistication was medium. It had never thought of bias even in day-to-day data curation; hence, the score on trustworthiness was low. It hired and developed relevant AI skills while building this chatbot and had a chief data officer to overlook the efforts, which meant that the score for AI skills was between low and medium. It did not reach out to build an ecosystem for AI as the focus was on just one process and making it better for scale.

FIGURE 1.3: Scoring AI Maturity Framework

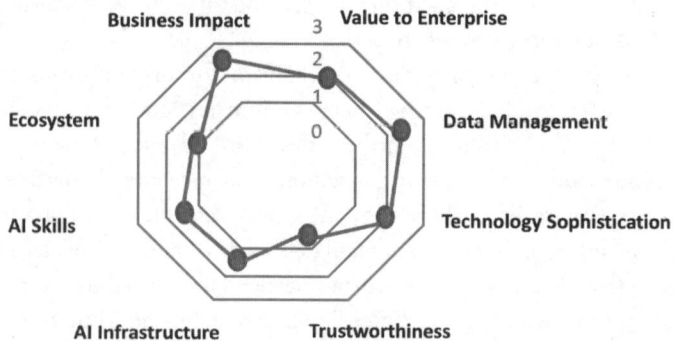

The immediate steps for this organization would be to check its models for bias as this is a client-facing AI, and a single misstep can mar its reputation in the industry. The other would be to build an ecosystem internally and externally which would help in taking AI to other business units. This will in turn set up an AI culture and, eventually, AI will have more value for the whole enterprise. This organization should not spend more money on technology and spending more time on it would also be a misstep.

Making the Flywheel Spin

We talked earlier about the AI strategy flywheel and how it must work and gain momentum for the organization to reap greater benefits from AI. Initially, employee trust in AI is low and the organization has to invest in smaller, achievable results to build credibility. The initial small but complete results then motivate more employees and especially senior management to throw their weight behind the flywheel, which in turn helps in building momentum for the flywheel. This leads to the breakthrough moment we spoke about, when the entire organization gets aligned, several independent results work in tandem and power each other, and greater impact is seen at all layers of the organization. This is a breakthrough moment of the AI strategy flywheel as now it has gained full momentum.

In his book *Turning the Flywheel*,[22] Jim Collins mentions that there are three things that are needed to make the flywheel spin: disciplined people, disciplined thought, and disciplined action. For AI to be infused and adopted across the organization and the right mindset to be enabled, all three are requirements. Moreover, this needs to be signalled from the top leadership.

> *When we started off, when we were a small company, we obviously did product listing by employing humans to do this. Every image was being seen by a human and there were dozens of checks done on each product. When you list the product on Flipkart as a product listing, the product will go through a bunch of curation stages. There is a moderation and data quality checks stage involved.*

To give you an example, when you first upload a product image on to our platform, we need to check for any policy issue, we will need to make sure that the images are of superior quality, we need to make sure that it is not offensive, obviously it is not an NSFW [not safe for work]... We need to make sure that it is not breaking any local laws. For example, that the Indian flag is not being used in any derogatory sense in this image, so all these checks must be run.

Now, the product listing can be exceptionally long. For example, we need to list more than 50,000 sarees even though the customer may not look at all of them, but the listing must happen, and each product needs to go through all checks. Now imagine several product categories like frying pans, T-shirts, bedsheets, shoes and books and each category carrying thousands or lakhs of products. With more than a million listings, there is a long tail of products which needs to be curated. The cost per listing was small but when multiplied with millions it was huge. There was no way we could have continued to do it manually we cannot afford to spend so much on product listings, which means that if I had not put in AI/ML techniques to automate it, the cost of running our operations would have become untenable. There are many other factors that go into the cost like logistics but we cannot pass on these costs to the seller. So we have to keep the cost low for the simple act of listing a product on our platform. So, in other words what we are saying is that this is how our business is being enabled by AI/ML, if we did not have AI/ML, we would not have been able to reach this scale.

—Mayur Datar, chief data scientist, Flipkart

Jim Collins talks about his research with several organizations where he was trying to find 'the one massive thing' which made transformation happen but could not find it. It was the sustained effort over a period of years which led to the final transformation. Several failures, small successes, multiple initiatives in the same direction, nudges, pushes, transitions, course corrections—all in the same direction—made the big transformation possible. So, the breakthrough moment does not happen due to a single large initiative but several smaller ones towards the same goal.

Several AI projects, PoCs, hackathons, failures, and infusion attempts would make this journey from AI PoC to AI transformation possible. Research in AI has followed a similar pattern. AI was an established field by 1960 itself but it took several small innovations and a couple of AI winter periods of several years to reach a point in 2012 when deep learning became a force to reckon with. IBM Watson won *Jeopardy!* and the Alpha Go software showed deep learning research which were turning points in AI and led to immense amounts of research funding and investments in AI.

Kotak Mahindra Bank: Setting the AI Strategy Wheel in Motion

Kotak Mahindra Bank's journey into AI began about a decade ago, with a small business unit comprising data analysts and business analysts, armed with a case study in retail liability. Today, the bank's analytics unit is 350-strong, cutting across a broad range of roles like data science, computer vision, ML, data mining, and data engineering, and solely serving the myriad needs of Kotak Mahindra's four major verticals spanning consumer, commercial, wholesale, and affiliated operations.

> *At Kotak, we are actively nurturing a culture of informed decision making through data democratization and an extensive application of data science. AI and allied technology is critical in ensuring this. We have been extensively investing in AI and driving usage across multiple engines.*
> —Shanti Ekambaram, group president, consumer bank, Kotak Mahindra Bank

As Ekambaram says, the bank has taken up the Herculean task of transforming itself to become a data-driven organization. This transformation is one that's driven from the core, with every employee, business unit, and leader embodying the transformational power of AI and analytics in modern-day banking.

Being an AI-Led Organization

Kotak Mahindra Bank as an AI-led organization has charted its own AI strategy, including tactical adoption strategies, identifying mission-critical and relevant business use cases, upskilling, data gathering, and more.

With over 70,000 employees to bring on board this new train of thought, Kotak Mahindra's AI team, led by Devendra Sharnagat, senior EVP, data analytics and customer value management, had a monumental task ahead. During our interview with Sharnagat, he told us that it simply wasn't enough to whip up a plan to leverage AI, hire some data engineers, and run ML models—it was imperative to rally the organization together to believe in one premise: a data-driven, scientific approach to problem-solving, improving outcomes, and enhancing the bottom-line revenue.

As per Sharnagat, some of the broad-stroke strategies and ideas that Kotak Mahindra Bank pioneered as an AI-driven organization was broadly divided into three pillars:
- Technology and platform
- Skill and development
- Application and adoption

The bank built each pillar over the past decade, each seamlessly flowing into the other, providing momentum and becoming a self-serving model for AI-driven success.

Kotak Mahindra Bank faced some tough questions. Conventional user acquisition methods provided stable profits but was this enough in the face of rapid economic growth and digital transformation? Were the bank's relationship managers—the most important people that customers interfaced with—fully equipped to serve the customer's needs in the present and the future? Did they have all the information they could possibly need to cross-sell/upsell the bank's various products and services?

The core AI/analytics team in 2010 believed that even if there was a 10 per cent increase in outcomes, driven by data, they were on the right track, and, hence, started identifying business use cases that could benefit the most.

In 2012–13, the AI team started out with a retail liability PoC as their first use case, supported by desktop predictive analytics and an operational data store, and driven by business analysts and data analysts. By 2014–15, all core products in retail liability as well as investments and third-party products were brought into the use case fray, while the technology was ramped up to enterprise-grade predictive analytics and group-wide analytical customer relationship management (CRM) implementation. By this time, they added statisticians, campaign analysts, developers, and quality checkers to the roster. In 2016–17, channel and regional analytics in retail liability were added as use cases to solve, along with omni-channel DTC and fraud analytics, while data scientists, fraud analysts, and reporting analysts were also hired.

By 2019, Kotak Mahindra Bank's AI flywheel had started spinning—retail assets, car finance, credit cards, and digital analytics were the coveted use cases being tackled by the AI team, but this time on an upgraded platform of enterprise data warehouse and an on-premises data lake, ably supported by data engineers, risk analysts, and data modellers.

Since 2021, it is using AI to solve challenges in wholesale banking, commercial banking, and has even extended to support functions like HR, IT, and operations, with data virtualization and ML operations for these use cases thriving on a multi-cloud data lake. The organization has also kick-started the conceptualization of a data governance platform. The team of 350 employees now boasts of data architects, cloud experts, and data stewards.

The three pillars have seamlessly merged to create an integrated data platform that can scale AI/ML operations and limit data duplication, while enabling inputs from multiple cloud locations, on-premises offerings, and different coding languages.

The AI strategy flywheel is truly in motion now. And this is made evident from the advancements being seen in AI to solve mission critical business use cases. For instance, credit risk challenges were largely addressed by reverting to bureau or banking data and statistical scorecards. Today, the bank uses advanced ML applications like Random Forest, XGBoost, and NLP, and real-time decisions are made on the on-cloud data lake. Another example is how the bank is approaching fraud detection using AI. Earlier, interventions were rule-based and would be analysed after the occurrence. Now, ML provides graphs and predictive analyses of malicious behaviour, enabled by real-time intervention.

One of the biggest successes to emerge from this self-sustaining AI strategy is the bank's recommendation engine—it provides multi-dimension data, advanced ML algorithms for collaborative filtering, and runs across multiple channels, all synced to the main recommendation engine.

It Takes a Village to Raise a Child: Building an Ecosystem

It takes a team of people bound together by the same spirit and ethos to make this change a reality. People have always been and will continue to be at the core of the bank's AI strategy—be it to build an idea, adopt it, scrutinize it, or further advertise it. Let's see how:

Power Users: These include business intelligence executives in product, credit, risk, compliance, and audit, and they rank as high-volume adopters of the AI being rolled out. Their feedback and participation in the AI building process is extremely critical, so much so that Kotak Mahindra Bank is investing in upskilling them and enabling them with data platforms.

Kotak Analytics Academy: This academy focuses on the core upskilling of employees in AI and allied fields. Skill development spans the organization, so, every employee is engaged through learning programmes based on their job profile. The aim is to equip employees with deep domain knowledge and critical thinking so they can understand the nuances of AI and get thoroughly involved in the product life cycle. Specifically, the Academy plans to train 6,000 large power users across the organization.

Partnership with IISc: In September 2021, IISc Bengaluru and Kotak Mahindra Bank announced a partnership to set up an AI/ML centre at the IISc campus. The centre will offer bachelor's, masters and short-term courses in AI, ML, deep learning, fintech, reinforcement learning, image processing, computer vision, NLP, speech understanding, robotics, computational finance and risk management, cyber security, fraud analytics, blockchain, biomedical engineering and technology, and healthcare. The centre is intended to be a hub for AI researchers to solve societal challenges using AI and grow a talent pool of problem-solvers for the future.

As the banking and fintech space continues to grow exponentially, Kotak Mahindra Bank is now confident of exploring new-age collaborations, thanks to the power of AI. While the bank remains bullish about payments, transaction data and alternate data streams are the focal point for its AI dreams, along with building more intuitive and demand-oriented customer experience journeys in the future.

2

AI and Innovation

Innovation provides the means and opportunity to an organization to infuse new ideas into its offerings, to become a thought leader in the industry, differentiate itself from competitors, and provide value to customers. With a fast-changing technological landscape, continuous innovation is the only way for an enterprise to stay relevant.

In every industry, the market leaders stand out due to their capability to innovate, plan for future features, and provide innovations to their customers. While historically innovation has been deemed necessary for sectors like pharma, IT, chemicals, etc., the trend is fast-changing. Now, companies in more businesses like banking, construction, and home improvement have started to invest in innovation-based offerings. Moreover, investments in innovation are no longer a trait of large organizations with R&D units. In fact, almost all companies now have innovation budgets and dedicated teams, albeit with different names—big data, AI, applied science, and so on. However, their goal is the same—to infuse innovations in their enterprise's offerings, products, services, and in engagement with customers.

Innovation can mean different things to different organizations, and even in different departments within the same organization. In concept, innovation is a process which the organization goes through to come up with new or improved offerings. It can be specified in the following ways:

1. Operational Improvements: Improving existing business processes, products, and services by adding new components

or drastically improving existing components. This often results in improving efficiency, quality, and effectiveness, helping companies grow their business reasonably as long as it is done continuously. This is the easiest way to innovate. For example, eBay wanted to send personalized messages to its millions of customers. Instead of opting for standard mail merge features which produce standardized (almost like spam) mails, it turned to AI, which used natural language understanding and generation tools from Phrassee— an application which can learn the brand language and create the content. The tool was trained on existing emails available with eBay and then it generated personalized text for millions of customers.[1]

2. Strategic Improvements: Developing a completely new product, service, and process which opens new channels of revenue. If done in conjunction with technology trends, market research, and due diligence, this can be a game changer and can serve the company's interest for decades. This type of innovation requires more investments, but the returns can be exceptional. Humana, a healthcare insurance company, receives around 1 million calls every month. The majority of these calls were routed to an outsourced call centre even though 60 per cent of them were standard plan-related questions. Humana partnered with IBM[2] to train and deploy a voice assistant system which was able to handle the requests. The solution leverages AI algorithms to understand a provider's call, verify if they are authorized to access the data, and then determine how best to provide the information requested.

3. Mindshare Improvements: This does not immediately generate revenue but creates mindshare and establishes the company as a thought leader in its sector. It acts as a magnet for talent, new ideas, prospective customers and starts the process for the next revenue cycle. Development of AI algorithms for self-driving cars is one such area. Companies like GM, Ford, Apple, and Google have spent millions of

dollars to build large teams, platforms, and data collection to build the technology.[3] Once the technology is perfected and regulations are in place, this investment will generate multifold revenue for the companies.

We have witnessed multiple examples where innovation was the cornerstone of industry-wide disruptions.

- Uber changed the entire car hiring and rental industry by providing location-based real-time car booking, availability, and tracking. This simple (in hindsight) innovation has already been adopted and repurposed in other delivery platforms including food delivery, courier services, etc.
- Tesla revolutionized the automobile industry by introducing electric cars to reduce dependence on oil and it is considered more environment friendly.
- Amazon has changed the way we shop. The company has the vision of becoming a one-stop shop for everything. Their search and recommendation features are very accurate which increases their sales and enables cross-sell and upsell.
- Netflix is another example of how innovation helped a business not only survive (unlike Blockbuster and other video rental companies) but also leap-frog the competition and be a market leader in the streaming video service.
- The IBM Hybrid and multi-cloud platform is yet another example where IBM innovated to bring the capability to enterprises to host their infrastructure and services anywhere but manage it via a single pane through IBM services on OpenShift. This capability frees up enterprises from a vendor lock-in and enables them to pick the cloud which is best suited for their needs.
- IBM invested heavily in their research teams to build state of the art algorithms for automating AI with trust. Over the years, the team published multiple publications at top venues, generated IP, and was at the top position on several leader boards. Many of these innovations were included in

products which helped them gain market share and emerge as a leader in the AI and ML space.
- Generative adversarial network (GAN) is something that has captured the attention and imagination of the AI community in recent years. GANs provide a sophisticated way to generate new samples which come from the same distribution as training data, but they are not a part of the training/seen data. The core ideas from Ian Goodfellow have been expanded and adapted in various applications areas: generating photographs of human faces, image-to-image translation, designing new fashion accessories, and deep fakes.[4] There is some way to go before GANs can be monetized but this is an example of an AI algorithm fuelling many applications.
- The innovations are not always algorithmic. Take the case of NVIDIA's GPUs. NVIDIA released the first GPU GEForce256 in 1999 to augment central processing units (CPUs) for compute-intensive graphics and gaming applications. CPUs can offload more mathematical operations to GPUs. Over time, GPUs became more powerful, flexible, and programmable, which allowed developers to use them for non-graphics use cases. Owing to the large number of cores and the capability to do parallel jobs, GPUs were found to be incredibly useful to significantly scale up the performance of compute-intensive AI tasks like image recognition. It will not be an overstatement to say that interest and progress witnessed in Deep Learning would not have been possible with GPUs.
- AI is being increasingly used in the healthcare sector to provide better, faster, and cheaper diagnostic and prescriptive services. Renowned names like Pfizer, Biocon, and Harvard Medical School have set up dedicated departments to use AI for early detection of diseases, discovery of new antibodies, understanding the trend and impact of medicines, etc. Bengaluru-based Sigtuple has developed AI 100 and AI 200

products[5] which provide AI-driven automation to do blood screening, pathology image analysis, etc., via cloud-based services. Paris-based Owkin[6] provides a federated data AI system which allows access to high-quality data sets to researchers across the world in a safe and compliant fashion.

The list of innovative companies and innovation is long, and one can see the impact of innovation on the economics of these companies. On the other hand, there are companies like Kodak and Xerox that were market leaders but failed to counter the technological shift with innovations and hence faced severe deterioration in their market value.

Facets of Innovation

In this section, let's look at different aspects of innovation, like size of the innovation, how to innovate, risk versus reward, etc.

Size of the Innovation

Going by the examples of Amazon and Uber, one may think that innovation only matters when it is ground-breaking. Nothing can be further from the truth. Innovation can come in any size, from bite-sized innovations like infusing AI in business processes to full-blown enterprise-level turnarounds successfully done by companies like Microsoft and Netflix.

Let's look at a simple but ubiquitous process of résumé selection and how an enterprise can go about infusing AI-driven innovation in it slowly. In its most simplistic form, the process has the following steps (after the résumés have been received):
- Reading the résumés and filtering out the ones which don't meet necessary conditions like the minimum years of experience.
- Filtering out the résumés which do not fit the job description (JD). For example, if someone sends a résumé which

doesn't list Go language skills but the application is for a Go language-based blockchain platform development.
- Then the résumés need to be ranked. This will be very subjective, even for one reviewer. For multiple reviewers, there is no way to maintain or even pretend to maintain objectivity.

Now, let us see what innovations or new ideas can be brought into each step by infusing them with AI, and what can be the expected benefits.

- *Filtering*: Instead of manually reading résumés, one can build AI models to first extract the text from PDFs or Word documents. Once the text is extracted, the filtering can be done via a simple keyword-based or rule-based matching process to filter out the résumés which do not satisfy the basic criteria. Conservatively, this will prune around 50 per cent of the résumés which will directly result in 50 per cent less work for human agents, directly impacting productivity.
- *Matching*: The résumés from the previous stage need to now be compared to the actual JD which requires the two documents (JD and the résumé) to be compared directly. This comparison can be done at a document level or by extracting important information from the résumés. Additional complexities like the programming language JAVA being closer to JavaScript as compared to C# needs to be factored in. Looking beyond the actual algorithm, AI will help in reducing the number of resumes by around 50 per cent. This directly saves the interviewer time and effort.
- *Ranking*: In this step, the résumés are ranked in some order so as to reduce the interview cost and on-board the candidates quickly. Apart from technical fitment to the job, there are other factors which can be included here. For example, one can estimate the probability of the applicant passing the interview, accepting the offer, and the eventual on-boarding.

This ranking also helps to focus on candidates who will join the organization as opposed to those going offer-shopping.

Of course, *all* these innovations (and more) will make processes better and more streamlined. However, even if *one* of the steps is transformed, there will be quantifiable benefits. Therefore, the enterprise should not adopt an all-or-nothing approach for this.

Formats of Innovation

There are multiple different ways to innovate in an organization, and it will often adopt a wide range to establish an innovation culture. We have already talked about innovation in offering and services. Let us now look at others:

- *Patents*: This is one formal and legal way to protect any IP which the organization may develop. Getting patents granted from the United States Patent and Trademark Office or other countries is an expensive process. It will require the organization to hire an external attorney and pay the patent fees. However, the patent can also be a revenue stream, assuming the organization can monetize it by licensing to other companies. Market leaders like IBM and Microsoft take patent activity very seriously. In fact, IBM has been the market leader in patents for the last twenty-five years and generates a significant revenue from IP licencing.
- *Publications*: Articles in peer-reviewed publications is another form of innovation. The organization should encourage employees to submit manuscripts to top-class peer-reviewed conferences, AAAI conference on Artificial Intelligence, International Conference on Machine Learning, ACM SIGKDD International Conference on Knowledge Discovery and Data Mining, Conference on Neural Information Processing Systems, etc. These conferences provide a great platform to showcase cutting-edge research

and innovation and host industry demos. These venues are also the best recruitment places.
- *Social Media*: Yet another relatively cheap but effective way is to publish blogs on social media sites like LinkedIn and Medium. The daily readership of these platforms is huge, and with appropriate amplification across other platforms like Twitter, it can be a game changer. The article topics can range from new ideas, a work in progress demo, or even a tutorial. Some of the most widely read articles are tutorials, like step-by-step guides to create docker images from a code repository.
- *Local Ecosystem Engagement*: Yet another way to announce a company's innovations and culture is through partnerships with local universities. Prominent leaders of a company can teach courses, give lectures, and mentor students in relevant areas. One can form working research groups with students and faculty to make quicker progress on the innovation agenda. The students can join the company as interns or full-time employees and, thereby, provide access to a constant pool of talent.

Note that incubating a culture of innovation and telling the world about it needs to be a continuous and gradual process within the organization.

Steps to Innovation

How do CXOs operationalize innovations in their organizations? As mentioned earlier, innovation requires a cultural shift. There is a simple three-step process for this.

1. *Innovation Discovery*: There can be many diverse ways to generate ideas from employees which will result in innovations. The idea generation can happen in short, focused groups. For example, a team of ten people can be

asked to look at trends, opportunities, and risks in batteries for electric vehicles. The team can decide to spend two whole days in a room discussing various aspects or spend two hours together while devoting maximum time to reading. For large, diverse companies, it is important to hear different perspectives. Therefore, a social or collaborative platform might be the best way to do this type of exercise. Typically, the idea generation session should last at least three days to cater to different time zones and give people enough time to think. In many companies, there are top-down initiatives where the senior leadership asks the technical community to come up with trends and opportunities to shape the company's investments.

IBM's Global Technology Outlook (GTO) is one such programme. It is a comprehensive analysis that looks three to ten years into the future, seeking to identify significant, disruptive technologies that will change IBM and the world. After a year of intensive work—generating ideas, gathering data, and rigorously debating issues—the final GTO report is submitted to the IBM chairman and CEO. At each step in the process, the team considers the societal and business implications as well as the technological aspects of each trend.

The organization needs to create a culture of openness and encourage everyone to share their ideas. In fact, a rewards-based system also works. Finally, it is the combined responsibility of all employees. At the same time, the organization should provide tools, support, encouragement, and a conducive environment for this exercise.

2. *Innovation Feasibility:* One of the side effects of unconstrained thinking is that it can generate ideas which are infeasible and/or not the right thing to do. Such ideas seem very promising and are difficult to let go of. The infeasibility can come from prohibitive costs and efforts or due to the need

for components which either do not exist in the company or exist in very early stages. In fact, ideas building off other ideas is a red sign. Let us look at two examples.

i. A business analytics team in a company realized that it takes the data analysts a few hours to generate a sales report based on the brief from the leadership. The team came up with the idea of a natural language interface where people can ask questions in a language they are comfortable in and the back-end system, which can understand the natural language, generates the report. The idea looked extremely promising. However, to fully realize it, the components needed were an advanced natural language understanding system, an advanced translation system to convert the natural language into queries which can be run against the data, and, finally, an advanced formatting system which can format reports based on the request. It is hard to understand that the idea may be a good one and yet may not be feasible because it relies on the availability of many other components which are not yet available with the desired quality.

ii. The HR team of a company was really distressed by the rate of attrition. It wanted to build a system which could tell if certain employees were going to attrite. An idea was floated to start looking at employees' LinkedIn profiles and watch out for signs of sudden activity, like the addition of head-hunters and recruitment officers of other companies. This could be a good indicator of whether the employee has started to look for jobs. While the idea seems reasonable, it was a clear breach of privacy of the employees. Someone in the HR team rightly pointed out the potential of the huge negative publicity as well as the possibility of a lawsuit if such a technology was built and put into production. This is an example of how a seemingly good idea can have extremely negative connotations.

Yet, another important aspect of feasibility is to get stakeholder concurrence. Each stakeholder will have a different viewpoint and different KPIs. For an innovation to be successful, each stakeholder needs to see and agree on the benefits. Due thought needs to be given to this, and many times the stakeholder inputs help to identify new requirements for the innovation. Let's say the innovation identified is to build demand forecasting to stock a retail store. The AI team analyses past data and builds a prediction model. The model predicts a low root mean square error (RMSE) on historical data. The business leader, while analysing the model, gives feedback and states the requirement for adding extra inputs on external events. For example, events like the FIFA World Cup and the Olympics take place once in four years and this will be a very important input for stocking merchandise when those events come around. This is a simple example of how the process of getting stakeholder confirmation will lead to better innovation.

3. *Innovation Inclusion*: Once the feasibility of the innovation is established, one should very quickly move to include it in the company. We revisit the key three stages of the AI mindset and note what innovation and innovation inclusion mean for these stages. Let us walk through these stages through an example. Consider a 'Customer 360' application where the goal is to link all customer data to create a single, cohesive profile. Apart from data integration, the challenge also includes resolving the entities so that John Doe, John D., and J. Doe are linked, assuming they are the same person. An innovative solution will use linking algorithms to connect entities across databases. Graphs are the most natural and intuitive way to model such entities and their relationship.

AI PoC: In this step, the innovation could focus on developing the core entity-matching and relationship discovery algorithm. The algorithm can then be used on a subset of the company's customer data to see if the results are in line with the expectations. The results should also be validated with business users to quantify the usefulness of the insights. Since the new idea was around the creation of a 'Customer 360' database, the core idea of linking profiles was tested. This could vary from case to case and context to context. But the rule of thumb is to focus on the core idea and show its technical feasibility, its value to business stakeholders, and, finally, proof of its worth to the sponsors.

AI Infusion: This is where the rubber hits the road. The team will now harden the core asset by following the project management methodology and engaging with other teams, including IT, to procure and provision the hardware and software teams to get the licences of required components, the development operations team to on-board the core solution on the platform, the learning team to create education material, business teams to start monitoring the usage and compute RoIs, etc. All these teams will work together to launch the new AI-infused Customer 360 service.

AI Transformation: Once the business starts to see the value of how this application allows them to approach customers in more meaningful ways, the next obvious step is to replicate it for other entities like 'Employee 360', 'Product 360', and so on. While all the hard work and investments are already in place, it is still necessary to go back to the innovation PoC to filter the 360 concept through the same process. It will be much faster in subsequent attempts as the path to scalable production is already there. However, without the PoC step, there is no guarantee that transferring innovation from one area to another will indeed provide similar benefits.

Across all these steps, the enterprises will also need innovation champions. These are employees who will share details of the innovation and its benefits in the organization. This is important as it will help everyone understand why a certain innovation is useful and motivate other employees to think about the innovation process.

Risk versus (Unexpected) Reward

Innovation does involve risk-taking. Organizations need to invest in the right talent, rewards, and culture to bring innovation to the centre of their operations. Additional capex/opex investments will be needed to build innovative products, engage sponsored customers for feedback, etc. Many times, stakeholders will have to take a call to not pursue certain innovations and hence suffer an investment loss. This is part of the game. With due diligence, some dead ends can be avoided much earlier, but it will not always be the case.

On the positive side, the RoI on innovation often exceeds the expectations of the original team. Who would have thought that the iPhone would end up having such a massive impact on Apple's bottom and top line!

Let us look at another example. IBM Watson was built using state of the art NLP algorithms which were highly scalable, and were able to sift through millions of documents and provide the correct results in a few milliseconds. The first public demonstration of the system was during a *Jeopardy!* episode on television. The Watson system put up an impressive show, defeating the all-time champions (Ken Jennings and Brad Rutler) very convincingly. However, a lot of people asked why IBM would want to participate in or win a game show in the first place.

Fast forward a few years, and there are a wide variety of IBM products and services today which are built off components of the Watson *Jeopardy!* system. IBM launched state of the art services like Watson Discovery and Watson NLU, which leveraged the core Watson system. The consulting arm of IBM successfully engaged with multiple customers in the text understanding, social media mining, and sentiment mining arenas. All in all, the Watson system resulted in developing a large business for IBM over the last ten years. This was not by chance or coincidence. A similar pattern was observed when IBM Deep Blue (which won a chess match) resulted in active research in the area of high-performance systems and IBM Blue Gene. Google's AlphaGo is yet another example where deep reinforcement learning techniques were developed which are now being used in other areas, including self-driving cars.

Inter versuss Intra-Enterprise Innovations

What will be the catalyst or driving force behind an enterprise's push to start innovating? It could be internal or external. Internal reasons could be to catch up with competitors, reaction to market needs, and a desire to get a higher share of the market. This strategy can work in the short term but restricts the organization's ability to truly transform itself.

External innovation is all about striving to be the market leader or even becoming a single player in the market due to high quality products and services. This form of innovation is proactive and is guided by the enterprise's quest for excellence. Internal innovations can often be incremental, aiming to fill the gap between a company's own offerings and that of the competitor. On the other hand, external innovations are disruptive because there is no set benchmark or precedent. They can also fuel other external or internal innovations.

A great example of external innovation is the introduction of usable interfaces in iPhones. When the iPhone was released, there was no benchmark in the market. Its launch had two major effects: it drove a lot of competitors out of the market (like Reliance, Nokia, etc.) and it made Apple Inc. the market leader. This also resulted in a series of innovations within Apple which were part of subsequent iPhone releases. It also forced other companies like Oppo, Huawei, etc. to innovate to catch up with Apple via internal innovations. Even Nokia relaunched its phones after some of its own innovations.

Ways to Innovate

Till now, we have talked about one specific and commonly used form of innovation, that is, through internal employees. However, there could be other ways:
- Acquisition: This might be the fastest strategy, in which an organization acquires the talent and IP from elsewhere instead of growing it internally in organic fashion. While this may be the fastest way, it may not be that simple because of integration and cultural differences between two companies.
- Partnership: As an alternative to acquisition, the company can decide to outsource or set up a partnership with a research organization or individual academics. This can provide access to a talent pool with the cost of ownership. The issues with this often lie in the ownership of IP, the fact that the partner can go and work with competitors, and, of course, internal resistance to an innovation which was built outside the company.
- Dedicated Teams: Many companies like IBM, Microsoft, and Amazon set up their own dedicated research labs which are responsible for developing cutting-edge technology. These labs usually do not have a direct profit and loss responsibility but are measured via the impact they have had on other business units in the company.

In most cases, a single strategy may not work, and a combination of approaches will be used to reach the innovation goal. For example, look at the hybrid innovation strategy of BigBasket.

It leverages a different partner to manage innovations. Some partners manage AI infrastructure. Functions like storage, computing, provisions, optimization, and the data pipeline is managed by a third party. The in-house analytics team builds the core algorithms while the third party provides the systemic part, like Kubernetes, scalability, and resilience.

PoCs are done in-house and then, after value assessment, partners are looped in, if needed. The in-house team's bandwidth is constrained, so that is also considered if partners are bought in.

To reiterate, the key tenets of a company embracing the culture of innovation are:

- Executive support
- An atmosphere devoid of fear
- Collaboration tools for faster idea generation
- Fast path to AI PoC
- Find/hire/train right talent
- Incentivize
- Long-term commitment

It is also very important for an organization to do some soul searching of sorts and figure out their DNA for innovation purposes. One good way is to map the organization's aspirations to a scientific quadrant model. The model specifies three types:
- Bohr's Quadrant: These are the organizations which do fundamental research. Their innovations have a long-term investment and returns outlook. Typically, academia, government-funded agencies, and pure industry research labs go into this quadrant. In current times, quantum computing, where a lot of scientific progress is being made, will fall into this quadrant. The eventual inclusion of quantum technology for the end user may be decades away. However, scientific breakthroughs are needed now to be future-ready.

- Edison's Quadrant: These are the organizations which perform very applied innovations to solve the current problem at hand. While this model works, it may lack a long-term vision. However, this is a wonderful place for an organization which is starting its AI journey. It need not masquerade as AI-led or AI-born but should focus on seeing the value of AI. Being in Edison's quadrant is liberating in some sense because the path is clear, investments can be low, and value assessment can be fast.
- Pasteur's Quadrant: These are the organizations which perform user-inspired basic research and innovations. They keep users in mind while innovating. The innovations are fundamental but keep practicality and usefulness on their radar. Practically, this is the best quadrant to be in, where the innovations are fundamental but at the same time provide benefits to the enterprise in the short term.

In practice, organizations will cycle through these quadrants. Consider an organization that wants to roll out chatbot services for its customers. In the first attempt, it may want to update the existing chatbot APIs via transfer learning and platforms to engage with customers. This will put the organization in Edison's quadrant. Next, based on user experience, it may discover gaps in current chatbots and start a focused research and development effort to fill those gaps. This will put the organization in Pasteur's quadrant. Finally, the team figures out an exciting agenda around collaborative chatbots where the chatbots can work together to solve the customer problem. This collaboration requires new algorithmic innovations but investing in it may help the organization to leapfrog the competition in a decade.

Technology Trends

Throughout the book and this chapter, we have provided multiple examples of how companies have innovated using

AI. Now, let's look at some of the core AI areas which provide opportunities for innovation and are extremely relevant for organizations.

Federated Learning

Traditionally, AI pipelines were built on the assumption that all data is available at a central location. The learning algorithms can access the data to learn the model structure and parameters. This centralized model works well on relatively smaller data sets but is not practical for big data. Centralized learning takes too much time, resources, and advanced programming methods to handle tera bytes of training data.

To alleviate this, researchers proposed introducing distributed learning algorithms where the data is split into small parts, and then training a local model on each partition. These local models are then aggregated into the final global model. Studies have shown that the global model learnt via aggregation of smaller models performs very close to the true global model. The data is split across multiple compute sites such that all the sites get the overall global distribution to learn the local model. This makes the aggregation of local models easier. In this paradigm, the engineering team has full control and visibility into each compute site, including its configuration, whether it is up or not, what is the current resource utilization, etc. One can think of distributed learning as a completely managed service. This looks pretty good. The data can be divided into smaller chunks and models can be learnt faster. So, what else do we need?

To answer that, let's look at a couple of technology trends first:

1. *Rise of the Multi Cloud*: Multi cloud refers to the architecture where an enterprise uses more than one cloud service provider to manage their IT infrastructure. As per recent studies, on average, companies use five different cloud systems, which results in data being collected and managed

at different sites. This partition of data is very different from what we do in a distributed case. There, one has the flexibility to divide and then ship the data to different sites. However, in this case, the data at each site is what it is. It cannot be changed or merged with other sites. Statistically, this means that each site can have different distribution and hence the local models may not represent the global characteristics. Let's take an example of a global online retailer which operates in India, the US, and Europe. Now, for efficiency's sake (and governance), they may store country-specific transactional data locally, creating three data sites. In the local models for, say, shopping and sales, prediction outlook will only learn from the country-specific models. It will not be trivial to aggregate the models across the countries. At the same time, data from one country cannot be moved to another country. To handle such cases, we need to innovate and extend the notion of distributed learning.

2. *Rise of Low Computational Devices*: Mobile phones and smart sensors are in the category of devices which can capture data and moderate processing on data locally but cannot do heavy AI learning. Let's look at an example of a smartphone keyboard and assume that its task is to predict the next word as a suggestion. Assuming availability of the data from hundreds of users, one can easily build such a model. However, collecting so much data on a central server is not feasible due to the sheer number of such devices and constant new data streams. Coordination and management will be a nightmare. Privacy is yet another constraint. Who would be comfortable sharing all their typing history, including passwords, credit card numbers, and other keypad entries with a central server? Identifying and removing such sensitive data before sharing requires training another AI model entirely. Finally, these devices are not reliable or always available. Sensors can

develop errors; mobile phones can be switched off or go out of internet coverage, among other things.

Clearly, we need a more advanced paradigm of thinking to handle these challenges. This is where federated learning can help. First, the device learns a small model based on local data. Then, this local model (its parameters) is sent to the centralized server, where the centralized server merges local updates into a global model. Finally, the global model is then sent to all the local sites.

This way the data never leaves the local device and alleviates privacy and data transfer concerns. This allows multiple devices across clouds, enterprises, and geographies to collaboratively train models without sharing data.

Even with advancement in core algorithms, there are still open questions which need to be answered for federated learning. The algorithms need to be robust enough to handle the low number of devices which will be active (switched on) at a given point in time; those devices also keep changing. One needs to build advanced aggregation algorithms which can reduce the number of iterations and hence the communication overhead between the local and global servers. While the data is not explicitly shared, an intelligent adversary can still learn data characteristics when local models/updates are sent to the server. So, encryption and privacy-preserving algorithms need to be developed for future-proofing.

Overall, federated learning is the future of AI training, especially in multi-cloud and multi-device settings. Immense progress has been made in the last few years, but a lot of questions need to be answered before it becomes as mainstream as the centralized training paradigm. Interested readers are pointed to resources in the bibliography[7] for deep dive on federated learning.

Multimodal Learning

Most of the examples and case studies deal with tabular/CSV (comma-separated values) data or text data. However, other data types like images, videos, audios, etc. provide an extremely rich source of insights. Think about self-driving cars, where the car is mounted with cameras to sense the surroundings. The on-board AI system analyses the feed in real time to navigate through traffic, stops signs, pedestrians, etc. With the advances in deep neural networks, the AI community has made tremendous progress in understanding such data types. For example, we now have very robust speech (audio) to text, image recognition, and video understanding systems which are used in commercial settings with high RoIs. These applications usually leverage one type of data at a time, which is suboptimal. Ideally, AI systems should use all the data types to provide better business outcomes. The use of multiple signals also helps in reducing the noise and uncertainty in a single source. Moreover, if multiple signals infer the same outcome, then the confidence in the outcome is also much higher.

Before outlining the areas of innovation, lets us look at a very popular multimodal task of a 'visual question answer' session to understand why this area needs more innovation. The task usually has an image and a natural language question, and the system can answer the question by analysing the image. For example, if there is an image of an outdoor scene, the question might be: 'How many people are there?' or 'Is it sunny?' Answering these questions is a complex task which requires natural language understanding (NLU), reasoning, image understanding, natural language generation (NLG), etc. And this is when we *just* have one image and one question! Now, scale that up to millions of images. How about adding audio and video as another source of data? Let us articulate some areas where innovation will be crucial to solving such problems.

- *Different Data Types*: The multimodal AI system should understand how to make sense of different data types which represent the same physical event. In a manufacturing setting, can the images of the final product and the sound the machines produce be correlated to predict if a machine will face a downtime soon and if proactive/predictive maintenance should be done? Joint learning across data types is one of the holy grails in AI and will need innovations over the next decade to reach a reasonable solution.
- *Different Storage Types and Location*: There are different kinds of specialized data storage for each type of the data. For example, Amazon Web Services Time Stream can be used to store temporal data while RDF (Resource Description Framework) can be used for storing linked data. While individual storage choices are optimal for reducing costs, they create additional challenges when it comes to joint learning and inferences.
- *Different Query Languages*: For a minute, let's forget about learning tasks and look at the simpler task of data retrieval. Given a user query, we want to get the relevant data back to the user. Is this simple in a multimodal setting? For starters, different data is stored in different formats, databases, and possibly at different locations. Now, we need to break the user query down, come up with an execution plan, send the smaller pieces to individual data sources, and finally aggregate the results from these sources to return a result to the user. Each of these tasks is non-trivial and requires research and development efforts. Let us explain the complexity of the problem with a simple example.
- The user's query is 'Extract images and sales numbers of the top ten selling shirts'. Clearly, this query needs to be split across the sales database and image database. However, can these queries be executed in parallel? No, because the query only wants top-selling shirts which will be retrieved from the sales database and then the corresponding images will

be fetched. Although this process seems very simple when discussed, it requires a lot of sophisticated decision-making for query-splitting, coming up with an execution plan, passing the partial results around, and finally integrating all partial results. All this for a seemingly simple query!

Natural Language Interfaces

Making computers understand and talk in natural languages is an active area of research. While tremendous progress has been made in this direction, there are tons of exciting problems and pressing issues to be handled. A detailed discussion of this topic will require a book on its own, but here we describe areas which organizations should think about.

Information Retrieval: IR simply refers to the process of finding the correct information, documents, or parts of a document to solve a user query. A rudimentary IR system can be implemented by taking a search term and matching it with every word in the document and returning the document which contains the word. This scheme is neither scalable nor accurate. Various indexing schemes like inverted indices and partitioning are used to store the document for fast scanning. What about the query? If the user types 'New Delhi' versus 'Delhi', should the results be different? Computationally, one can argue that the search phrases are different and hence the results should be different. However, let's look at this from the user viewpoint; the two search terms are the same. So, the IR system needs to have the intelligence to understand such variations. What about something like acronyms or misspelled words?

A lot of existing IR systems already take care of these cases. They can handle acronyms, spelling errors, variations, and much more. So, why are we still talking of IR as a trend to focus on for an AI enterprise? IR is graduating to the next set of problems. In multilingual societies, it is imperative that customers are served in the language they are comfortable with. How can we build a retrieval system which can work across cross lingual documents and also handle transliteration.

Cross-lingual: Can the IR system take a simple English phrase like 'coffee cup' and show results from Spanish documents even though the phrase 'taza de café' is not part of the user query?

Multi-language: Does the user have the ability to specify the query in multiple languages, such as: India का president कौन है (Who is the president of India)? This type of query is common in countries which have multiple languages.

Transliteration: Yet another complexity comes from the very common phenomenon of transliteration. For example, the same query can be asked as: India ka president kaun hai?

Natural Language Understanding

NLU deals with AI algorithms and systems which help computers understand and interact with human languages. NLU systems can understand the intent of a text and can handle grammatical, spelling, and other types of common errors. NLU uses AI algorithms to extract entities, relationship, intent, and other important information which can then be used to answer a user query. For example, a simple query like 'Book me the cheapest tickets from Delhi to Bengaluru for later today' will go through a series of AI components, including lexical analysis, syntactic analysis, semantic analysis, intent mining, and so on to understand that Delhi and Bengaluru are entities; the intent is to 'book' and there is a temporal information on when the booking needs to be done. The chatbot or assistant technology understands entities and the intent to take appropriate action.

Now, one might argue that we already use Siri and Alexa so why is NLU still an interesting area to look at? We argue that typical enterprise setting is far more complex and critical than saying, 'Alexa, play me a song'. Let us look at a bot for providing IT and HR support to employees and what issues we need to solve before such bots can function like human experts.

- *Managing Incomplete Information and Context*: Many times, users do not provide enough information about the issue at hand which then requires the NLU system to go back and forth with the user. This results in a fairly complex dialogue which is not easy to analyse. For example, the user may say, 'My laptop is not working', and now the system needs to ask more questions to get to the core problem. The system needs to maintain the context and history to even ask the right question. If the user specifies that the 'laptop is not progressing beyond the boot-up screen', then it will not make any sense to ask, 'Is the laptop plugged in?' As one can see, a much more complex response system is required than one which gives the standard response: 'Sorry, I don't understand, please try again.'
- *Inclusion of Domain Information*: Enterprise NLU needs extensive domain-specific knowledge. A generic NLU system will perform very badly in enterprise setting. Building an HR chatbot to answer employee queries on taxation will require the bot to understand all tax rules. Understanding taxation rules or other legal documents is still a big open problem for NLU.

  Domain knowledge inclusion faces multiple problems—in many industries, this information is not available in a consumable format; many out-of-the-box NLU systems do not provide customization points to retrain using domain knowledge; and the domain knowledge can change over time or even across countries.
- *Multiple Questions in a Single Sentence*: Typically, users will ask all their questions in a single utterance. For example: 'I am unable to log on to VPN and cannot check my enterprise email.' While this is a simple task for human agents, it poses a big challenge for an NLU system because there are multiple problems listed in the same sentence, the problems are correlated, and the problems have a causation. The inability to log on to a VPN is causing the mail problem and not the

other way round. Moreover, the email access may not be a problem if the VPN access is solved. However, this will confuse many NLU systems. The system may prioritize the email-access problem first, which will result in a disastrous customer experience.

These are just some sample problems in the context of an enterprise IT bot to illustrate why the problems with NLU are far from solved even if we interact with NLU every day through assistants. Enterprise NLU needs much more innovation to be able to perform at human accuracy. As of now, enterprises handle this by building intelligent and collaborative workflows where humans and machines work together. If the NLU system cannot handle a query confidently, it will seamlessly bring a human into the loop. NLU as an active area for innovation will be around for years to come because the human language is very complex and constant innovation will be needed here.

Natural Language Generation

NLG is an AI system which aims to convert machine-understandable information into a human-understandable format. So, in a sense, it is the exact opposite of NLU.

Traditionally, NLG has been approached via templates and slot-filling algorithms. These templates are predefined and have some blanks which are filled using contextual data and hence natural text is generated. While this method works fine, it is also manual because a person needs to define these templates. Moreover, no new scenario can be handled without someone creating a new template. This method works fine for simple cases and generates high-quality text.

The other approach is a pure learning-based approach which is adopted by GPT-3. It is trained using billions of tokens taken from books, the web, and Wikipedia. The resultant model is extremely accurate in producing content which is indistinguishable from what is produced by humans. The model can be used to converse more accurately with customers. But does it solve the NLG problem? Unfortunately, no. Since GPT-3 learns from public data, it also picks up biased views. For example, Nabla, a French start-up specializing in healthcare technology, tested GPT-3 as a medical chatbot, though OpenAI itself warned against such use. As expected, GPT-3 showed several limitations. For example, while testing GPT-3 responses about mental-health issues, the AI advised a simulated patient to commit suicide.[8] Similarly, studies have shown GPT-3 to be biased against certain religions.[9]

NLG is still an open area of research with many in academia and industry labs working on it.

Now let us look at a realistic use scenario with NLG.

Almost all executives and analysts spend a lot of time making sense of data using Excel sheets, charts, diagrams, etc. They then use these insights to come up with a strategy for the organization. Wouldn't it be great if there was a system which took an input on an Excel sheet and produced natural language explaining the data? If we can marry NLG with business analytics, systems can not only explain data but also provide data-driven actionable insights. Think about the life of a CXO with such data-driven and AI-led technology which analyses the previous day's sales data, generates insights, and delivers it all to a mobile phone—and all before the CXO has had their first cup of coffee in the morning!

Local Language Support

Most NLP models are trained in the English language, considering the availability of a vast amount of text, concentration of researchers, and funding in English-speaking countries. However, with increasing customer bases in non-English-speaking countries, there is a growing realization that the economics supports the creation of models in local languages too. For example, Alexa now supports Hindi and IBM Watson supports more than thirteen languages apart from English.

There are a lot of technical challenges in this area; the biggest among them being the non-availability of training data in local languages. Collecting, curating, and annotating the local language data is an expensive and time-consuming task. However, it provides an excellent opportunity for enterprises to build innovative systems and interfaces to prepare the data. The availability of the data will also enable expediting research in NLP, NLU, and NLG for local languages. For example, Arnab Kumar, who was one of the contributors to the NITI Aayog's discussion paper on the national strategy for AI, provided us a creative example. NITI Aayog was trying to handle the issue of lack of training data for Indian languages. It started its team off with Rajya Sabha speeches which were already translated into multiple Indian languages. With this move, the research community had access to training data for NLP and also a parallel corpus across languages. This simple example shows that, while local language support can get tricky, there are ways around it.

Apart from the data, one needs to build techniques to understand grammar, syntax, semantics, metaphors, and sentence structure, etc. to make significant progress in this area. A lot of this information may already be with local language experts which needs to be elicited in proper fashion.

There are existing toolkits, like iNLTK, for Indian languages which provide text normalization, word segmentation, transliteration, translation, and other capabilities. However, there are still a lot of languages spoken and understood by millions of people which need more attention. Enterprises which can serve in the language understood by customers will eventually be the market leaders.

Quantum Computing

The first thing everyone understands about classical computers is that every piece of information is stored on them as a series of 0s and 1s. All algorithms including those with AI manipulate these bits to generate insights. Quantum computers change this fundamental principle. Instead of bits, the basic unit is qubits. A qubit is able to simultaneously store 0 and 1 using the superposition principle. One qubit maintains the state until it is observed. Two qubits can maintain four states at the same time and computations can be done on all four states simultaneously. As the number of qubits grows, the computation improvements will grow exponentially. The largest quantum computer is a 127-qubit IBM one.

Because of laws of quantum mechanics, including superimposition, quantum computers can perform computations much faster than the fastest classical computer. Below are some kinds of applications of this breakthrough which illustrate why it will be necessary for companies to embrace a quantum way of thinking.

1. *Faster AI*: As we know, learning AI models is a compute-intensive task. However, with quantum computing, such computations can be done trivially, because multiple data elements can be processed directly. While still in the early stages, the initial results are encouraging. IBM researchers have developed a series of quantum algorithms that show how entanglement can improve AI classification accuracy. Readers can get a hands-on experience at https://ibm-q4ai.mybluemix.net.
2. *Molecule and Drug Discovery*: New drug discovery is a fairly complex process which needs to go through trial and error with different combinations. ProteinQure is one such company which is using quantum computers for molecular dynamics simulation to discover new drugs.
3. *Route Optimization*: Volkswagen is working with D-Wave to solve some of the oldest and NP (non-deterministic

polynomial) problems like the travelling salesman problem which cannot be solved using classical computers but are tractable by quantum computers. The teams have already used the solutions to do real-time traffic-aware route planning in many cities across the world.
4. *Modelling Financial World*: JP Morgan Chase (JPMC) is partnering with IBM to model stock movement using quantum computers. A 2019 paper co-written by IBM researchers and members of the JP Morgan's quantitative research team included a methodology to price option contracts using a quantum computer.

There are numerous other efforts around weather prediction, quantum safe encryption, and improving simulation algorithms like Monte Carlo algorithms. While all the applications are at a nascent stage, the promise is immense for organizations, society, and AI. Even if enterprises cannot invest in quantum research, learning and keeping updated is essential. Enterprises can choose other options outlined earlier, like partnering with companies such as IBM or D-Wave or academic centres to make progress in this area.

Viome: Pushing the Boundaries of Science via Innovation

Viome Life Sciences,[10] founded in 2016, is a US-headquartered biotechnology company which uses RNA to analyse health conditions and predict future occurrence of health-related issues. Its mission is to provide data and AI-driven insights to individuals to enable them to take control of their wellness.

Guruduth Banavar, founding CTO of Viome, notes that scientists have now established a clear link between one's health and the microbial organisms present in the gut. Viome translates insights from the body's RNA into personalized nutritional recommendations to help address the root cause of inflammation, biological ageing, and chronic disease. Its AI has analysed data from over 350,000 samples from people across more than 100 countries and can match the molecular patterns from an individual's data with data from people of different ages and give one's biological age. A person's biological age may be very different from how old their body's microbes say they are. Predictive models are learnt to uncover mechanisms of ageing, obesity, irritable bowel syndrome, inflammatory bowel disease, diabetes, colon cancer, oral cancer, and more. Understanding the biology of chronic diseases requires connecting a lot of data points. This is where AI comes into the picture.

Viome's core technology makes sense of data based on RNA gene expression within samples of blood, saliva, and stool to decode the mystery of the human body. According to Guru, the work is 99 per cent reliant on AI, including bioinformatics algorithms, biological pathway analyses, biomarker, and disease target discovery. He says, 'An understanding of chronic diseases started only ten years back. Each sample is hundreds of thousands of rows. Add to it millions of columns where each column represents a gene of the micro-organisms present in our body, like a bacteria, or a yeast, or a virus.' That's the tree of life for him, where he runs his algorithms to find a new pattern every day on tens of thousands of such samples, often doing 10 million reads into about 10,000 features. Dimensionality reduction presents a huge set of algorithmic issues. The 10,000 features that they get are mapped to various biological processes. It could lead them to a metabolic disease, an autoimmune disease, a neurological disease, or a chronic disease like cancer. 'I don't know how we could do this without AI.'

Guru said that he and his team are working with meta-transcriptomic technology which again is a brand-new area of science. The company is breaking new ground towards analysing the RNA data as opposed to the traditional DNA data. RNA data is much richer and larger. Extracting critical information like disease prediction with confidence requires innovative-domain infused algorithms which are scalable and fast. In fact, Guru asserts that, although Viome is a data first company, there are few companies which do more AI than Viome!

Building algorithms to handle such massive data requires innovation at the very core. The Viome team has built a fast and scalable algorithm to analyse, index, and search millions of individual and billions of data points for each individual! One level of innovation is algorithmic innovation to build predictive models. The algorithms are developed by a diverse team of chemists, biologists, AI researchers, and core engineering teams. This close collaboration is the reason why the algorithms are domain-knowledge-infused and follow the best of AI R&D practices. However, think about the computational cost of running AI at this scale.

Viome used to pay exorbitant amounts to cloud service providers for using out-of-the-box AI offerings. It innovated on this front as well and, using open source and custom code, the engineering team redesigned the whole tech stack. By adopting and adapting the best DevOps and MLOps practices, they were able to bring their hosting and running cost down by 90 per cent. Viome has embraced AI and innovated at all levels—platform, algorithms, people, domain knowledge, and scale—to build a new-age bioinformatics company.

It comes as no surprise that Viome is called the Google of RNA metatranscriptomics.

3

AI and Technology

If data is the oil for AI, technology is the engine which converts that oil into energy to propel the organization forward. One needs to invest in acquisition, maintenance, and upgradation of technology to keep the AI relevant and functional. We will go over the different aspects of the data and AI life cycle, how to infuse trust in AI, and multiple other topics. However, let us first look at some of the impediments in the successful adoption of AI, which can be simplified using the technology.

In recent times, we have seen a euphoria around AI models where each AI leader is publishing, publicizing, and (almost) boasting about the models which achieve human or superhuman performances. Examples include image recognition tasks on ImageNet, chatbots, language generation (GPT), etc. One aspect common across all these models is that they all leverage a state-of-the art technology stack for training. For example, GPT-2 takes X weeks to train on Y CPU/GPUs. Imagine if OpenAI had not built the training platforms, would we even have such models in existence? Unfortunately, while everyone wants to reap the benefit of AI models, the platform requirements and investments are often overlooked and undervalued. This could prove to be a costly mistake. All successful AI companies like Amazon, Google, and Flipkart have built and managed fast, scalable, and robust platforms which fuel AI to serve millions of customers and billions of transactions. When in doubt, do remember, there is no AI without IA (information architecture).

The second-most undervalued aspect of AI is investment in getting the right data in the right format. Many business owners (including well-established ones) believe that just because they have sensors and data collection hooks in the applications along with cheap storage media, they are ready for AI. Unfortunately, this is not true! All data is not equally important or even useful. Therefore, one needs to carefully select data which is business critical. It must go through multiple processing steps before it can be used for generating actionable insights. But, for now, let's remember that data must go through a lot of pre-processing, cleaning, and standardization before it can be used for downstream applications.

Gone are the days when the technical team would sit in a dark room and develop an application. A successful AI journey requires multiple people to work in close coordination. A team can include any number of people, including but not limited to data collector, data steward, AI scientist, a DevOps team, a governance officer, a business owner, etc.

Is communication more of a soft skill? Why is it being clubbed under technology? We believe that, with the right set of tools and automation, communication ceases to be *just* a soft skill and, in fact, becomes a tangible and trackable skill. Communication is meant to enable full transparency and access to information as per the role. We now have multiple tools which enable this, for example, Slack/email for group discussions, Github for code collaboration, JIRA for bug tracking, project management and other collaboration tools like Google Docs, Box, and so on. If the tools are used properly, everyone will have access to information about the progress, roadblocks, and decisions. Wrong decisions can be caught and corrected much earlier. Moreover, all team members have a sense of ownership, shared responsibility, and a common goal to make the project successful.

Journey to AI: From PoC to Transformation

Our purpose is not to scare CXOs into believing that a huge upfront investment is required, but rather to provide a blueprint of best practices through different stages of the AI journey so that the focus is at the optimum level. Let us now look at the role technology would play in these stages.

AI PoC

The technology needed for this stage is on an as-needed basis. There is no requirement to extrapolate the future requirements of the technology and plan for it. The AI team should on-board the bare minimum components that are needed to demonstrate the AI value and RoI. However, choosing the right components and configurations remains critical.

Assume that there are two teams in two different enterprises, A and B, trying to build a system to use social media feeds to understand customer sentiment and to generate a list of potential customers. Team A decides to use text files to store the few hundred social media messages offline, read the messages in bulk in a Python programme, and use a ten-word positive and negative sentiment dictionary to flag a customer as satisfied or unsatisfied. The output is stored in a CSV file and mailed to the business team. Team B, on the other hand, decides to use a streaming technology like Apache Storm to read the messages in real time. It uses a crowdsourcing platform like AMT[1] or F8 to get messages labelled as 'positive' or 'negative' to create training data and then train an AI model. The team also spends effort on building a simple UI which can be accessed by business users directly.

Team A did the PoC at a very low cost and fast pace. Was that the best approach? Did it choose the right technology stack to provide confidence to stakeholders about the future success of the effort? Did Team B overinvest in the PoC? There is no right or wrong answer here. Depending on the context and business need, both approaches are valid. The key thing to note is that the technology during the PoC should not only think about the returns but also the investments to support the

PoC. Questions like what the expected value is and what will it take to roll out the PoC in terms of production-level capability should be explicitly asked, answered, and documented. As Mani Subramanian, former head of analytics, BigBasket, says, 'PoCs may reflect benefits at not the expected level but better than current situation. The benefits may be realized over a longer period of time.'

AI Infusion

This is the stage when enterprises build a specialized and focused AI technology and platform team. The team advises and gives recommendations to stakeholders on the correct components for infusing and scaling AI. Ideally, the enterprises should build a horizontal team with architects and technology visionaries to chart out the technology roadmap. This stack has a few different layers and each one requires focus. Let us see four important aspects and why they are critical in the success of AI.

1. *Hardware*: AI often needs specialized hardware like GPUs and fast interconnect switches to scale AI to serve millions of requests per day. The team also needs to suggest the topology of the hardware, keeping in mind the non-functional requirements of fault tolerance, back-ups, performance, etc. It is important to have a knowledgeable team which understands current and future trends. For example, companies which decided to move to a PaaS model to leverage hardware through cloud saved a lot of upfront investments to buy on-premises hardware, AMCs, and support teams. The team should always think if the current decisions will be valid in the coming five years. Of course, it may need to go back to the PoC stage to test new technologies.
2. *Software*: As the name suggests, the correct software, frameworks, and tools are essential for any enterprise. The software landscape is constantly changing. For example,

the industry has gone through a sea of change from simple in-memory graphs (JGraph)[2] to triplets (RDFs) to property graphs (Titan,[3] Neo4J[4]) for modelling linked data. There is no way one can prepare for all-new programming models. However, the technology team should make sure that the architecture is flexible where components can be plugged in and out with minimum changes. Microservices and APIs are among the options. In general, the intercoupling between different components should not be tight and hard coded to make the transition to new software easy.

3. *Development Tools*: Once the hardware and software are ready, the AI developer is brought on board for building the AI model. As mentioned previously, AI talent is a costly resource and, therefore, there should be productivity and automated tools available on the platform so that the focus of the AI developer is on the right tasks. Ideally, the platform should natively support the CI/CD[5] pipeline, automated governance and policy enforcement data, and AI life cycle management, automated testing capabilities, and a variety of other automation tools. These tools not only improve productivity directly by reducing manual and repetitive tasks but also indirectly by reducing errors in the development cycle.

4. *Security and Governance*: Imagine having an efficient platform which hosts enterprise data, applications, and processes without any security or in-built governance! This could be a nightmare and enough of a problem to derail any AI initiatives in an organization. Therefore, there needs to be a Chief Information Security Officer (CISO) team with the right tools for policy management, identifying security risks, and enforcing governance and auditability.

While we have presented the four layers in sequential fashion, the components will work in tandem. For example, some security requirements can be pushed into the hardware. Similarly, not all combinations of software and hardware are equally optimal and the choice of one component may guide decisions in other layers. As per Dr Mayur Datar, chief data scientist, Flipkart,

> *Data engineering actually plays a far bigger role than data sciences or AI/ML. The organizations that have been successful at it are the ones who had invested earlier on and have invested properly in the data engineering platforms, in the data architects because if you get that part of your engineering right, in fact, you make life very easy for your data scientist. And you don't need the top of the line or the best data scientist out there because your data does most of the work for you. So, that is the biggest impediment that I have seen or a roadblock to good adoption to AI/ML.*

AI Transformation

The AI transformation primarily has three aspects related to technology:

1. *Amortization*: The organization starts to build more and more AI-infused applications, discovers new patterns, establishes new business lines, and, in general, begins making heavy use of the technology platform built during the infusion stage. The stack remains the same, so the original cost gets amortized, and the organization sees high returns on very low net new investments. For example, an online food delivery company wants to build a platform to provide multiple options to end users to order food, find the fastest route, deliver the food, and eventually capture customer satisfaction ratings. The initial investment would be for managing restaurant data, setting up CRM systems, tying up with mapping APIs, and real-time notification systems. The company has to invest substantially to build the platform. It can then start using the same platform to open a new business line to let customers order grocery from local shops

and run errands. There will be a sales and marketing effort to on-board local grocery shops to the platform, but, from a technology viewpoint, there is no change required and a new revenue stream can be realized using the technology that already exists.

2. *Calibration*: The amortization pattern is the best-case scenario. In many realistic scenarios, one may need to do some calibration of the stack. This calibration can be on-boarding new components or upgrading to the latest technology. The technology stack is ever-changing, and the enterprise will need to constantly upgrade the stack based on new developments. However, if the platform is correctly constructed during AI infusion, the incremental changes to the platform should be low-cost and not result in too many big changes for the developers, and absolutely no change for the end user. Let's look at the payment component. The earlier payment modes were 'cash on delivery' (customer pays once the food is received) or registering a credit/debit card online. However, newer payment modes like UPI[6] and online payment wallets have since emerged and become the customer's first choice. Therefore, these payment modes must be integrated into the platform by adding new APIs. This is a simple example but such calibration will always be there to leverage the best available technology.

3. *Re-factor*: This is the hardest aspect where, due to technology change, one might have to redesign a part of the platform. It could mean addition of a totally new component which was not envisioned or planned for in the architecture or it could mean (a more painful) replacement of an existing component. For example, in early 2002, RDF and Triplet stores were very popular to model relationships between entities; however, around 2010, knowledge graphs provided a (arguably) better alternative. Such refactoring or replacement can be very costly if the platform is not modular where components can be swapped in and out.

We expect to see all these patterns coexist for an enterprise. For a platform with sound architecture, these changes should not be too complex. We hope that, after understanding these patterns, readers can better understand why we said that there is no AI without IA. Together with open-source projects and embracing the cloud, organizations can really build a super flexible platform which is robust, scalable, and also economical because of the pay as per usage paradigm. This is exactly what Viome did. 'We were able to reduce our compute and storage cost by re-architecting our infrastructure on Open Source and moving it to AWS,' says Guru Banavar, founding CTO of Viome.

Here is a slightly more detailed take on how to take PoC to the production stage from Mani Subramanian, formerly of BigBasket. BigBasket has developed the methodology with the following six steps, referred to as EMBEDD methodology.

- Evolving a hypothesis and KPI
- Mapping the model: I/O, data sources, time horizon of data, etc.
- Building the model: Scala and Spark
- Evaluating the model with respect to multiple metrics
- Deployment: Production platform finalization, scalability, responsiveness
- Deepening the model: Iteration of model 1.0 to 2.0. Establishing RoI of the improved model.

Data and AI Life Cycle

So far, we have seen different stages of AI infusion in an organization and how factors like strategy and innovation impact its life cycle. In this chapter, we will go over the AI life cycle which will hold true for all phases of AI infusion and will help organizations to move towards AI transformation. From a bird's-eye view, the AI life cycle can be broken into three phases, with governance being enforced throughout the process.

FIGURE 3.1: Bird's-Eye View of AI Life Cycle

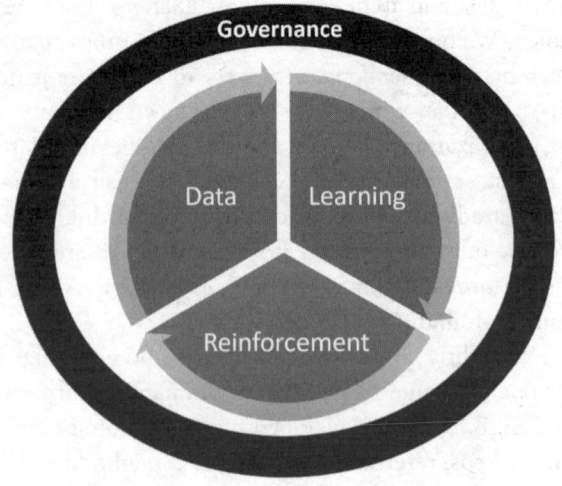

Phase 1: Data

This phase prepares data for upstream modelling tasks. This is the most important step for ensuring the success of any AI project. Availability of data is not a necessary and sufficient condition to go on the AI journey. The data needs of AI are significantly different from that of business analytics systems. For example, tabular representation may be the best and easiest to run business intelligence queries and develop charts; however, for many AI tasks, a tensor representation might be most suitable and compact. Moreover, AI has shown significant progress in areas of images, videos, audio, etc., which are traditionally not used for business intelligence. Therefore, the management of such data sets will require fresh thinking, infrastructure, and talent. Some common steps during this phase include data collection, quality assessment, selection, cleaning, normalization, labelling, redaction, deletion, etc. While these operations have been around for decades, for AI tasks, many of their aspects need to be reimagined. What if the data is not pattern-rich for effective modelling or if the data has bias? To solve this problem, new-age quality metrics like Bias, Label Skew, or Feature Sparsity need to be introduced to assess if the data is good enough for AI. Siloed data poses yet another challenge for extracting optimal value from it.

Phase 2: Learning

As the name suggests, this phase deals with task-specific model learning from the data. Ideally, the model needs should be grounded in the business requirements and constraints. Unless there is a tight integration across the two, it is very difficult to build a model which will generate business outcomes. For example, consider the case of building a model for deciding if an applicant should be given a loan or not. There are two ways to approach this problem. One is to take historical data and build a highly accurate model based on it. Accuracy is one of the most common metrics and often the most used one. However, in this example, one of the other business constraints could be to make sure that the model is fair and does not discriminate based on, say, gender, skin colour or religion. This additional constraint will require the AI scientist to do things very differently. First, she has to check if the historical data is unbiased. If not, then she must work with the data steward and the content team to fix the problem. Next, in the model-learning phase, she must take care of balancing and optimizing both accuracy as well as fairness. There may be a trade-off between the two and hence a continuous dialogue between the AI team and business team will ensure that, out of the many possible correct models, the one which satisfies the business need is picked. This is a simple example to show how the AI team needs to be fully integrated across different business functions to make sure that the learning phase is productive and in line with business expectations to produce usable models. The most common learning tasks are classification, clustering, prediction, anomaly detection, etc.

The learning algorithms strive to meet the business goal by optimizing for the corresponding technical objective or loss functions. Examples of objective functions include root mean square errors, entropy, area under the curve, etc.

Phase 3: Continuous Reinforcement

One of the key differences between AI and traditional business analytics lies in the fact that an AI system keeps updating itself by learning from its environment: new training data, user feedback, or payload data. We refer to all these tasks collectively as a 'feedback loop', and it is critical to keep AI models up to date. The model update to account for feedback can primarily happen in two ways. First, the new feedback can warrant that the current model should be discarded, and a completely new model be built from scratch. The second option is that the knowledge from the new data is absorbed into the old model by fine-tuning its hyperparameters.

Each of these options has benefits as well as shortcomings. For example, when the new model is built from scratch, one has to ensure that the decisions made by the old model are still valid. The new model cannot significantly change the decisions made by the earlier model. In highly regulated use cases like compliance, the requirement of old decisions still holding could be even stricter. The option of upgrading the current model comes with its own challenges, such as incorporating all the new data into the old model. Many times, new data conflicts with old data, in which case updating the model will be a complex task. Continuous reinforcement helps keep the model up to date. However, we should exercise extreme caution in this process. Many times, the feedback could be wrong or noisy. In such cases, blindly going through the feedback loop will do more harm than good.

Many AI researchers and practitioners mistakenly equate AI with the learning phase. While it is true that actionable models are built in this phase, the responsibility that the models are of high quality and always up to date falls on the adjoining phases.

The above three phases will guide an AI practitioner to build and run a model in a controlled environment like a laptop or with very restricted usage. However, the teams will face an impediment when convincing others to use their model. The key element missing in this is governance. To realize the full value of an AI model, each phase should be governed, audited, and trusted.

What Does the Term 'Governance' Really Mean?

1. Data governance is a set of rules, policies, and roles which are defined to make sure that the data is used in a safe and compliant fashion. It can be as simple as having access control policies or as complex as enforcing regulations. Global Data Protection Regulation or GDPR[7] is one such regulation. It describes how the data should be stored, how it should be used, and how it should be managed. One of the other goals of data governance is to make sure that the data is usable for AI learning. This implies that the data should be usable, searchable, of high quality, and sharable in a policy-compliant fashion. For example, data governance tools are responsible to make sure that the data is unbiased. Data which has sensitive personal information like credit card numbers or addresses needs to be handled with even more care. Typically, either the sensitive information is redacted, or the data is encrypted on the disk to protect against any leakage. Data governance also covers the process of acquisition of data. For example, any data collected should be accompanied with a signed consent form from the subjects. Moreover, data lineage— the ability to track how the data changes or flows through the enterprise—is an important aspect of data governance systems. Data governance, if done right, can provide an organization the maximum value by enabling policy compliance, sharing, providing data scientists with

high-quality data and auditors with all the information required for regulatory audits.

2. Governance during learning ensures that the model is trustworthy. The most commonly used principles of trust are fairness, generalizability, explainability, and availability of audit trails. Let us briefly go over these.

- Fair or unbiased models do not provide systematic advantage or disadvantage to certain sections or individuals. Many use cases warrant that certain attributes are not used in the learning phase. The input training data may contain information about a person's age, gender, location, and other sensitive personal information. If this data is directly fed into a learner system like AutoAI[8] or AutoML,[9] there is a high probability that the model will give more importance to some of these attributes to learn the decision boundary. It is obvious to see that the model will be biased and show unintended side effects if used in production.
- Generalizability[10] refers to the ability of the model to handle the noise or different distributions in training data. In essence, the models should be generalizable and not overfit the training data. Overfitting is a learning artefact where the model performs very well on training/seen data, but the performance deteriorates significantly on payload/unseen data. One common way this problem is handled is by creating a hold-out set from training data. During the learning phase, the hold-out data is not used in estimating the parameters. Once the AI scientist is satisfied with the model, it is evaluated on the hold-out data to get an estimate of accuracy, fairness, or any other metric on unseen data.
- Explainability[11] is the ability to explain the outcomes of the model. This is a very important aspect as more and more AI is put into practice. Why will anyone trust an AI model? The complex part is that explainability has

different meanings for different personas. For example, consider our AI-infused hiring system. An applicant is interested in knowing why he was rejected and how he can improve his chances. The recruitment officer is interested to know if the model is indeed selecting the best candidates. The developer of the system wants to understand the performance numbers and why they are not up to the expectations. So, as we can see, there needs to be a different form of explainability to satisfy all queries. In highly regulated industries like healthcare, legal, workforce, etc., the presence or absence of explainability may be the deciding factor for a model to be used in production or not. We have seen what audit trails mean for data. Extending the same line of thought, auditability for a model seeks to answer for the model. The questions like what data is used for training the model, how the model is tested, who built and approved it can be easily answered if proper audit trails are maintained.

To provide this level of trust in the model, it should be tested by generating test cases and evaluating various metrics like fairness, robustness, sensitivity, etc. Both white-box and black-box testing should be performed. White-box testing is when the internal mechanics/parameters of the model can be accessed and used for testing. It is usually done by developers of the system. Black-box testing refers to testing the API of the model. No internal working, architecture, or parameters can be used in it. Irrespective of the testing form, it should be performed outside of the data science team to avoid any potential conflict of interest.

3. Governance for a deployed model is essential to guarantee that the model, firstly, scales and is able to serve millions of incoming requests with reasonable latency, and, secondly, the quality of the outcomes do not deteriorate. Model metrics like accuracy, fairness, performance, and throughput, among

others, should be continuously monitored and relevant alerts should be raised in case of any deviations in the metrics. Policy compliance is yet another important aspect for run-time governance. For example, in a typical deployment where the same system is served via multiple geographies and the requests are routed to the available system, care should be taken of local regulations. For example, the policy may mandate that payload data from one country cannot be sent to another. Moreover, many times, the payload data is stored to run diagnostics and improve the model. This storage should be done after getting consent from the users and should follow strict data protection and encryption methodology.

There is also a need to secure AI models from a newer class of attacks like 'model poisoning' where an adversary sends 'bad' samples or 'bad' feedback to the API with the intention that, during re-learning, the model will learn from them and misbehave. Such attacks have gained a lot of importance in recent years due to the evidence that carefully crafted noise can fool AI systems. An example of this is an attack on Microsoft's Tay Twitter bot[12] which was 'taught' to tweet racist tweets. In 2016, Microsoft launched the bot on Twitter. It was supposed to interact with the Twitter user and engage them in a dialogue. The bot also had a feedback loop where it constantly learnt from the ongoing dialogues to improve itself. However, a bunch of adversaries got together and started to converse with the bot using bigoted and racist language. Within a matter of twenty-four hours, Tay started tweeting extremely racist tweets.

Similarly, Eykholt, et al.[13] show that, by injecting noise in traffic signal images, image detection algorithms in self-driving cars can be fooled to not recognize stop signs or red lights. A not-so-robust model in production can have a catastrophic impact.

AI AND TECHNOLOGY

Henceforth, we will use the term 'AI governance' to include all aspects of trust in data and the AI life cycle. In later sections, we will cover more intricacies of trustworthy AI and also point to tools which can make it easy for an enterprise to embark on this journey.

Data Life Cycle

Figure 3.2 shows the important steps which need to be performed on data before it can be used for generating insights.

Please note that we do not show these steps in a cyclical fashion because in all practical scenarios they are not performed in a specific order. For example, if a data set is found to be of poor quality, it can trigger a new data acquisition step. Similarly, if the data cannot be discovered, then it should trigger metadata assignments to generate better searchable terms.

FIGURE 3.2:

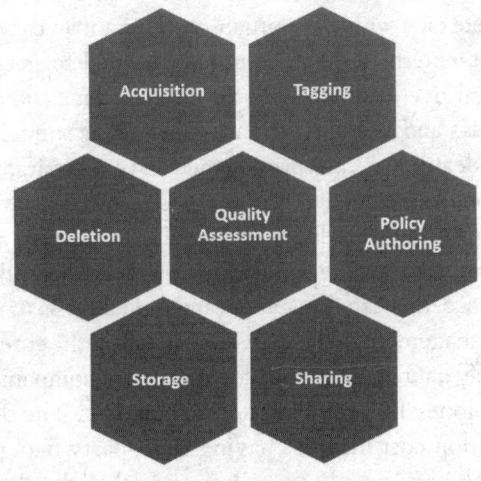

Let us look at each of these steps in a bit more detail:

1. *Acquisition:* This is perhaps the simplest step to understand how we get the data to fuel downstream AI processes. It is a critical step in the enterprise data life cycle. All forms of data, including transactional data, operational data, text, images, sensors, videos, and anything in between need to be collected, managed, and used. The data acquisition comes in two forms: from within the organization and sourced from external parties.

   One may imagine it should be very easy to make internal data available to the AI team. Unfortunately, the truth cannot be further from this. In big organizations, the data is often managed by a line of businesses with their own management, control, and policies. This control is mandated by security (sometimes perceived and misplaced) or technology: for example, a line of business (LoB) using Virtual Storage Access Method (VSAM) to manage the data which cannot be easily consumed by RDBMS (Relational Data Base Management System) practitioners. Breaking these silos to acquire the complete data within the organization is not an easy task. Lot of intra-enterprise work is usually needed to get it. While the legal overhead is lesser for internal data, the enterprise processes and LoBs' reluctance often act as stumbling block here. Ideally, the enterprise should have a separate business function like a chief data office (CDO) which serves the entire company's data needs. This unit should be responsible for managing, governing, and providing access to other users. In essence, one can think about individual LoBs to outsource data management to the CDO and focus on the core business.

   Since data is so valuable, there are companies which make money by providing and selling data. The direct data acquisition cost includes paying third-party data providers or employing people to collect and label the data. While the immediate cost of buying data is well understood, there are multiple other costs which should be considered. For example, data which contains sensitive information on individuals will require organizations to invest in setting up strong governance mechanisms. Other costs include specialized storage costs, data deletion policies, keeping the data up to date, etc. Similarly, the data might be available in non-standard formats like PDFs or MP4s. Processing such data before usage can be an additional cost.

Consider a stock recommendation company which wants to access the financial records of all publicly listed companies. It can go two ways—either get the free PDF from each company's investor relation webpage or pay specialized companies like Dun and Bradstreet that provide APIs[14] to get access to clean and curated data. In the first case, the enterprise would need to clean the data on its own before it can be used. This will be an ongoing process to clean the data every time quarterly results are declared. On the other hand, one will need to pay for the Dun and Bradstreet subscription service. So, one needs to factor all this in before deciding on the best mechanism to get external data into the company.

As readers would know, many of these costs can be recurring in nature. Nowadays, many organizations have a dedicated content acquisition team which looks at various factors before bringing the data in. The other critical aspect of acquisition is adhering to regulations. For example, while purchasing third-party data which contains personal information, it is essential to evaluate if the data comes with the consent of the individuals. If the consent is not available, the data should not be acquired. The other way to acquire data is to look for free public sources like social media, newspapers, blogs, etc. However, do remember that not everything public is free, so, extreme caution needs to be exercised while getting this data and the terms and conditions need to be carefully understood before bringing the data into the organization.

2. *Tagging:* There are two seemingly conflicting phenomena at work when it comes to data. The first is that organizations spend a lot of energy and effort to manage huge amounts of

data. The second is that users or employees cannot find and use the data they need quickly.

This paradox is often the outcome of an absence of a robust metadata[15] assignment methodology. If the data cannot be found, then it cannot be monetized. Metadata assignment is targeted towards alleviating this problem. Ideally, every data set should have associated metadata which captures key properties of the data. Metadata includes:

- Data properties including distributions, minimum value, maximum values, unique values, variance, etc.
- Data tagging to see if the data is sensitive or personal in nature.
- Advanced data features like associations,[16] correlations, bias, noise, missing values, etc.
- Business terms which assign business meaning to the data. For example, a column named CID is assigned the business term 'customer identification number'.
- Audit-related metadata like lineage[17] to store where, when, and how the data came into the enterprise.
- Data quality metrics for AI[18] which helps users know the usefulness of data for downstream AI tasks. These metrics include label noise, data richness, etc.

Broadly, the above-mentioned metadata can be grouped into two classes.

Semantic or Technical Metadata: This includes metadata which is purely a property of the data without any external context. For example, the technical metadata for the column 'Name' may include data type as string, minimum length, maximum length, sensitive personal information (SPI) flag. The metadata may also include a link to another table which has a column of the same/similar semantic name. In many cases, the data lineage information is also a part of the metadata.

Business Metadata: This captures the essence of the data from a business process viewpoint. Continuing the same example, the business metadata will map 'Name' in the customer table to the customer's name in business ontology while 'Name' in the product table gets mapped to the product's name.

If done in the correct fashion, the metadata will provide the fuel to an organization's data discovery process which is an enabler for optimizing value from data. This metadata can make data discovery in an organization very easy.

Typically, metadata-tagging is done by a specialized data steward. However, the next generation of metadata systems include automatic metadata generation. These systems can go over the data lake and generate very high-quality metadata. Similarly, data discovery using natural language interfaces is yet another hot area of investments. Metadata together with advanced discovery algorithms can enable optimal value generation from the data. For example, a business user can simply request data in the natural language: 'Give me sales data for North America where the customers have spent more than $100,000 for the last two quarters.' Using metadata, one can really point to the right tables, including CRM, orders, location code, etc., to get the answer to this query. Even if the system cannot provide an exact answer, reducing the search space from thousands of tables to tens will help tremendously.

3. *Quality Assessment*: The cliched idiom of 'garbage in, garbage out' is apt for AI applications too. If the training data is not of good quality, then the resultant model cannot be good enough to be put in production. As a rough estimate,[19] 80 per cent of the time is spent in data preparation as opposed to 20 per cent on AI building and managing. Moreover, low-quality data will have a multiplicative impact in an enterprise. Think about the increased effort the data scientist team will need to put in to develop a good model from bad data. Historically, data quality assessment has focused on making the data ready for business analytics, reporting, and building the dashboard. The relevant quality assessment

includes missing data, standardization, normalization, etc. However, data quality takes a very different view when the downstream application is AI modelling. We need to look at a new class of metrics which directly influences AI. For example, what if the data is biased, has a class skew or a wrong label? Unless the aspects are detected and handled in the data, the modelling or any other use of the data will be suboptimal and result in bigger issues in the later part of the AI-infused business process. Let us look at some of the common data quality issues:

- *Data Format Issues*: Due to different processes of collecting data, or if the data is a from combination of multiple sources, it is highly likely that it will have different formats. The most common example is the date column which can be represented in multiple formats including dd/mm/yy, mm/dd/yy, dd/mm/yyyy, etc. All the formats are correct but, if they are not converted to a single format, the downstream tasks will suffer.
- *Data Recency*: In many applications, real-time data is more important than old data. For example, consider an IoT application of predicting energy consumption per hour in a building based on the number of occupants. If the application is not fed the most recent occupancy data, the model's prediction will deviate a lot from the actual consumption. As you can see, this is not a problem with the model but the data which is used by the model.
- *Different Representations of the Same Data*: A typical problem in enterprise data integration is entity resolution, where the same entity is being represented by different values in different data sets. A simple value-matching exercise will not help in resolving these entities. For example, one data set may have the name stored as John Doe while the other one has J. Doe. Advanced entity resolution algorithms need to be used here to see that

J. Doe is indeed the same as John Doe ... or can it be Jane Doe? Advanced algorithms, which can collate information from multiple sources and infer the correct matching entities, are required to handle such issues.
- *Outliers*: Outliers[20] are simply the data elements which look very different from most of the other points. These could come in due to wrong or careless data entry, mistake in data transformations, or simply a measurement error. For example, the sensor shows a temperature of 40 degrees Celsius on a December morning in New Delhi. Outliers are somewhat easy to detect because they look very different from the rest of the data. However, a related phenomenon of concept drift should also be considered. Concept drift refers to a slow and gradual change in the data which could be mistaken for an outlier locally, but it is not. Let's look at a clothing store as an example. The store wants to analyse shopping patterns for inventory management. The analysts observe that 98 per cent of their sale is of summer shirts and 2 per cent of winter jackets. Now, this 2 per cent can be treated as an outlier and more summer shirts are ordered. The next day, the distribution is 97 per cent and 3 per cent, and the same model from the previous day is applied. However, over time, the distribution changes to 80–20. Suddenly, the winter jackets are not outliers. Looking back, the pattern is clear that this was the end of summer and the start of winter and hence people were starting to buy jackets. The first 2 per cent was not an outlier but the starting point of a concept drift. This is a difficult situation to handle but one that is encountered frequently. The AI team should keep an eye on this, especially in real-time data applications.
- *Erroneous Data*: While outliers can be detected and corrected, another class of wrong data exists which is much more difficult. For example, consider census

data where we encounter the following data: 'Age: 13, Education: Master's'. This is clearly wrong, but the difficulty is that we do not know which attribute is wrong. Is the age supposed to be thirty-one? Or is the education level incorrect?

- *Label Noise*: This metric is specifically useful for supervised AI tasks. In supervised tasks, there is a feature vector and a class label for that feature vector. For example, the applicant data in our résumé-screening example is the feature vector while the decision of whether to hire is the class label. What if the class label is wrong? In such cases, the model cannot confidently learn the decision boundary to differentiate between 'hire' and 'don't hire' candidates. According to an estimate, the popular data set of ImageNet has approximately 100,000 wrong labels. Unless these details are corrected, they will show up as misclassification errors in the model.[21]

One important aspect to note is there is no 'correct' way to clean data for AI. For example, what one application considers a data bias may be a prerequisite for another application. This is a departure from traditional data quality where missing data is considered unwanted property, irrespective of the upstream Business Intelligence task. Therefore, in some cases, we should look at quality assessment for AI as the generation of more metadata. If bias is detected in the data, then, instead of auto-cleaning, we can add the details of a data bias as metadata and different users can decide to clean the data based on their requirements.

4. *Policy*: Data provides a great opportunity and leverage for enterprises. However, with this opportunity comes the big responsibility of using the data in a compliant, safe, and governed fashion. In fact, it might be better to not use the data at all than to use it in a non-compliant fashion. Therefore, it is non-negotiable that organizations have strong policy

enforcement. Let us look at some of the common types of policies.

- *Access Control*: This is largely self-explanatory. Only authorized users should be able to use the data. Apart from access, the policy should also note the kind of access—read, write, append, etc. This is simple to understand but tough to operationalize. Everyone in an organization would request access to all the data. Therefore, a proper process needs to be there to vet requests and only clear valid ones. Please note that the organization should not put an artificial upper limit on the number of requests; instead, all valid requests should be approved. Moreover, a complete audit trail of the access requests should be managed.
- *Data Use Policy*: Simply controlling access to data may not be enough because the same data could be used for a variety of applications and some of those applications may be in a grey area and not strictly compliant. Therefore, the data access request should be accompanied by the intended use of the data. The approver should carefully look at the intended use before clearing the request. Let's say that the use of face recognition technology to mark employee attendance is a valid use of data. However, using the same technology to monitor if employees are attentive or not during office hours will be a clear breach of privacy. Please remember that the data is only as good as the application it is used for. The same data which opens multiple revenue streams for a company can also turn into a PR nightmare.
- *Fine-grained Policy*: So far, we have looked at the policies which are enforced at a data-set level. Now, consider a data set which has one sensitive column, such as date of birth. How should we define the policies for such a data set? It should ideally be restrictive because it has one sensitive column. To handle this situation, we have

fine-grained policies which are enforced on a subset of columns. One should be able to define a policy to say that the data set can be shared if the sensitive column is either not shared or is only shared in an encrypted fashion.

The enterprise policy engine should be rich enough to encode and enforce diverse policies. Some standard policy classes include access control policies based on roles, access control based on location, further sharing and distribution of data, deletion of data, etc. With the proliferation of hybrid cloud and multi-cloud, location-based policies are also becoming important, such as ensuring that data about employees in India is not accessed by a compute site hosted in Europe. Readers will appreciate the complexity in even authoring such policies. This is an ongoing area of research and development.

5. *Storage*: There was a time when most data was tabular and there were highly efficient and scalable relational database management systems to store and index such data sets. SQL was the query language of choice to extract information from such databases. Now, there are multitudes of data types including text, images, video, audio, graphs, etc. Each one of them requires a specialized database for storage and a specialized language to retrieve the data and run analytics. To add to the complexity, the data is never static and data updates are either in real time or in batches. The requirement is amplified during multimodal AI learning. For example, simultaneously learning from text and images will require data to be fetched from multiple databases.

Choosing the right data format and data storage can help accelerate the AI journey for a business. Therefore, proper due diligence should be done in this step. A good data engineer will make the wrong choice work as well (at least initially) but soon it will become unmanageable.

Let us look at an example. While advising a set of master's students of a prestigious university in India, we picked up a problem of link prediction. The students did not know any graph or RDF store like DB2 RDF or Titan, so they decided to mimic the graph through relational tables. Sure enough, it started off easy, as the end point of each edge were stored as two columns of the table and the graph was modelled. To browse such graphs, we had to write complex self-join queries. However, the team was convinced that they had to write and optimize this function only *once*. How wrong they were!

Soon, we got extra information about the type of relationships—friends, relatives, co-workers, etc. Suddenly, the simple two-column schema was not enough. So, more columns had to be added and access functions had to be rewritten. As soon as the team settled into this, we got more information about the people, including their names, location, interests, and so on. At this point, the team gave up on extending the schema and instead decided to learn knowledge graphs (Titan). Within two weeks, we had a graph database which was able to accommodate all incoming data. Tasks like browsing, path finding, and other graph algorithms were a breeze to write using native GREMLIN commands.

Choosing the right database is one part of the solution, but the database should be configured correctly with the right indexes, fault tolerance back-ups and the geography to host the database. For example, if the text data and graph data are used frequently in many applications, then they should be physically co-located to get maximum performance and throughput.

Finally, a micro services architecture should be adopted so that the data is always accessed through APIs and not directly. APIs provide an extra layer of security and governance. Moreover, with API, back-end systems can be replaced without changing the downstream applications as long as the API remains the same.

One area which any organization with AI inspirations should invest in is building a data management middle layer. This layer is composed of APIs and utilities which can be used by AI scientists to access any slice of data without writing complex queries, going to different data sources one by one and then merging the data sets post hoc. For example, a query like 'Get all logs tickets for customers in New Delhi for the last month and for those customers get the average account balance' should be done via collection of APIs. In the absence of each layer, the scientist will need to get access credentials to each data set and write complex nested queries. An added advantage of a common access middle layer is that auditability comes for free.

6. *Sharing*: Now we have some great high-quality data which is stored in the most efficient fashion and is governed as per regulations. Is this enough? NO! Unless the data can be shared and used by multiple people, all efforts to make it good is not worthwhile. How do we enable data-sharing? The answer is by cataloguing data. A data catalogue is the binding glue which brings together all the aspects we have discussed so far. The catalogue is an index of all data sets available in an organization along with its metadata and quality metrics. Policy enforcement is also one of the core responsibilities of the catalogue, which serves as a single point of entry for all data needs.[22]

All the data and associated metadata are indexed in this catalogue. Please note that the catalogue may not be a physical data store but store pointers to actual data sets. This way the catalogue can be thought of as a layer between physical data assets and users. The catalogue should also manage the credentials to data sets so that they are not shared over email or phone (which is a rampant practice). One of the other important functionality which the catalogue should support is effective search. This functionalities should be able to search the metadata and other descriptions associated with the data to provide the user a shortlist of data they may be interested in. With the right catalogue, organizations would have strong governance and credential security and be able to identify duplicate data assets. The other advantage of a catalogue is lineage data with which commonly used assets can be identified and virtualized or rarely used assets can be spotted and a root cause analysis can be done to see if the quality of data is an issue.

7. *Deletion*: The AI team is often hungry for more data and does not believe in deleting data. More is always better is the unofficial maxim. However, deletion or archiving of data is essential for three reasons:
   - *Operational Efficiency*: If the older and redundant data is not removed, then, over time, data access APIs will get slow and result in overall slowness of business processes.
   - *AI Efficiency*: For tasks like the next best action, demand prediction, etc., recent data is much more important than older data. If older data is not removed, either the data scientist will need to do more modelling work, or algorithms will suffer due to data which contributes less but still needs to be modelled.
   - *Regulations*: Finally, regulations like GDPR[23] mandate that organizations should have a data deletion capability and a customer can request organization to forget her data. This becomes a legally binding contract between a data owner and the enterprise.

   Deleting or archiving old data is a simpler task because one can just select the data by date and archive or move it to a less expensive storage option. However, deletion of data as per individual consumer requests or needs is a bit hairy. It should first be possible to extract the data at the customer level. Remember, we are still at a point where the organization does not even know what data assets it has. To accomplish this, one needs to manage a very fine-grained data lineage and data tracking.

Model Learning

In this section, we will go over different aspects of model learning. We will not cover the learning techniques but instead provide a step-by-step playbook which can be followed by enterprises for the successful infusion of AI.

1. *Business Goals/KPI Identification*: The primary goal of any AI infusion tasks undertaken in an organization should be to improve a business KPI. The target business goal or KPI should be identified on day zero. Ideally, this process should start from a business user and then the AI team should be brought on board. Conversion of the business metric to AI goals is a non-trivial task and can take significant time. But, without this, one cannot compute the RoI of AI infusion. The goals can be a functional requirement which map directly to the business problem and non-functional requirements which may not contribute directly to business but are essential for successful deployment like latency.

   For example, an HR team wants to build AI models to rank résumés for their interview process. The business KPI to improve is the number of candidates hired versus the number interviewed. The functional metric is to build a model which can predict with high accuracy if the given candidate will clear the interview or not. The non-functional metrics are that the model should not have any bias against the candidates, be able to handle thousands of résumés every day, and so on. As it is clear, converting a high-level business goal to technical metrics will take multiple iterations with business users. Often, these iterations go through expedited processes, resulting in a half-baked understanding of business goals. This results in a huge expenditure for enterprises when the trained model does not pass the business quality assurance test and the whole process either restarts or is shelved. Finally, the business discussion should also document the existing information architecture in the organization. For example, if the organization does not support a graph database but graphs are required, this should be discussed with stakeholders before starting the development.

2. *Training*: Once the goals are established and the data needs are satisfied, the development of the model starts. The AI team will train multiple models, each differing in architecture, hyper parameters, and objective functions. However, the data scientist should also keep the non-functional requirements in mind so that she can take the correct modelling choices. For example, there will be a trade-off between a highly accurate model and the associated running/inference time. A seasoned developer will be able to manage these choices. While the functional and non-functional requirements provide a good handle on model choices, the AI team should also keep an eye on complexity. Often, complex models will take more effort to manage and update when new data comes in.

Since model training is iterative and the data scientist will go through multiple choices of architecture and techniques before arriving at the final model, it is important to keep track of the different choices tried and what impact it has on model metrics. Without meticulous bookkeeping, the process can soon become unmanageable and ad hoc, resulting in a loss of compute resources and development times.

3. *Model Testing*: Just how in the traditional software development cycle the developer tests his own code in the development environment before handing it over to the next phase, in model testing[24] too the AI needs to test and verify if the model satisfies the original goal. Since the developer

has access to internals of the model, this phase of testing is known as White Box Testing. Apart from following the standard train-test-hold-out set methodology, it might be necessary to generate additional test data to do focused testing.

Let us look at an example: consider a three-class classification model where the model learns to predict one of the three classes: A, B, or C. Using standard hold-out validation, the AI team observes an accuracy of 95 per cent. At first glance this looks very good. But let us dig deeper and plot the confusion matrix[25] for the same problem. The confusion matrix estimates per class accuracy. Looking at the confusion matrix, the AI tester realizes that the model does very well for Class A and B, almost reaching an accuracy of 99 per cent. However, it does very badly for Class C. Upon further analysis, he realizes that the number of samples for Class C in the training data were very less (and even lesser in the validation set) and therefore the model's performance for Class C is not statistically valid. The team needs more Class C samples. Now there are two options:

- It can go back to the data content team to request more data for Class C.
- It can generate more Class C data.

As we can see, careful testing, especially around corner cases, can stop promoting the wrong/suboptimal model to production. The testing can also generate very actionable insights not just for the data science team but also for the data steward. The outcome of testing could trigger model retraining or in some cases even the data acquisition step. The AI model is more or less useless in isolation. Shocked? Let us explain. No one will commission an AI model with requirements like 'Build a face recognition model'. The goal will be: 'We want to automate the attendance system in schools and hence let us use face recognition technology.'

The business requirement is the genesis of the AI model. Therefore, the model needs to be tested in the context of the business process and application.

4. *Business Process Testing*: To close the loop of business requirements, it is critical that the AI model should be tested within the actual business process. This can be thought of as a parallel to integration testing in the software engineering world. Many times, while individual models perform satisfactorily, getting them to work together for a common goal requires some work.

   For example, consider the HR use case we outlined earlier. For résumé ranking, we need two models:
   - To process the unstructured résumé to extract key value pairs like name, age, education, previous experience, etc.
   - To predict the hiring or no-hiring decision based on the key value pairs.

   Now, each model will have its own error rate. However, the error introduced in the first model will have a severe impact on the dependent second model. Individual AI teams may claim around 90 per cent accuracy in their models but then applications will have much lower accuracy due to cascading errors. Individually, each model performs within the agreed upon error ranges but collectively the pipeline will not meet the goals.

   Therefore, an end-to-end AI-infused business process testing is a must before drawing up production plans for the model. It may not be important to monitor metrics like accuracy when doing this testing. In fact, the focus should be to measure the change in business KPIs. In our hiring example, business users should measure if the AI model helped in improving the quality of new hires, reducing the time taken to process candidates or any other hiring-related metrics. Individual model metrics become less important in business process testing.

5. *Model Documentation*: As discussed earlier, AI models will constantly be updated, and it will not be prudent to assume that the original team will always be around. Just like documentation plays an important role in traditional software engineering, we need to follow AI documentation with the same rigour. We may need to do more for AI models. For example, the choices of architecture tried and discarded during model development need to be thoroughly documented so that the work is not repeated by new team members. Ideally, the documentation should also maintain negative results. If some technique was tried and it did not yield good results, it is important to document it. Without this, the next data scientist will take same decisions and reach the same conclusions. Similarly, the testing methodology and actual test cases need to be managed. In fact, organizations should invest in tools to automate the generation of such documents. IBM proposed FactSheets[26] for Model documentation, whereas, Google released Model Cards[27] for this purpose.

Over time, these model documents could be quite useful. For example, one can discover important patterns, frequently used testing methodologies and useful information out of a collection of these model documents which can be then used to streamline further processes. There is a clear parallel between data-specific metadata and model documents. In fact, model documentation is metadata about data. All this metadata itself could be managed to provide an enterprise catalogue for AI models. A combined data and model catalogue will propel the enterprise towards the next gear for the AI journey.

Finally, this documentation is not a one-time activity. It is a living and evolving asset. Anytime a change is made to the model, it needs to be documented.

Deployment and Continuous Reinforcement

There is a proverbial slip between the cup and the lip when it comes to AI initiatives. Roughly, around 80 to 90 per cent of

AI projects never see the light of day in the production phase.[28] They simply end at the PoC stage, which leads to scepticism in the business leader's mind on the usefulness and RoI of AI. Moving the model into production is a tough task that often needs a close working relationship between the AI team and IT team. Now, let us look at some of the conditions the organization needs to fulfil to move models to production and then keep in place deployed in-production models.

1. *Compatibility between Development and Production*: One of the biggest headaches for any enterprise is managing incompatible environments. The AI team, while building models, likes to use the latest and greatest of libraries and code to make the model efficient and in sync with the latest developments. The IT team, however, must do a lot of due diligence before adding a new component or upgrading the older version. Let us understand the core reason for this. The AI team will be making local decisions that are best for the task at hand, whereas, the IT team will be looking at the broader picture and making sure that any change to the hosting platform will not create issues for other developers or applications which are already in production. Since commercial tools always provide backward compatibilities, new versions should not pose a major issue, but the same may not be true for open source. Even if the requirement is to on-board a completely new package, the new package may have certain dependencies which cannot be resolved without messing with the existing set-up.

    Unless the dependencies can be resolved by adding the correct versions or new components, it will require the data scientist to go back to the learning phase and repeat all the steps. Apart from being time- and cost-ineffective, it will be very difficult to convince the team to redo the model learning.

However, not all is lost. With the increasing use of Kubernetes, Docker, and cloud technology, this problem is somewhat handled. As a good practice, the organization should adopt these technologies which allow developers to bundle all relevant dependencies into containers which can be integrated into the pipeline. In fact, with technologies like Red Hat OpenShift, the model can now be executed anywhere: on premises, or on any cloud provider. However, it is still prudent to make sure the development environment and production environment are in sync and that the AI team is aware of this.

2. *Strong DevOps Tools*: There needs to be availability of enough investment and the right tools for data science and deployment managers to move AI to production. As soon as the code is ready, one of the team members needs to download all the code, compile the application, transfer the compiled application to the server (it can be cloud, or not), and then start the application. There is a high possibility of errors in this manual process. Another important point is that the new application can be deployed a couple of times a week through this process. All the changes are compiled in one go. This compilation itself can be challenging since there is no way of knowing if all the changes are compatible with each other! Resolving errors between the changes can itself be a project. This is where DevOps tools are helpful.

The AI team needs to imbibe CI/CD (continuous integration and continuous delivery) methodology which enables continuous movement of models into production. CI is the coding methodology which asks each change to the code to be pushed to a central repository (often managed through Github) so that all changes can be easily integrated and validated. The CI philosophy does not stop at code integration but extends to building and testing the application automatically as soon as the new changes come in. Jenkins is one common open-source tool used for continuous integration. CD picks up where CI ends, allowing rapid, automated, and easy deployment of new packages to the production system. Together, the CI/CD pipeline allows extremely robust and automated processes to include any code-level changes in the production environment without manual intervention.

The other thing enabled by the CI/CD pipeline is that one doesn't have to wait for a week to push a new version of the application into production. Instead, any small change can be pushed into production automatically. In this fashion, there is always an up-to-date copy of the application or the model running in the production environment. Now, imagine how the CI/CD pipeline can make the whole process smoother, especially in the case of hundreds of developers working across the geography on a common application.

While some DevOps tools like Github are already commonly used, utilization of other tools like Travis, Jenkins, Dockets, and Ansible is limited, which encumbers the overall AI process. Many organizations do not invest adequately in acquiring the right skills in these areas and focus too much on model learning skills. This is one of the primary reasons for models not moving to production.

3. *Security*: The security of the deployment model is an important issue to deal with. While there are enough tools and methodologies available which can take on traditional attacks like Denial of Service, AI models are susceptible to a new class of attacks. For example, an AI team spends months working with the content team to curate the training data and building a state-of-the-art model, which is then offered as-a-service/API, such as a face recognition service. The user will be able to send images of faces to the service and the service will return results with labels like male, female, young, old, etc. Before the model gets to be served at API, the team would have passed through multiple gates of governance officers,

IT, and the legal team. New attacks can undo all efforts astonishingly fast. Let us discuss a few kinds of attacks:

- *Stealing Attack*: In this class of attack, an adversary tries to learn the model behaviour. If we look at a face recognition service, the user will send a lot of images to the service and get corresponding labels back. What if this is a ploy from the user to get more and more training/labelled data so that she can learn a new model based on non-obtained training data? There are several studies which have shown that the model can be stolen within a matter of a few days and the user (now an adversary) can learn the model behaviour in one day within a 5 per cent accuracy. This poses a real economic threat because the creator would have gone through the whole data and learning life cycle spending considerable time, money, and effort on it. However, the adversary can steal it in a few days and create a competitive service at a fraction of the cost. A seemingly simple solution is limiting the number of requests per user. These attacks are fairly sophisticated. How do we deal with colluding adversaries where there is a group of adversaries trying to learn different parts of the model and then reassemble it on their own? These are ongoing problems and various teams in academia and industry are innovating in this space. One thing is for sure: as long as open APIs exist, there will be some form of attack. All attacks may not be stopped, but proper guardrails can be built so that they are minimized.
- *Poisoning Attack*: In this class of attack, the adversary feeds either wrong samples or wrong feedback to the model. These incorrect inputs, when passed to the retraining module, will cause models to misbehave. Let's look back at our example of face recognition API. The API will take an image as user input and send the results back to the user. Along with the results, the

API will also ask the requestor whether the results are satisfactory or not. Now, assume that the results were indeed correct; however, the adversary masquerading as a legitimate user provides the wrong feedback. In this case, the model will retrain itself to make sure this mistake is not repeated, even though it wasn't a mistake. Over time, such wrong feedback can deteriorate the quality of the model. This is what happened to Microsoft's Tay bot that we spoke about earlier in this chapter. That was, in fact, a well-meaning experiment which went wrong and also exposed the vulnerability of online systems to poisoning attacks. These attacks are even more difficult to handle than the stealing attacks because it is difficult to distinguish between bad and good feedback unless there is a manual intervention.

- *Evasion Attack*: In this attack type, the adversary tries to create samples which will fool the model. This can be done by observing input and output to the system and trying to learn how the model works and then creating samples. Let's go back to our hiring example and say that the hiring system was triggered to identify candidates who have a background in artificial intelligence. Now, the adversary can create a résumé with a lot of hidden text to enumerate AI skills. These non-existent skills will now match the positive word list and hence the applicant will be called for an interview. Imagine this being done by a large set of candidates. Suddenly, the model performance is very bad, and business users will be suspicious of the model usefulness and RoI. So, this simple evasion attack could mean that the model will be moved from production back to the development stage.

Protection against such attacks is an active area of research and development. The IBM Adversarial Robustness Toolbox (ART) 360[29] is an open source offering which provides state-of-the-art attack detection and mitigation algorithms. Readers can try the toolkit from: https://github.com/Trusted-AI/adversarial-robustness-toolbox.

4. *Testing and Validation*: During the AI learning stage, the testing is done by developers who understand the model and can tweak the parameters based on the testing outcome (white-box testing). This certification is essential but not enough. The AI development team cannot certify their own model.

   There needs to be an AI governance team which independently tests models before they are deployed in the production. This team, typically, has business users and not technical or data scientists. This type of testing/validation is known as black-box testing. The team will test the model from all aspects including but not limiting to fairness, performance, accuracy, scalability, etc. Therein lies the problem. This is the team which has to give the green signal to the model, but it is composed of business users only.

   Recall that the common way of carrying out testing is via test case generation. However, this is an extremely challenging task, especially for testing AI applications. In software testing, test cases are generated by looking at the variable types and then enumerating multiple values for that variable. For example, all values between 0 and 65,535 are valid test cases for a variable of type integer. But for AI models, there is an additional constraint that the test cases should be realistic and plausible. Consider data where the age ranges from five to eighty years and education ranges from primary school to the graduate level. Now the test cases must be carefully generated so that the combination of age and education makes sense. One cannot have 'Age: 5' and 'Education: Graduate'. While each attribute is taking a valid value independently, when put together, it's wrong. For most testing, the number of test cases are in millions so there is no way cases can be manually generated or verified for plausibility.

The organization should invest in building tools for this team so that it can test the model from a business viewpoint without knowing anything about its internals. In the absence of such tools, the governance team cannot confidently check and approve it. The legal and governance teams will always err on the side of caution and hence the model will not be deployed. Enabling governance teams with the correct tools to test, validate, and certify the models will result in much higher deployment of AI models.

5. *Continuous Monitoring*: The deployed model needs to be continuously monitored to make sure that its performance is as expected. As we have discussed throughout this book, there could be many metrics which need to be monitored, including accuracy, fairness, scalability, robustness, etc. Therefore, the organization needs to on-board a good monitoring system for this task. Just monitoring the model for performance is not enough. The monitoring data needs to be fed into an alerting system which would then analyse the signals and proactively generate alerts if it senses that the model is going to perform suboptimally in the future. And the last piece of the puzzle is the actual action. The monitoring data, along with the payload data, needs to be shared with the data scientists so that they can correlate the model's performance with the payload data and take corrective action. The corrective action could be retraining or model upgradation or in the worst case a rebuilding from the scratch.

    IBM Watson's OpenScale[30] is one such offering. In the hybrid cloud world, the models can be running anywhere; however, the administrator would want to monitor all models from a single pane of glass. OpenScale has the capability to monitor models in the IBM cloud, AWS, or any other cloud provider.

6. *Payload Data Analysis*: Payload data refers to data which is sent to the AI API for scoring or decision-making. This data is a gold mine of information and can be used for multiple optimizations,

including business decisions. Let's assume that our AI application recommends to users what clothes they should buy. Users can also give a thumbs up or thumbs down based on whether they like the recommendation or not. Now, simply counting thumbs ups or thumbs downs may give a false sense of utility for this service. Its real value can only be understood if the thumbs-up data is correlated with the actual sales data to see if users are indeed acting on the recommendations or not. And this is where the payload data would come in handy. The user inputs and model recommendation coupled with actual sales data will give the business owner a very clear picture on the effectiveness of the AI model.

Here are some more examples of use cases:
- *Drift Detection*: Many times, payload data shows very different characteristics from training data. For such data, the model performance decreases. Identification of data drift helps the data scientist fix the issues during retraining.
- *New Class Detection*: The payload data can also point to the emergence of a new class label which needs to be accommodated in the model.
- *Leverage as Training Data*: An intelligent sub-sample of payload data can help in improving the model. We don't advocate using all payload data because the data can contain outliers, poisonous samples, or samples which are already part of the training data. Therefore, a good data-selection algorithm should be leveraged to slice the payload data. Needless to add that, while the payload data is a goldmine of information, proper security and compliance protocol should be followed to store it. In many cases, explicit user consent might be mandatory.

One of the innovative AI-first organizations in India is BigBasket. It pays special attention to model monitoring and correlating the model performance with actual business KPIs.

Everyday performance is tracked on two fronts. First, at the infrastructure level, for instance, response to the client has to be in 50 microseconds.

Second, the business metric track: when model is deployed we measure KPIs, for forecasting it is minimizing order stock, minimizing wastage for recommendation, the number of clients who bought the recommendation. We try measuring if the test group performs the same as the control group.

We at BigBasket have tools for both. We monitor these regularly: response times, how many pods are used; we get alerts if it's breached. We also analyse logs and have predefined mechanisms to capture performance data and other observability metrics.

—Mani Subramanian, former head of analytics, BigBasket

Building Trust towards Enterprise AI

One of the biggest impediments for enterprises to close the gap between the promise of AI and the realization of its benefits is to make AI trustworthy. Different stakeholders in an enterprise would have a different understanding of the concept of trust. Therefore, it is essential to build trust from all different stakeholders' viewpoints. In this section, we go over the core components to make AI trust-ready. Let us look at the key aspects of what constitutes 'trust' in AI.

1. *Auditability*: In simple terms, auditability refers to the capability for tracking all actions and operations which were undertaken to build the AI model or applications. This is an essential and almost a hygiene factor for all governance and audit officers in an enterprise. The audit trails can be broken into three parts, corresponding to three high-level steps in the AI life cycle.
    - *Data Audits*: These audit trails capture the key events from data acquisition to the point where data is shared within the organization. The key aspects are data acquisition

(who, when, why), metadata tagging, setting access control policies, data storage, data preparation, and data movement across different zones in the organization. The audit trails do not include real data. This is the simplest of the audit trails to broadly understand the key events in the life cycle of the data asset. This is a coarse audit which tracks data assets as an atomic unit. The most common governance use cases this audit supports are: Who used the data sets? When was it used? When was the data set acquired or transformed or deleted? This seemingly simple audit data is an organization's first step towards governance and regulatory compliance. Consider a situation when a data set needs to be deleted; it is not enough to delete the original data, but the subsequent copies and derivations of the data should also be deleted. The audit/lineage/provenance data is essential to find all copies and derivation of the data.

- *Learning Audits*: These trails capture data transformation from raw data to insights. While data audits provide information on data assets as a whole, the learning audits capture the fine-grained lineage of each transformation event which goes through in the analytics pipeline. Consider an example where credit approval data is used to build a prediction model on who should get the credit. The audit events will include events for data preparation such as missing data imputation, bias removal, date normalization, events for learning the model, events on how the model was tested, and so on. Such audit data will help show evidence of the data going through the debiasing process, show that a thorough testing on hold set was performed, as well as demonstrate that SPI was removed and not considered in the model building, and many more such questions.

Let's take an example where the AI pipeline was built to analyse the financial filings of companies. Text extractors were written to mine information like the key people in a company, its financial results, risk statement, etc. Such a pipeline will have upward of 300 extractors. These extractors will not be independent and will feed into each other, resulting in a very complex data pipeline. This data is then provided to end customers via data APIs or as a natural-language-enabled interactive environment. For instance, if in May 2020, someone queries, 'Who is the CEO of IBM?', the answer generated is 'Virginia Rometty'. Now, this answer was correct until April 2020, till Dr Arvind Krishna took over this position. The user flags this as the wrong answer and the feedback, along with the question and answer, goes back to the development team. Consider the enormity of the problem. Without any extra metadata, the team now needs to sift through a complex pipeline of operators to find out the source of the error.

If the lineage across all extractors has been recorded, then suddenly this problem is more tractable. For example, now the extractors who have nothing to do with names can be avoided for any further analysis. Similarly, the extractors who extract names or operate on names can be easily identified for any further analysis.

This lineage is also very useful to figure out which part of the pipeline needs more efforts to upgrade or maintain.

- *Deployment Audits*: Once the AI model is deployed, it is critical to track the operational lineage. This lineage specifically notes how the model is being used and what the feedback is from users. The lineage trails should be utilized to do smart metering as per usage, perform root cause analysis in case of bad feedback, and move the most used/accessed services to optimized infrastructure. This aspect of the lineage is arguably the most important for computing RoI, improving operational efficiency, and identifying new revenue generation opportunities.

Now that we understand the use of lineage for governance and trust, let us look at the simple concept of metering and pricing of data APIs. One way is to price each API the same but that may not be too effective. The other is to price APIs factoring in the cost of cleaning, curating, and preparing the data. Using the data, learning and deployment lineage data, we can get answers to questions such as:

- What was the data acquisition cost?
- What kind of processing was done on the data?
- What is the cost of the infrastructure the data is hosted on?
- How many times is the data being asked for?

While the end-to-end lineage, starting from the data capturing event all the way up to deployment is the end state, organizations need to develop an iterative plan to get there. The collection of this data will require instrumenting the toolchain so that appropriate events can be generated. This instrumentation can be a costly exercise to undertake. Next, the audit data will grow at a fast rate and the organization will need to plan for dedicated infrastructure and the associated team to manage it.

2. *Fairness*: Discrimination is a necessary and desired property of AI. This may seem like a contradictory statement, after all that we've talked about so far, but it's really not. By definition, AI models learn to differentiate between two (or more) classes. This is desired except when the discrimination is systematically targeted towards a specific segment in the data. For example, say résumés need to be classified into 'hire' versus 'don't hire' categories. If the

decision is made based on a candidate's suitability for the job, then it is a good decision. However, if attributes like location and gender are influencing the decision, then this results in a biased or unfair AI. The need for fairness can be driven by regulations, or the market and PR posture. In fact, no organization will want to be unfair in their business practices. In the case of AI, it becomes more difficult because outside of a handful of deep technical people, no one understands how it works. With the advent of deep neural networks which employ non-linear learning mechanisms, the check for fairness becomes more difficult.

While the data scientist may care mostly about accuracy and performance, the risk officers and marketing officers will want to focus on fairness. Any unfair behaviour of a deployed AI model will be catastrophic to a business financially as well as from a branding viewpoint. Fairness in AI has three important components:

- *Data Fairness*: Data which shows unfair characteristics will often result in a biased model. The simplest way to detect bias in the data is to employ metrics like a disparate impact across sensitive attributes like gender, religion, age, etc., and evaluate how these attributes impact outcomes like hiring decisions, credit approval, and so on. If they do, then the data is biased. Unfortunately, this simple setting does not always work. In the real world data schema, the bias often manifests itself through a combination of attributes and a sub-segment of the population. For example, the data can show a bias against women in non-metros but not in metros. Such intersectional data bias detection is a computationally expensive problem. Data bias mitigation is an even trickier problem. One may think that if the 'gender' and 'location' columns are removed, the resulting data will be unbiased. Unfortunately, such seemingly correct methods do not solve the data bias. The data bias can be there due to strongly correlated columns. The location and ethnicity/religion/race can be tightly coupled. In this case, removing one of the columns has a minimal impact on increasing data fairness. Very often, sampling strategies are used to handle data biases. We point the readers to Trustworthy Machine Learning book (http://www.trustworthymachinelearning.com/)[31] for an excellent survey on the techniques for bias detection and remediation.

- *Model Fairness*: Fair data is not a sufficient condition for fair models. Non-linear and advanced learning algorithms can discover hidden and sometimes biased patterns from the data to minimize the loss function and hence increase accuracy. Just like data fairness, it is important to detect model bias. Primarily, one needs to check for two classes of model bias: group bias and individual bias.

In the case of group bias, the model displays bias towards a sub-segment of the population. In simple settings, the segment can be identified by simple conditions like 'Gender: Female'. However, in realistic settings, the conditions can turn out to be very complex. For example, Buolamwini and Gebru[32] showed that many commercial face recognition APIs are able to recognize White women with high accuracy but not Black women. So, the model demonstrates bias for a small cross-section of the data.

Individual biases surface when an individual is treated unfavourably, and the decision is based on sensitive attributes. Let's take an example of Jane Doe, who applied for a home loan. The home loan application model analyses the important information and rejects her application. However, the model accepts the same application after only one value of the application is changed while all the other parts remain exactly the same. Now, if the change is related to demographics or personal data (age, gender, race), then one infers that the application showed an individual bias against Jane Doe.

However, if the change was in a column like salary, job, etc., then it might be okay. As readers would understand, the absence of an individual bias is more critical for end users, whereas, group bias detection is needed for the governance team to make sure the model is good to be put into production.

- *Fairness during Retraining*: As noted earlier, the AI life cycle has three phases: data, training, and retraining. Till now, we have seen fairness in the context of the first two stages. Let's now look at what fairness entails in the last stage. Please recall, what differentiates AI models from other analytics is the ability to continuously learn from the environment. Consider a loan approval model which is put into practice to approve loan applications. Over time, some customers start to default on the loans, and this feedback is provided to the model for retraining. What if the model discovers patterns that 90 per cent of loan defaulters live in ABC neighbourhood? Or that 65 per cent of loan defaulters are Black men? It would then adjust parameters accordingly. In this way, a fair model can over time turn unfair and biased due to an ungoverned feedback loop. Therefore, fairness is not a static property (cite Google Paper) and will change over time.[33]

    There are a number of open-source toolkits like IBM AIF360[34] and commercial products like IBM OpenScale and AWS Sagemaker which can enable organizations to fast-track the journey to build, deploy, and use fair models.

3 *Explainability*: Explainability is arguably the most important factor which infuses trust in the end users of AI

tools. In simple terms, explainability allows users to ask the reasoning behind a decision. Let us look at the two variants of explainability:

- *Global Explainability*: Global explainability assures that the model makes sense at a high level and encodes domain-specific rules and constraints. This is useful for business users and regulators to make sure that the model has correctly learnt the domain rules. Similarly, the AI scientist can be asked to update the model if any 'wrong' rule or pattern is inferred. For example, in the credit approval model, the governance team can examine if the model paid attention to credit score, salary, and past defaults, and not to factors like location, race, or gender. The explainers can also discover the weightage for each attribute which can further infuse trust into a business user.
- *Local Explainability*: While global explanations are good for business users, it falls short of utility for the end consumer. The consumer will not be interested in the model's behaviour on an average but would require a personalized explanation which provides insights for a specific case. For example, if someone's loan application is declined, the insights should be able to tell that the majority of people with a credit score of 700 are approved, whereas, the applicant's credit score is at 690.

This can help the applicant know exactly where to focus for the next submission. Note that explainability will have different meanings for different personas and one explanation will not fit all.

For example, let's reuse our loan approval scenario and see what possible questions could crop up for different people. An AI scientist might want to know why their model isn't performing well, and why the prediction is different for the very similar-looking inputs. A governance officer would wonder how to prove that the model is fair and safe. A loan officer would want to find out why a loan got rejected and if the business rules were correctly learned by the model. Lastly, a consumer would probably just be interested in finding out why the loan was rejected.

Since the definition of explainability varies across personas, it is important that enterprises on-board different tools or technologies to serve all needs. There are multiple algorithm implementation and toolkits available which can help to get started. LIME and SHAP are two widely used algorithms for global explanations. Explanations via counterfactuals are a popular way of generating local explanations. At a high level, the counterfactual techniques explain the minimum change required to the input data to change the decision. For example, suggesting to a user that, if the credit score is updated by 10, the probability of loan approval increases by 40 per cent is accomplished via counterfactual techniques.

There are a number of open-source toolkits like IBM AIX360,[35] LIME,[36] and SHAP[37] which can help organizations get started on AI explainability. AIX360 is a comprehensive explainability open-source toolkit which supports multiple personas and algorithms for local and global explainability.

4. *Benchmark*: Imagine going to a retail outlet to buy a bag of chips and seeing hundreds of options at approximately the same price point. The decision to buy one of them is made by looking at the nutrition label on the packet and deciding which one is the healthiest. This is possible because chips manufacturers have tested the product to come up with these labels. Drawing the analogy to AI, enterprises will always face the issue of which AI models should be used in production. The answer to this lies in having a robust AI testing framework. There should be an AI tester persona which can test AI models and come up with the equivalent

of nutrition labels. Business owners can just look at these model labels and pick the correct model. To generate these labels, the AI tester should be able to generate and manage test suites. The generation of these test cases for AI testing is a very difficult task. Apart from satisfying properties like coverage, scalability, etc., AI-specific test cases need to satisfy the following two properties:

- The test cases should be realistic and not violate business rules. For example, let's take a CIBIL score which ranges from 0 to 800. Any test case which has a CIBIL score as an input cannot violate this range. This is a simple range constraint on a single dimension, but the constraints can get really intricate, involving multiple dimensions. For instance, the delivery date should be within five days of the dispatch date. Now, all test cases need to adhere to this rule. The rules can also include correlation and causation and span multiple dimensions.
- The test cases should be focused, which means they should be driven towards testing a specific metric. For example, testing an AI model for fairness would result in different test cases than testing for robustness. The metrics on which the AI model needs to be tested should come from business users, and the AI tester should be able to generate a report on how the model behaves specific to the metric at hand.

Readers would agree that generating millions of test cases which satisfy these properties is not a feasible manual task. Therefore, we need tools to generate such test suites. Not only do the test cases need to be generated but also stored and managed. The reason for storage is to be able to run the same test suite on different models or different versions of the same model for easy comparison.

5. *Safety*: For an enterprise, it is very important that, apart from the AI being governed, fair, explainable, and accountable, it

is also safe and responsible. AI models should not be used for tasks which put humans or society at risk. Similarly, the AI should not be used to breach individual privacy. The purpose of AI models should be well established and agreed upon. As per Responsible AI Licenses, AI should not 'detect or infer aspects and/or features of an identity of any person, such as name, family name, address, gender, sexual orientation, race, religion, age, location (at any geographical level), skin colour, social or political affiliations, employment status and/or employment history, and health and medical conditions'.[38]

Typically, it requires thorough thinking to articulate if AI models can have unintended side effects. For example, researchers as Stanford University built an AI model to predict if a person is homosexual on the basis of the image of the face. While the researchers would have developed advanced data collection and preprocessing techniques and advanced training, the final application was a bad choice. Not only does it infringe on privacy and basic human rights, if the technology falls into the hands of regressive governments, it can have catastrophic consequences for the queer community. While it is very difficult to predict all the different ways in which AI can be used in a 'bad' fashion, conscious thinking can help catch some of these issues early on.

Niramai Health Analytix: AI Transformed Healthcare

Niramai Health Analytix[39] is a Bengaluru-based deep-tech start-up which has developed software that uses innovative AI algorithms to analyse thermography images to detect breast cancer at a much earlier stage.

Thermography is a method of measuring the temperature distribution on the surface of a body. A visual heat map of temperature distribution on the surface of the human body is called a thermogram. From the perspective of breast cancer screening, the activity in the blood vessels surrounding a developing cancer is almost always higher than the normal breast tissue which shows up in the thermograph. However, there are only over 500 clinicians with an ability to interpret these thermal images to identify patients with likely malignant lesions. The analysis of the thermal images is very complex and requires deep knowledge and skills to look at the massive correlated and connected data. This task is nearly impossible to do manually. Doctors doing the interpretation have to use about 400,000 data points and 32,000 colour shades, resulting in many false positives and subjective interpretations. Niramai's core innovation, Thermalytix, solves this problem by developing novel AI algorithms which can interpret these thermal images with extremely high accuracy and low false positives. This is a perfect example of disruptive AI-led innovation which solves an important problem in a non-traditional fashion. Just like Viome, Niramai works closely with thermologists to interpret and come out with a certified diagnostic report after following all clinical protocols.

According to Niramai Health Analytix, its trials have demonstrated:

- Accuracy rate higher than mammography by 27 per cen
- Positive predictive value higher than the visual interpretation of thermography by 70 per cent

The success of Niramai is due to the focus on innovations which help solve the pain points of stakeholders: patients and radiologists. The benefits for patients are:

- Age-agnostic technology: Thermal imaging is effective even for women under forty years, for whom mammographies are not recommended.

- Early detection: Detects tumours that are significantly smaller (5 cm) than what can be detected with physical examination (25 cm).
- No side effects: No use of radiation of any form; it only measures temperature on the body.
- Non-contact, private screening: The equipment is placed 3 feet from the patient. This no-touch, no-see screening makes it a painless procedure.
- Affordable: Niramai's cost per screening is significantly lower compared to other modalities.

The other critical stakeholders are radiologists who need to be on board with the analysis of Thermalytix. Some of the positive aspects are:
- Ease of interpretation: Niramai's patented solution processes 400,000 temperature values per person to make an accurate and automated diagnosis of the patient's condition.
- Complements sono-mammography: Since Thermalytix provides information about the location of possible lesions, it helps perform targeted breast ultrasounds, which saves precious radiologist time.
- Complements mammography: Interpretation of mammography images for dense breasts is somewhat difficult. Using the Thermalytix test as a complementary modality helps increase confidence in diagnostics.

The final stage of inclusion of the innovation is done via hosting the application on Google Cloud. The team has broken the monolith application into smaller microservices architecture and used the Kubernetes container orchestration system to deploy, manage, and scale the production application seamlessly. Using modern architecture and cloud technology, bringing innovation into the field has become very easy.

To reiterate, Niramai Health Analytix went through innovation discovery to zoom in on the use of thermal imagery for early breast cancer detection, innovation feasibility by building highly accurate AI models and managing stakeholder benefits and, finally, using a state-of-the-art technology stack to make it easy to deploy and manage.

4

AI and Talent

People are essential to make AI successful. Technology alone will not cut it, and it is the people and their role in the technology that defines the success of AI. It is the people who are learning and making it better; it is the people who are fearing it and rejecting it; it is the people who are causing it to fail. If the people do not believe in AI, it is bound to fail.

How to Make Your People Learn AI

Learning happens through our experiences and our reactions to all that is happening to us. Experiential learning has been a much-researched topic. For young kids, this is the best way to make them understand and become adept at skills. On the same lines, if we want an organization to learn about AI, it must be experienced by the people working there. People learn through experiences, through observations, what they see and what they hear. The five senses are critical in these observations as the brain consolidates and assimilates all that we hear, see, touch, smell, and taste. Our sensory organs have receptors which enable our brain to learn. Once our brain learns, it is almost impossible to forget, and the learning soon reaches the deep-rooted memory. So, it is essential that we expose people to those receptors when we want them to learn AI and imbibe it deep in their hearts.

Let us look at a framework called ' The Five senses of AI' to understand how these five sensory receptors work to contribute to learning AI.

FIGURE 4.1: The Five Senses of AI

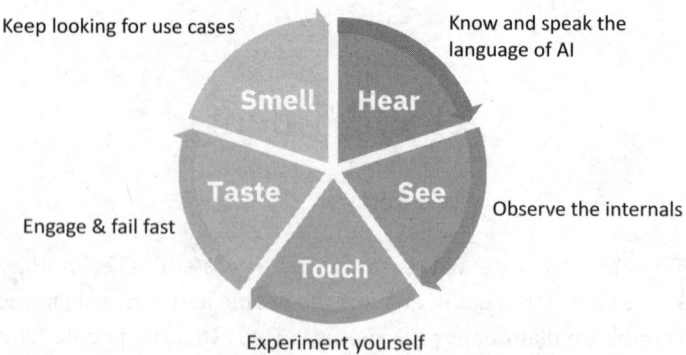

Hear

Everyone needs to speak the language of AI. If employees hear their leaders speaking this language, they will start adopting it. Now, what do we mean by the language of AI? Each employee needs to understand the foundational concepts of AI: How does AI learn? How is it built? What are the successful use cases, and how does it fail? What are the kinds of problems it can solve—forecasting, optimizing, or predicting? Not all employees will need to undergo technical training, but they will need to understand the basics and imbibe it in their day-to-day lives. They need to get familiar with AI terminologies and the lingua franca. They need to get comfortable routinely using phrases like 'the model is learning', 'the model is not trained enough', 'predictions will improve over time', and so on.

The way learning to use a computer became so fundamental that all roles in an organization became dependent on it, understanding the basics of AI is just as vital. A doctor or nurse, a reliability engineer, a store planner, an inventory manager, a loan approver, and even a credit card agent needs to understand the basics of AI. Once the organization speaks a new language and hears successes and failures, it will improve and make AI succeed.

Let us take the example of BigBasket—one of the largest online grocery stores, which has now been acquired by the Tata group. Mani Subramanian, their former head of analytics, says they are a data-first organization. They were born with the idea of using data to attract and retain customers. BigBasket is a digital business in which everyone needs to speak and hear AI, right from the CEO to the warehouse manager, otherwise they cannot survive. The warehouse manager needs to understand how AI can help detect rotten mangoes through image analysis to improve efficiency. Everyone at BigBasket speaks and hears the language of AI. It will always have a vast edge over a brick-and-mortar organization which performs a small PoC exercise to prove AI. At BigBasket, the CEO talks about client retention improvement through analytics. He is aware of which AI models are succeeding and showing improvements in client satisfaction and can easily pair up with a warehouse manager to explain better product quality through image analytics.

See

Seeing is believing, and that is perfectly applicable to the journey of AI too. When employees see the relevant use cases succeeding, their receptibility to AI grows automatically.

In a hospital, when doctors and nurses witnessed the head of the ophthalmology department using an AI model to detect lazy eye syndrome and used that to prioritize and refer patients to various doctors, they started believing in AI. The order of sending patients to doctors and hence queue management was dependent on this initial screening outcome. The doctor could see more patients, and the administrative staff was not as hassled with crowds visiting the hospital. The hospital staff needed to 'see' the head of the department trust AI and moreover 'see' the actual success of the use case manifested by reduced queues.

In continuation of this theory, employees in an organization need to *see* more than the benefits of AI. They need to understand the internal working of AI models which means learning the basics.

A product manager can always discover the benefits of using AI in his/her product. Further, if they see the internal functioning of how an algorithm works and how it uses data, a more significant benefit is achieved. The product manager would then know which data makes the algorithm perform better and what kind of data would make it fail. The product manager can then suggest ways of removing bias in the data and making algorithms more explainable to end clients.

Similarly, why should a doctor remain oblivious to the AI model that detects lazy eye? She should know what kind of data the model is trained for. The doctor should fully understand the model building, training, learning, and monitoring cycle. If the data model is trained on men forty to sixty years of age, it will not be as accurate for women in the fifteen to twenty-five age group. The doctor's confidence in the model would be different in such a case.

Interestingly, knowing how much productivity enhancement she gets from this model, the doctor will start providing feedback to the model about her newer patients. The doctor knows the more she gives feedback, the more the model will learn. It is a partnership that gets established. Over time, the nurse will have to learn the same skill, because why should this learning and training be restricted to the doctor?

Touch

How well do we remember science concepts by theory vis-à-vis by practice? Experiential learning for employees, irrespective of the role, will make them understand AI and make it a way of life. 'Touch' here means doing experiments on tools, undergoing training programmes, and even doing as simple a task as collecting and sorting data for an AI problem that will benefit the organization.

Suppose organizations outsource the entire AI business to technology partners and believe that they will get a miracle answer to their business problems. In that case, they will completely miss the experiential learning phase of AI. AI is not a three-to-six-month project. It takes more than a year to realize its actual benefits. For that to happen, the employees need to be walked through each AI stage. This could be via courses or data fed into AI models, and through cost-benefit analyses which take place before any technological intervention. Employees need to realize what works, what does not work, and the reasons behind failures and successes to make AI even better. It is not a technology implementation; it is a cultural change that we are attempting until the organization transforms.

We talked to an organization where people in every role were taking an AI course. The CEO was taking a simple Stanford course on Coursera to better understand AI strategy. The lead risk manager was undergoing a free AI course which came bundled with their cloud subscription, and the risk analytics head had enrolled herself in an online course from the University of Texas, Austin. The organization had employees in all its layers and roles undergoing AI courses, making them experience AI from different angles. Not all the employees were doing so, but the exposure of several roles ensured that AI was being diffused through the organization. The mindset was getting prepared, and employees were getting ready to embrace AI.

Taste

Our taste buds define our experiences as sweet, bitter, sour, and salty, and that is how we should correlate our AI experiences.

First, a caveat: all experiences will not be sweet. In an organization, employees need to 'taste' AI by getting deeply involved in AI projects. They need to have experiences on their own and decipher small successes and failures. AI projects cannot be thrust down employees' throats before they experience them on their own.

We talked to an organization where the HR leaders resented AI models for predicting the right compensation for employees as it took the decision away from them. In another organization, where HR teams contributed to developing that compensation model, the adoption rate was much higher as the HR leaders felt accountable for everything the AI model was predicting. In the same organization, the HR leaders pushed for salary revisions for 'high-potential' employees who were highly underpaid based on market analysis and what the competition was paying. Their proposals were shot down due to a lack of belief in data. The same HR leaders created an AI model based on employee attrition due to salary issues and used it to predict new salary levels. This time, the leadership team believed in the AI model and agreed to revise salaries. This was a situation where an AI model carried more credibility, mainly because the HR teams created it, and it was not thrust upon them.

Taste is also about the kind of experiences you are having. Failed AI projects can teach you a lot if you do a proper analysis, learn, and reinvent yourself. Many leaders abandon AI if a three-month pilot isn't successful, and they never come back to it. AI is a journey that tends to get better the more you stay on your path. Taste AI by actively engaging in projects across the business functions and become better at it. Failures are not because AI has failed. It's because someone would not have followed the basic AI methodology, or something was lacking. We will continue the discussion on failed AI projects in a separate section.

Smell

Don't we say food is good if it smells good? The 'scent' of AI travels far. People can smell success and failure much faster.

Let us discuss the success of chatbots, which is a splendid example of the scent of AI success. Advancement in conversation technology and its successful application as virtual agents in the customer service industry is an example where the scent of AI travelled faster than expected. Several sectors are deploying text-based chatbots, including banking, insurance, healthcare, and retail. Steve Worswick's chatbot Mitsuku,[1] now called Kuki, has won the Loebner Prize[2] for four consecutive years, and it is now proven that chatbots can appear humanlike. The Loebner Prize is an annual AI competition that attempts to find the most humanlike chatbot based on the Turing test. The judges cannot distinguish whether it is a bot or a human texting with them. This success has pervaded the industry, and there is a proliferation of chatbots that act as virtual agents and help organizations reach their client base.

Alexa is an example of a burgeoning voice assistant in homes, and, smelling its success, several car manufacturers are also embedding voice assistants inside vehicles for navigation.

Yes, clients are smelling AI success through chatbots, and, in most organizations, deploying chatbots is the best and only usage of AI. Chatbots have proven that they are scalable, have 24/7 availability, cut costs, automate work, and reduce human errors. The realized business benefits make the scent of its success spread faster than any other AI use case. A chatbot is a mix of several AI technologies at the back end, using information retrieved from vast data sources already existing in the organization, and conversation technology, which has been perfected in the AI world for years.

Perception of AI

Combining the above five senses makes an organization learn AI and imbue it in its people and culture. When we talk of people, we should also talk about what all they should know about AI. As we have argued in other sections, distinct roles need their own learning maps.

Beyond our five sensory organs, the brain interprets our experiences and applies logic and memory to arrive at conclusions. Individual experiences define our perceptions, and each person has a different interpretation and perception when given the same set of facts.

AI needs and benefits are perceived differently by individuals in an organization, which is evident as we realize that all people do not think similarly. Everyone is wired differently, and the leadership team needs to understand that tweaking their messages based on the benefit to a particular person is more acceptable.

We talked to an organization that was evaluating workplace analytics as an AI tool for employees. So, the example goes like this: A bot would collect data on one-on-one meetings from a leader's digital calendar and then analyse it to see if the leader were spending enough time with his immediate subordinates on their career progression. Further, another bot would collect data from the email inbox and measure each leader's email response time. It would then prompt them if they were too fast in replying to emails and hence not reflective enough or too late in responding and therefore procrastinators. As an outcome, a good 70 per cent of this organization's employees perceived this bot to be a great productivity enhancer. In contrast, 30 per cent of employees stated that it was an invasion of their privacy and derailed creativity by measuring insignificant things. Further, HR found this an excellent tool as they discovered that many frontline managers were not spending enough time with their team members, which was a cause of employee dissatisfaction. Many leaders felt that one-on-one meetings were not the right measure of time spent with their teams as it didn't account for the innumerable working sessions the team was in together, when the team members felt more cared for as the leader was *with* them always.

Well, both sides are right in this situation because people are wired differently. AI adoption of this bot in the organization would highly depend on whether it is seen as an efficiency enhancer or an intruder of personal space. To enhance the complications, some of the leaders who found it a creativity killer were strong proponents of AI for customers but found it difficult when AI intruded in their own work lives.

As AI perceptions are different for different people, organizations should focus on individual learning paths for each role. If the same training course of a data scientist is shown to a business unit head, he will shun AI for sure. The fear of AI will creep in, and it will be considered too complicated an application, only meant for data scientists. We will discuss a plan to create individual learning paths in the next section.

Talent Map for an Organization

There is a war for AI talent going on right now. We keep hearing and reading about the need for data scientists, their scarcity, and, of course, the huge salaries an organization needs to pay to hire them. Seeing this trend, data science has become a skill in high demand, and there are thousands of people rushing to enrol in data science courses. Data science needs domain expertise; hence, there are financial analysts, retail consultants, operations SMEs, and healthcare professionals jumping to upgrade themselves.

The need to be future-skill-ready has never been more urgent. Organizations need to re-engineer their skill plans to align with AI strategy. Reskilling the workforce for tomorrow's jobs is the number one priority for most organizations. Not all skills can simply be hired, and, hence, the impetus on reskilling employees becomes a strategic imperative. Reskilling is not easy, and many organizations undertake it just for training, or ask simple questions like which courses should be introduced for the best return on investment. While there is no single answer, we highly recommend creating a talent map for your organization.

A talent map has three main components: 1. Learning ladder for all; 2. AI skill compass; and 3. Hire, buy, or reskill decision. The following sections explain these components in detail.

Learning Ladder for All

The learning ladder should be designed for all roles in an organization—anyone who is keen to learn about AI! There should be a comprehensive and well-structured programme designed by the core AI strategy team in conjunction with the learning and development teams to take employees through a complete journey, from discovery to learning and then applying their knowledge to become an AI expert. By going through this structured learning ladder, employees can achieve the following:

- Learn AI tools and methodologies relevant for their role.
- Maximize application of their learning through hands-on experience on AI projects.
- Get coaching from AI experts to turn their ideas into a prototype and potentially into a minimum viable product.
- Participate in innovating with AI and infusing AI into their own product or offering.
- Gain experience by participating in cross-business unit projects to infuse AI.
- Get industry-recognized badges and certificates.

The learning ladder should have sufficient mentors to assist and enable employees through the journey. There should be an internal communication and messaging channel available where employees can discuss their doubts freely and collaborate with mentors.

The learning ladder should have a name which establishes a brand and is also catchy. It should be made familiar in all internal communications and be launched by the CEO or head of an organization. It should be supported by the chief analytics officer, the CTO, the chief data officer, or even the chief transformation officer, depending on which role is most relevant in an organization. The focus needs to be on 'you', in this case, the employee.

There are three stages in the AI learning ladder: explore, learn, and practise.

FIGURE 4.2: Learning Ladder for All

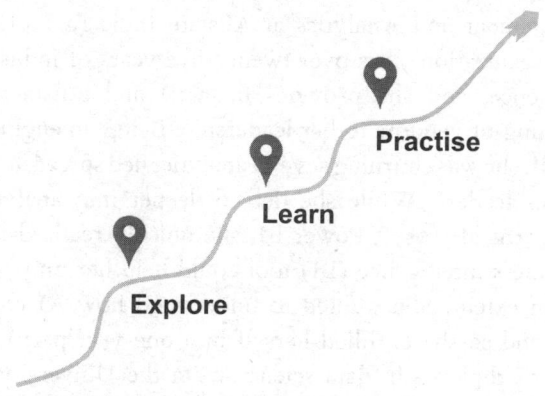

EXPLORE

We all come from different educational and work backgrounds, follow different learning paths, gain different skills, and use different tools to execute our role in an organization. Each role is distinct and will be impacted differently in the journey to AI. That's why there should be a customized 'learning AI' pathway based on the persona in an organization. Employees should be able to explore and choose a persona that resonates with their current role and understand what basic concepts they need to learn as they undergo the AI journey. So, this phase is about discovering your own role and the right courses, learnings, people, experiences, and examples based on it.

Different (AI) Strokes for Different Folks

Here are some real-world examples of individuals who embarked on their learning journey and re-engineered their skills to transform their roles in their respective organizations.

Amita Agarwal, who leads IT Outsourcing Category Management and Analytics at Allstate India (a Fortune 500 organization), has over twenty-five years of industry experience, and she provides financial and satisfaction reporting of vendors to her leadership. Being an engineer herself, she was churning several analytics-led spreadsheets for her leaders. While she delved deeper into analytics and learnt Microsoft Power BI, she quickly realized that a business intelligence (BI) tool could help her only to a certain extent. She wanted to understand how AI could help, and so she enrolled herself in a one-year part-time master's diploma in data science from the University of Texas, Austin. This new learning changed her mindset completely and she soon started applying what she learnt into her work, which empowered her to make better vendor decisions. She says that she even convinced her friend Sapna Chaturvedi, who heads finance at Xerox India, to take the course. Sapna too transformed into an AI-enabled finance professional and was soon building AI use cases for 'order to cash' scenarios at her workplace.

In another such case, Shilpi Jain, head of Bangalore Engineering COE at Envestnet Yodlee, has over twenty years of experience in the industry. She leads quality and testing for Envestnet Yodlee, a large fintech organization. As her organization pivoted towards AI and she grew into leadership roles, the need for re-engineering herself became larger. Her pursuit of optimization and efficiency in testing and automation required a fair amount of data analysis in order to identify initiatives and prioritize them based on impact. She soon realized the need for exploring the world of data science as traditional techniques became insufficient with the increase in complexity, volume, and velocity of data. As her team started testing data panels and data models created by their data science teams, she became interested in AI and realized its immense potential. Her love for the subject and passion to do even more made her enrol in an online master's of science in analytics from Georgia Tech University, US.

Usha Rengaraju, data scientist, freelancer, and Kaggle[3] grandmaster, has a similar story to tell. During a consulting assignment, she engaged with a retail organization which converted testers into data scientists! Is that even possible? Yes, according to her. She says, 'The organization hired fresh engineering graduates at ₹5–7 lakh per annum and asked me to train them for an intensive twenty-eight days on data science methodology and architecture. These young graduates soon became data engineers and architects. The organization then hired three data scientists from the market and their AI and analytics organization was ready at a much lower cost. There are very few data scientists required in a project; most of the heavy lifting is done by data engineers, front-end designers, and data architects, hence this model worked out perfectly for this retail organization.'

LEARN

After we have mapped roles in the organization, the next step of the learning ladder is to build the actual learning plan. A well-defined learning plan can be spread out over a year and will have courses and measurement mechanisms. And, most importantly, a budget for courses should be planned as all learning comes at a price.

Since there are several courses available on AI, there is often confusion on which course is relevant to the people undertaking the training. Further, several people quit the learning halfway as they find it too difficult or repetitive. We recommend creating three learning levels for each persona: essentials, experienced, and expert. The essentials level should include the core concepts required to begin the AI journey for that persona and be provided with several examples of a use case that reinforce those concepts. This expertise will help in kickstarting initial proof of concepts. At the experienced level, learning will continue with deep-dive courses aligned to each persona as it should include hands-on AI exercises. At the expert level, the persona should focus on deep expertise and mastery of all concepts. This should include advanced courses which explain the chosen topics in depth. It might also include implementing a capstone project with a cohort or a team.

Learning and training is an industry, and there are tonnes of courses available. We are intentionally refraining from recommendations on courses here and the choice should really be made based on individual preferences.

There are several learning options, like online courses through MOOC (massively open online courses) platforms, corporate training institutes offering tailormade programmes, academic institutes offering six-month diplomas to three-year master's programmes. It's important that a learner first discovers his/her persona and then chooses the course.

Cognitiveclass.ai is an example of a learning platform where one can choose amongst several learning paths, do courses, and earn badges.

Earning certificates to mark a period of learning is a great motivator for everyone to learn and share with prospective employers. The prospect of a certificate itself often triggers the demand for learning new courses. The online learning platform Coursera's courses are in high demand. Trends from 45 million learners show nearly 2 million enrolments in AI-related content in 2019 alone!

PRACTISE

Famous statistician and economist Ernst F. Schumacher once said, 'An ounce of practice is worth more than a ton of theory.'

Mastering AI requires augmenting learning with opportunities where they can be applied. There should be projects and exercises identified for employees across business units to let employees get their hands dirty.

There are several exercises and problems available on the internet and some can be easily created by the team assisting in AI learning. Some frequent problems and corresponding exercises are employee attrition prediction, stock trend prediction, bug triaging, defect fix date prediction, workforce transformation, app for prediction of health status based on ECG, blood glucose and heart rate, and many more.

Hackathons are a perfect way to engage the entire organization and have teams work on quick and dirty solutions. During a hackathon, The teams explore data sets, attempt to solve pressing problems, and learn from collaborations. Several large organizations conduct hackathons as it's the best mechanism to create a buzz and identify new and interesting ideas. When hackathons are done with a specific objective in mind, they reap better benefits. The objective could be identifying the most relevant start-up, hiring the best talent in the market, identifying the best solution for some specific problem, or even challenging the status quo of existing teams and cross-pollinating them with new ideas.

Usha Rengaraju, principal data scientist and corporate trainer, says she had to train executives, diplomats, and cybersecurity experts in AI in two hours at the Management Development Institute, Gurgaon. She had to trigger their interest, show them good examples of AI, and also give them a touch and feel experience—all in two hours!

She used Google CoLab[4] to make the executives run Jupyter notebooks and get a feel of the code. The executives were told not to worry about the Python code, but just to look at how to analyse data and visualize it. Using the browser, they imported an image data set and some more data from Excel sheets, trained an image classifier, and evaluated the model written for the purpose. At the end of two hours, they understood the cycle and the power of data, which was more than enough for them.

Learning AI is a journey, and just like any journey, a mentor is needed to help navigate it. The mentors should have worked on multiple AI projects in the past and/or should be steering important AI initiatives. They should be contacted for any queries about the 'explore' stage mentioned earlier in this chapter, technical challenges, use case definitions, course guidance, or while working on 'Practise' projects.

The Udemy[5] 2020 Workplace Learnings Trend Report shares a case study of Booz Allen Hamilton, a management and technology firm, and its AI learning journey. Jim Hemgen, senior learning associate, Booz Allen Hamilton, mentions how it set a goal over three years to employ 5,000 data scientists. Due to the talent shortage, it knew it couldn't rely only on hiring data scientists externally. As a result, the firm doubled down on training existing employees for new data science roles. Its learning and development (L&D) team played the role of 'learning experience architects' and set out to create a personalized learning programme at scale. They created online assessments and pre-work to tailor learning, personalized online learning pathways, blended learning models focused on hands-on projects in the classroom, and mentor circles to guide the learning journey.

The Need for AI Skill Compass

Building an AI organization is a time-consuming exercise. Whether it is about sourcing AI skills or reskilling existing employees, it needs thought, time, and, of course, a lot of money. However, effort and money can be optimized if there is the right plan and a clear understanding of the target. Across the board, AI is the topmost skill needed by all organizations, and the costliest. Gartner's TalentNeuron[6] data shows that, although the firm's IT department's need for AI talent has tripled between 2015 and

2019, the number of AI jobs posted by IT is still less than half of that stemming from other business units. This clearly shows that AI skills are needed across business units. With ever-increasing demand, reskilling current employees has become increasingly important.

According to Udemy's 2020 Workplace Learnings Trend Report, AI went mainstream in 2020. Udemy mentions, 'We're starting to see AI adopted in all parts of the business. Marketing is applying AI data insights on customer behaviour to tailor sales offers. HR teams are beginning to use AI to recruit, screen, and interview candidates. Finance teams are applying AI and ML to reduce company travel costs. The list of AI applications is endless.'

Udemy also predicts that organizations will have to build an internal talent marketplace. The report says that the old way of structuring a workforce based on fixed roles is not the optimal way to support a fast-moving business. Organizations will need to shift to more agile and flexibly networked teams focused on projects, instead of fixed roles. Like how consulting firms or the gig economy operates, team members should be selected for a specific project based on their skills, not their role. They may work on a diverse range of projects throughout the year and teams may change based on the project.

So, whether organizations build an internal marketplace or hire AI experts from the market, they need to have a skill compass in place. What is an AI skill compass? Let us try to understand it.

To build a successful AI project there are certain essential skills which are needed. An AI skill compass is a navigator which can guide an organization's hiring strategies, learning plans, and re-engineering roadmaps. This skill compass can be used by AI-led, AI-born, and AI-enabled organizations.

To cater to skill sets, we need several roles in the organization which might not be mutually exclusive. If we look at LinkedIn, we can see examples of these designations or job roles mushrooming daily. Let us understand what these roles are, what they do, the technical skills they need, and what mindset they need to have.

- *Head, AI, or Chief AI Officer, or VP, AI, or AI Centre of Excellence Head, or Chief Analytics Officer or Chief Data Officer*: There are several names for this leadership position, but the job description is typically to set the AI roadmap of the organization. An AI leader is needed to lead the whole AI mission. This person is most critical for setting up the AI mindset in the organization and will steer it through the PoC, AI infusion, and AI transformation stage. This person should report directly to the CEO and could even be the CEO herself for AI-born organizations. This person needs to have experience of creation as well as implementation of AI projects. The AI leader is the captain of the ship and sets the direction for innovation, culture, and technology decisions based on the organization's vision and business drivers. This leader sets the AI strategy and is responsible for setting the AI strategy flywheel in motion. She is aware of several successful and failed AI projects, understands AI trends in technologies, AI architectures, tools, and infrastructure. This leader also understands the need of AI governance and sets the AI ethics policies for the organization. Most importantly, she knows how to build the organization and sets the AI mindset by hiring the right people and managing stakeholder expectations. Knowledge of big data, the digital transformation journey of organizations, and deep expertise in a domain and/or managing AI at scale are desired skill sets.
- *Data Scientist*: Of course, this is the most important person in an AI organization. Glassdoor[7] has named this the best job for the last five years and Harvard Business Review calls it the 'the sexiest job of the 21st century'. A data scientist typically has a PhD in the computational field, understands maths, statistics, ML, business/domain, and has storytelling capabilities. Curiosity should drive a data scientist, hence, compelling him/

her to identify patterns which are non-trivial. A data scientist might have other people working with her to clean, visualize, and organize data so she can build the predictive model for the AI solution. A data scientist also does the algorithmic selection for a business problem and works with domain specialists to solve it. A data scientist with programming skills becomes much sought after and can command better salaries in the job market. A data scientist should also have several soft skills like analytical thinking, inquisitiveness, interpersonal skills, communication, and intuition.

- *Business Insights Analyst or Data Analyst*: Most organizations have this role as business analysts have been traditionally providing the analytics needed by an organization and it only gets enhanced with AI. These roles have a high 'figure-it-out' quotient—they solve business problems, do what-if simulations with several options, and conduct storytelling around data. They can come from a maths, statistics, finance or, operations background.
- *Statistician, Actuary, Biostatistician, or Risk Manager*: These are traditional roles in which employees develop or simply apply mathematical and statistical models to collect, organize, and interpret data for AI models. They have a mathematical and research mindset with the aim of solving problems, innovating, analysing, and interpreting data with statistical theories and applied mathematical techniques. They might specialize in certain areas like biostatistics, economics, finance, agriculture, or the social sector.
- *ML Engineer*: According to Gartner, by 2023, the role of an ML engineer will become one of the fastest-growing roles in the AI industry. Gartner also estimates that, in today's date, there is one ML engineer for every ten data scientists and it will increase to five and ten by 2023. An ML engineer designs, develops, applies, and runs ML and deep learning systems. She also runs tests and experiments on algorithms and checks the suitability of the most appropriate one.

ML engineers need to have a combination of statistics and programming skills and should try to bring the two worlds together. Training, retiring the system, understanding ML frameworks, algorithms, and tools are requirements for such a role.

- *Information or Data Architect*: This person has a love for data architecture design patterns and can create an architectural mindset and blueprints for data management systems to integrate, centralize, and protect data-storing systems. A person in this role uses spreadsheet tools, BI tools, database systems, and visualization tools. A data architect creates the roadmap for the data life cycle: extraction, organization, and transformation, and then decides the data storage and archival mechanisms.
- *AI Product Managers/Offer Managers*: They have a deep understanding of user behaviour and are responsible for their product being accepted by customers. They engage with cross-functional teams, and are involved in each stage of AI storyboarding, wireframing during design workshops, use case development, usability testing, focus group studies, and data analytics. At BigBasket, we were told that it's the product managers who decide which AI use case should be given priority over the other as they know what will bring better customer satisfaction.
- *Data Engineer or Model Testers*: Well, the entire responsibility of a model's life cycle does not lie on the shoulders of a data scientist alone. Data science is an exclusive skill and there is no need to fill organizations with data scientists. Data engineering is also a part of data science where there is a need for cleaning, collecting, and organizing the data. Sometimes, large data sets need to be annotated and labelled and that's where data engineers step in. They make the entire foundation of data ready to be fed into algorithms and models designed by data scientists. Data pipeline maintenance and testing is the realm of a data engineer.

A data engineer develops, constructs, tests, and maintains architectures like DBs and large-scale processing systems, database systems, data warehousing tools, data modelling, and ETL (extract, transfer, and load). There are some organizations like CrowdFlower[8] which hire only data engineers to collect, clean, and label data. Labelling data is labour-intensive and data scientists cannot be asked to do this. Data engineers help with data categorization, image annotation, and metadata creation, which makes the life of a data scientist easier.

- *Designer or Data Visualizer*: This is the most underrated skill required in an AI system and is sometimes the deciding factor for AI adoption in an organization. An AI system is made for users and an AI designer has a deep understanding of user behaviour. She engages with cross-functional teams, understands customer centricity, and does frequent playbacks to the stakeholders. The AI designer needs to be proficient in front-end design, storyboarding, wireframing, scenario development, usability testing, focus group discussions, and data analytics.
- *ML Operations (ML Ops) or DevOps Engineer*: This skill combines the traditional software engineering DevOps, ML, and data science. The ML Ops engineer takes the code along with data and deploys them so that the ML system can scale over a period and has least downtime. The ML Ops engineer ensures that the model pipelines are maintained and managed, that the model versioning happens, the models are continuously validated for drift or any other changes, the models are giving the desired results, and that the predictions are not degrading over time.
- *AI Ethicist*: The best description of this role is explained in the INDIAai blog.[9] As per the blog, this is the person who questions the fundamental issues of fairness and bias in every AI team that is building algorithms that will impact many people. As predictive models begin making

important decisions, from making hires to taking loans, it becomes paramount to ensure that they are built on the right values. Algorithms are prone to mirroring human biases, but given the pace and reach of technology, the implications of an algorithmic bias can be exponentially higher than that of a human bias. Ethicists promote accountability and the responsible use of AI. As the blog states, 'Anyone who isn't afraid to ask the tough moral, philosophical, and critical questions is fit to be an AI ethicist, regardless of their academic background.'

- *Conversation Specialist*: This is a skill needed while building chatbots and voice assistants, a design skill in which the designer needs to create intelligent virtual agents. Building intelligent and intuitive conversations across various domains is not an easy task and needs a person skilled in this area to engage end users. A conversation specialist needs to design several mock conversations, understand language usage, how creative question and answers flow, and the concept of content libraries. The nuances of how to build with 'intent' and the requirement of different utterances, entities, and business rules are needed by a conversation specialist.
- *NLP Experts*: Considering that most of the data on the web and enterprise warehouse is text, enterprises need NLP experts to make sense of it. NLP experts' skills range from building algorithms to understanding popular languages semantically, lexically, and syntactically. Building core grammar systems for local languages, building reasoning and inference algorithms to handle ambiguity, etc. is what they need to do. A team of good NLP experts can turn the text data of an organization into a gold mine by generating actionable insights. The automated ticket resolution area is expected to be worth $11 billion by 2023 (Transparency Market Research, 2021), and the core skill needed there is NLP to understand the tickets, identify problems, and generate resolutions without human intervention.

- *Analytics Translators*: As per estimates by McKinsey Global Institute, the demand for analytics translators[10] may reach 2–4 million by 2026 in the United States alone. They are the most important bridge between data engineers and data scientists and domain-functional people. So, if a model is predicting the failure of a turbine, then the translator has to explain this to the shop-floor people and the head of manufacturing. Translators also work with data scientists to ensure that business objectives are understood, and models have the right insights. Translators are needed when AI needs to scale, and the impact has to be felt across the organization.
- *AI Researchers*: This is the think-tank for the AI mission, usually comprising people with PhD and master's degrees in AI, ML, statistics, etc. They have deep expertise and are formally trained in AI. This team is and should be highly active in external conferences via publications, reviewing, and delivering tutorials and keynotes. Many times, the team is augmented with a set of software engineers who can take the core ideas and implement them in a scalable manner. Depending on the enterprise and area of research, the team can focus on core research, such as quantum or theory of computation or applied research like NLP, graph mining, etc.
- *AI Project Managers*: It is often said that project managers are the reason any software mission fails or succeeds. There is a need for AI project managers in the industry, those who can keep the army of AI resources together, manage their own and stakeholder expectations, and keep costs in control. The difference between a traditional project manager and an AI project manager is that the latter understands the AI life cycle and ensures smooth functioning of the project.
- *Domain Expert or Functional Consultant*: These are the doctors, insurance experts, wellness practitioners, mechanical engineers, structural engineers, store inventory managers, music composers, historians, etc. whom the AI functionality is

supposed to benefit. All these experts need to learn the basics of AI so that they can communicate and provide inputs to the AI team.

> ### Six Simple Rules for Building an AI Team
>
> 1. You will not get all AI skills in one person, so do not even try. At most you can aim for a person who has two skills.
> 2. Names of roles are misleading most of the time, especially when you look at résumés. Several résumés might state a role as data scientist, but the person may have expertise in ML Ops. So, you need to look at the skill compass mentioned earlier and then map it to your organization.
> 3. You need to look at the overall team composition and output while delivering an AI product. Do not fret and fume about certain buzzwords or roles which might be hot in the market but do not show up in your team composition.
> 4. If each checkbox cannot be ticked for a role while reading a résumé, it does not mean that the person is not fit for the role. Job descriptions are just a guideline. The power to learn can transcend role boundaries. We personally know AI project managers who understand data science models and their viability better than data scientists themselves!
> 5. Some roles can be outsourced, while some cannot. The decision depends on what you are trying to build.
> 6. Do explore some skills on contract whenever you need it. The advantage of a gig economy is hugely unexplored in India, though start-ups are setting a trend here.

Hire, Buy, or Reskill Matrix

Not all skills can be re-engineered—some need to be purchased from the market. Now, for those organizations which really want to hire, the question is *how* should they hire? Which roles are most critical to be hired from the market? Hiring the right leaders at the top who are agents of change and understand AI transformation is critical.

If you are looking for, say, an NLP expert, re-engineering an existing role would be an uphill task. You either need to outsource the NLP-related task to a vendor who has done several such projects or hire the NLP expert herself. But should you hire or buy? Or Reskill?

The answer is based on where you are in your digital transformation journey. If you are an organization which is born digitally or have a large digital presence already, it is better you hire a few NLP experts to do prototypes on your own on NLP. You would be keen on developing your own question-and-answer system based on your domain. You will have the NLP engine as a core of your strategy and reach out to users. You might not want to outsource this part as you are bold in your AI strategy and know that this might replace the traditional way of doing things. You will need to hire experts to experiment, develop, and eventually implement the AI models.

Let us take an example of an organization in the business of manufacturing gears. This organization wants to use AI to predict early failures and incorporate image analyses for product quality checks. It has all the required data but does not need a data scientist through the year. It will be difficult for it to maintain and manage a data scientist on the payroll. In this case, it could engage a vendor who can provide it with the right skills and models and work with it in tandem to deliver the required results. So, buy when you cannot maintain and manage the skills for a longer duration.

We talked to Coursera India and APAC MD Raghav Gupta, and he shared an interesting story with us. Bharathan, one of the learners enrolled on Coursera, was pursuing his Bachelor of Engineering programme at the Maharaja Sayajirao University of Baroda. He was able to use what he learnt on Coursera to land a ML internship. Bharathan was diagnosed with macular dystrophy and lost 85 per cent of his vision when he was just five years old. He was using a combination of Windows Magnifier and NVDA, a screen-reading software, to study his school material. He was exposed to programming in eleventh grade and to Coursera by a Boston-based NGO. He enrolled in Python classes and later in ML and deep learning courses. As a part of his project work, he developed a salesforce conversational analytics chatbot, and that gave him the confidence to launch his career in AI. He landed a data analyst job at a multinational firm in Chennai.

Reskilling existing employees is definitely possible and a must for organizations that are ready for a change. Reskilling is also aided by several learning academies both offline and online. Founded in 2013, with offices in Bengaluru and San Francisco, Springboard is an online learning platform that prepares students, mostly working professionals, for data science careers with comprehensive, mentor-led online programmes.

Its key strengths lie in its focus on data science projects for working professionals who are ready to level up or make a major career shift. The company has thirty-six projects in the form of case studies, guided capstone, and general capstone projects throughout the curriculum, all of them built to provide as much hands-on training as possible. In general capstones, students need to pick their own data sets and problems and work through them from start to finish with the support of mentors. The capstone projects are aligned to areas related to students' current professions. For example, a sustainability consultant used an ML algorithm to make hurricane damage assessments, a photographer whose jobs had dried up due to the pandemic built a model to revolutionize photography with an AI-based image classifier, a rock climber created a recommendation engine for rock climber using a Netflix-inspired algorithm, and a PhD physics student built an image-to-image transfer model for metamaterials.

On top of the curriculum and projects, Springboard provides a unique network of personalized support for each student. Students are matched with advisers and have weekly one-on-one meetings with them. Upon graduation, students are also matched with a career coach to support them through the job-search process. Overall, Springboard acts as a support system, coach and cheerleader for working professionals. Liudmila Khalitova (data science career track graduate in April 2021) was offered a $115,000 dream data scientist job at Advanced Dermatology and Cosmetic Surgery, one of the largest dermatology providers. Mengquin 'Cassie' Gong (data science career track graduate, 2020) was offered a place on the Facebook product team as a data scientist for the return-to-work programme. Though Cassie did not have direct experience as a data scientist, she passed all technical interview rounds with flying colours!

> *There's tremendous potential to solve some of humanity's biggest problems by harnessing AI and for that, we'll need many more skilled professionals than we have today.*
> —Parul Gupta, co-founder, Springboard

Envestnet Yodlee: Reskilling for Tomorrow

Envestnet Yodlee,[11] a leading data aggregation and data analytics platform, helps consumers live better financial lives through innovative products and services created for more than 1,400 financial institutions and fintech companies, including fifteen of the top twenty US banks.

Envestnet Yodlee offers a host of AI-powered financial wellness solutions that enable actionable advice and personalized financial coaching for consumers. The offerings include a financial data platform, AI-powered 'finapps', and APIs, which enable financial institutions and fintech companies to deliver financial wellness solutions. Core to these offerings is the data enrichment platform that provides highly accurate and easy-to-use data, enabling clients to drive insights, make smarter business decisions, and improve customer engagement.

Using new and advanced AI-driven techniques enables the identification of actionable patterns across massive data sets. Insights and financial advice based on insights mined via Envestnet Yodlee's platform can then be offered back to consumers via a plethora of channels including conversational ecosystems like Amazon Alexa.

Pramod Singh explained to us his journey as a chief analytics officer (CAO) while he led the change in his organization and transformed the talent to move towards AI. He mentioned to us during our interview that steering an entire organization towards such a change is equivalent to a big ship turning and changing its course. For Envestnet Yodlee, it was about changing the functioning of all departments. The firm had salespeople who were used to selling deterministic data solutions while AI solutions were probabilistic. The sales team had to learn the language of AI, including words like 'precision' and 'recall'—hitherto unheard of for all of them. The customer support team knew how to handle hotfixes when issues required immediate fixes. Now there was an AI model and the team needed to understand that the models would need to be retrained when issues/errors were reported. In an AI model, one could get 96 per cent accuracy, which meant that 4 per cent of the times things would go wrong. How would the team explain that known margin of error to customers? How would it set the right expectations? Would customer support reps be able to understand and explain coherently?

Pramod knew that the DNA of the company had to transform. He went about changing everything, from the development process to customer support, sales team, product management philosophy, sales support teams, and even the quality assurance (QA) teams. To deliver on the promise of AI-driven solutions, he built a team with three solid pillars: core data science, analytics engineering, and business analytics. These teams were underpinned by strong annotation capabilities and quality practices. To differentiate the notion of analytics/data science quality from typical QA in a software organization, he also renamed the QA team as the analytics solution validation team and staffed it with a mix of skills. With that, the capabilities to develop and deliver AI solutions were in place.

To set the pace and evangelize AI, he invited the entire sales team, including the CEO, to an internal analytics summit in the company headquarters. He flew down top data scientists and made them run the three-day summit for the entire sales team. Day Zero was a boot camp on orienting participants towards AI. Day One was on 'Why AI?', where they discussed opportunities where AI could be applied. Day Two was an event where the company leadership was asked to pitch their analytics/AI ideas to the CEO and a jury which could turn ideas into pragmatic solutions. This summit was a tremendous success, and the entire sales and product organization was now geared towards positioning AI as a game-changer that enabled cutting-edge solutions. The entire team had an unclouded vision of 'Why AI?' and had trust in the data scientists to solve the 'How AI?' part of the question says Smitha Suryanarayanan, senior director, Business Analytics, Envestnet Yodlee. Smitha was key in organizing this summit for Pramod and is herself among the top 150 AI leaders/influencers in India, as per 3AI.

For Pramod, it was particularly important to work with the sales team as it was following, in his words, 'the classical wine and dine approach'. He said this approach enabled the team to get a foot in the door of a client's office but did not prepare them for a second or third level of discussions on AI. The salespeople were not yet in a position to have AI-centric conversations with the customers. Moreover, the team was not engaging data scientists in conversations with customers as it felt the latter were too technical. This meant that while salespeople needed to become conversant with AI, data scientists too needed to demonstrate familiarity with business requirements.

He also gave us multiple examples of the data science team's involvement in customer conversations, which enabled meaningful discussions and helped in setting the right expectations. Today, the sales and customer support teams have an open line of communication where they involve the data science teams as early as possible in both pre-sales and client management conversations. This partnership has fundamentally changed the way the company does sales and account management of its new AI solutions and services to clients.

Today, Envestnet Yodlee touts its AI-driven solutions as foundational to its solution portfolio. The journey has come full circle, from having to 'sell' AI concepts internally a few years ago to AI now being embedded in several commercialized solutions!

HAMMER LOOKING FOR A NAIL

Data scientists love working on newer technologies and adding new frameworks to their résumés. Many times, what needs to be seen is whether the model makes sense. Pramod talked about saving millions of dollars by *not doing projects that do not make sense*. He cites an example where his team created some models that would have taken $2 million to create the whole project while the total market size was just $5 million. He also narrated a story to us about a data scientist he interviewed who seemed to have forcibly used recurrent neural network or RNN models because it looked good on his résumé, and another who used SPARK when all that was needed was Tableau visualization. All examples of an aircraft engine being embedded for a chariot.

5

AI and Culture

An interesting experiment called Mindset Matters[1] was done by Elissa Farrow, a researcher at the University of Sunshine Coast, Australia. It studied how mindset affects the ability of employees in an organization to anticipate and adapt to AI.

Mindset as a concept was first introduced in Dr Carol S. Dweck's 2006 book *Mindset: Changing the Way You Think to Fulfil Your Potential*.[2] This experiment by Elissa went further and studied people with growth mindsets and fixed mindsets and their respective reactions to AI. Participants were given a hypothetical scenario: 'If you are not technically capable or [do not] offer a unique "value add" you will lose your jobs due to AI in 2030.' The participants were oriented to two scenario settings and their reactions in each were collected as data. First scenario was of a fixed mindset and the second of a growth mindset and traits of both were provided to all participants. To introduce the scenario, role playing, experiences, and behaviours were explained. Participants had to step into each relevant mindset and document their 'immediate personal response, feeling or sense'.

When people were in a fixed mindset, they had strong expressions of 'fear', 'anger', and 'loss of self-worth'. People expressed anger or blame towards the leader or shared feelings of 'betrayal by the organization'. The fixed mindset expressed a 'loss of purpose', 'identity', and 'status' and most people described a condition of 'not being able to learn'. Other words were 'end, death, doom, inhuman' and 'feeling of powerlessness'.

The same participants were then shifted on to the growth mindset.

When this shift occurred, there was a positive change in energy and mood in the room, according to the researcher. Participants expressed a 'strong sense of self', 'determination', and 'self-belief in the ability to adapt and find solutions'. Several suggested that they 'could offer something that AI could not replicate' in the foreseeable future such as 'connection', 'physical touch', and 'empathy'. Participants were thankful for the 'reduction of boring' or 'dehumanizing' work. Many participants had a 'willingness to learn new skills' and 'explore AI technically'. One participant even wanted 'AI to be their new best friend at work'. There was definitely an excitement in this experiment group to use AI to 'bring better outcomes to the community'.

The findings of the above study[3] were clearly pointed out by Elissa, stating that: '1. Mindset embodiment enriches the ability to anticipate, plan and action future scenarios; 2. Mindset selection affects activation of higher order motivations and needs; 3. Open and willing frames of mind enable shared learning and insights.'

A mindset change is needed for a cultural transformation in the organization. A cultural change will not happen unless an AI mindset sets in. The above experiment had the same participants, but their responses differed depending on the mindset they had: fixed or growth. A growth mindset welcomes AI and wants to ride the wave of positive change. It does not see AI as a threat. Organizations need to drive the change of their employees from a fixed mindset towards a growth mindset. Driving change is not easy—it is like a huge ship changing direction while sailing on the ocean. For culture to change, you need a compass to define the direction, the true north. This is defined through an AI strategy where the flywheel is set in motion, as we explained in Chapter 1. It is also impacted by the team's mindset, which we explained in Chapter 4, where everyone needs to have a personalized learning roadmap. Additionally, it needs the right tools, as explained in Chapter 2 on AI and Innovation and Chapter 3 on AI and Technology.

The AI mindset is not the responsibility of any one department head, but must be owned and executed by the CEO directly.

According to a *Harvard Business Review* report, 'The AI-Powered Organization',[4] most organizations take eighteen to thirty-six months to complete AI transformations, while some take five years. The reason is that AI transformation is not a technology implementation project. It is a cultural transformation, and the AI mindset takes time to set in; it cannot happen overnight, for the reasons stated above.

Partnership with AI

Can we build a partnership with AI? Let us look at an interesting story.

An online insurance marketplace created an AI chatbot to help clients compare insurance policies across vendors and pick the right one. The chatbot was trained to capture the client's profile through data such as age, gender, need, financial history, and even medical history. Based on this, it would then pick the best policy in the market. This tool was also given to independent insurance agents to assist them during the client servicing stage. It was discovered that, while on the field, agents would introduce the chatbot to clients, but would then remark on its inadequacy and how the chatbot could never replicate the personal relationship they had. Sometimes, they would make fun of the chatbot and use failed scenarios to have a good laugh and build a rapport. Over a period of time, the agents managed to convince the marketplace that the chatbot was actually being rejected by clients. The insurance agents who never partnered with the chatbot and inherently saw it as a threat to their jobs ensured that it failed.

On the other hand, we worked with a cancer hospital overloaded with terminally ill patients where doctors had to work overtime. AI helped them put cancer detection models in place that started helping them take second opinions from their own personal advisers. The doctors partnered with AI to make it even better, and started giving feedback based on the actual decisions taken by them. The AI models improved and helped doctors. This partnership also helped clients and, of course, the hospital management.

This partnership is what is needed in an organization. In the above example, the doctors needed to learn how the AI behaved so that an outright rejection did not happen. Moreover, they needed to trust the AI output.

Treating AI as our own adviser and removing the inherent fear of it is of paramount importance. Employee acceptance is key for AI to take root in an organization. Employees in the business unit have to be convinced for a successful AI implementation, not the technical team.

An organization which has a culture of collaboration between those who possess domain knowledge and those who are implementing AI will be able to create AI which thrives. For this to happen, organizations should be open for collaboration. The leadership should facilitate diverse teams to work together for building the right AI content and methodology. We highly recommend setting up of an AI ethics organization that can serve as the conscience of the organization. Responsible AI is a must-have thought process which needs to be part of the culture. While designing AI systems, humanistic questions should never be ignored. The AI Ethics organization should delve into governance policies, principles, tools and methodologies of AI systems build. Fairness, robustness, bias, explainability all should be in the purview of AI ethics.

Predictive maintenance of machines would not be possible until mechanical engineers explain what makes a machine fail, the operations team captures all machine failure data, the analytics teams explain the relation between different parameters of the machine, and the data scientist collaborates with each one of the above to build the model.

For an agile, nimble, failure-prone, risk-taking culture, leaders should expect barriers to AI and explain them well. AI too needs feedback; hence, in this partnership, employee contribution is maximum.

How to Address the Fear of AI

Organizations need to confront this problem head-on and address the fear of AI lingering in employees' minds, as we also mentioned in the introduction. The fear of AI is present in several people across AI-born, AI-enabled, and AI-led organizations. The type of fear might change, and, hence, the fear mitigation plan should also be made according to that.

Multiple change transformation studies show that this fear of AI is felt only by a section of people—perhaps around 20 per cent. Everyone does not face the same fear, but it can permeate across employees, and, for a true culture change, it is vital that we talk about it openly.

There are five types of fear that people associate with AI. Here, we discuss the reasons for them and the methods to address them, in detail.

1. *Fear of Loss of Jobs*

    Let us look at what history teaches us about the fear of modern technology.

    Back in the 1980s, there was a large one-day strike by employees of all public sector banks against computerization in India. Computers were taking their jobs away, they feared. They realized that soon there would be no need for accountants who spent all their time tallying ledgers and books. There was paranoia among the employees that a huge number of them were going to be made redundant. Well, the impact of computerization on the banking industry is there for all of us to see. The number of jobs in the financial industry and the software companies which mushroomed over the last decade to handle online banking, core banking software, and ATMs are unimaginable. The fintech sector is worth billions of dollars in India alone, and is a trillion-dollar opportunity worldwide. According to Invest India,[5] a national investment promotion agency set up by the

Government of India, the overall Indian fintech market is currently valued at $31 billion and is expected to grow to $84 billion by 2025, at a CAGR of 22 per cent. Further, the transaction value in the Indian fintech market is estimated to jump from approximately $65 billion in 2019 to $140 billion in 2023. Invest India also mentions that India saw cumulative investments of $10 billion in the fintech industry in the last four years.[6] This phenomenon cannot be ignored and compared with the few jobs lost in the 1980s.

We all know how crowded India's Dalal Street would be, with brokers clamouring to trade shares. With computerization, everything changed. The industry saw a sea change when staff who used to work till late at night started going home early and had a holiday on Sunday. Further, the market grew in size, and, with the increasing demands of clients, the turnover of most brokers trebled.

The computerization of the Indian Railways reservation system changed the way we travelled. The railways had to spend two years evolving a system that took care of seven classes of travel, thirty kinds of fare concessions, seventy-five different types of coaches, and over hundred special reservation quotas—a previously unimaginable scale. Of course, there were doubts, cases of fraud by touts, and workarounds by people through the system's various loopholes. But over a period of several iterations, the system improved to cater to billions in India.[7]

Today, there is a fear of loss of jobs because AI promises to do away with some mundane tasks done by humans. Yes, some jobs which are highly routine might go away, but they will get replaced by higher-order thinking jobs which will come in plenty. The gap between job loss and job creation is not a subject of study, and not much research is available. But we can compare this trend to the computerization wave which happened several decades ago and only benefited humankind. A change is hitting us which will change our job conditions, and, as we have adapted to all changes, we will adapt to this one as well, by reskilling and going ahead with a growth mindset.

2. *Fear of Wrong Decisions*

The great power given to us by advancements in AI algorithms does indeed come with great responsibility. Trusting AI to make decisions for us brings a fear of whether those decisions are right, whether they are just, whether they can be trusted, whether they are valid or efficient.

As AI becomes all-pervasive and powers our cars, healthcare, homes, phones, and factories, it is important that trust in AI is established. That trust can happen only when human values are reflected in AI and it is taught to make human-type decisions.

It is important that we start building transparency and explainability in our AI models. We need our business and domain users to understand why algorithms take specific decisions and recommendations, the impact of previous choices, and the confidence score on the decisions made. We need explainable and understandable models which can power business users while they are running their businesses.

A clear brief of the domain user is vital for incorporating explainability in AI apps. Is the model going to be used by a retailer, space planner, or an aviation operations manager? The business user is the ultimate person who will benefit from the AI model; hence, explainability has to be in tune with him or her. Every business user has the right to know about the usage of data types, weightages given to each factor, and the contributing factors for specific recommendations or optimizations.

IBM has built an AI Explainability 360[8] toolkit which has a set of eight open-source explainability techniques which can be used by anyone building AI models in the industry.

When we go to buy a refrigerator, we check the power rating, and that governs our buying decision. Today's aware consumers want to pay more for sustainable and energy-saving appliances as they think about sustainability, green appliances, and the need for a better world. In similar fashion, there is awareness about what constitutes trustworthy and responsible AI, and IBM has published factsheets for increasing trust in AI services through the Supplier's Declarations of Conformity, which is a self-declaration mechanism to show that a product or service conforms to a standard regulation. As transparent reporting mechanisms are the basis for trust and safety in many industries and applications, including the food industry with its nutrition labels on each food item, the AI factsheet[9] is, as described by IBM on its website, 'a collection of relevant information (facts) about the creation and deployment of an AI model or service. Facts could range from information about the purpose and criticality of the model, measured characteristics of the data set, model, or service, or actions taken during the creation and deployment process of the model or service.'

3. *Fear of Bias*

Many big tech companies have struggled with AI, and this has made news for all the wrong reasons! Amazon scrapped their recruitment software as it was seemingly biased against women, and was choosing candidates based on ten-year-old data, with more men being selected. The software had downgraded the rating of two women-only colleges as potential recruitment sources. In another case, Cambridge Analytica was found to be using the personal data records of millions of people on Facebook which contributed towards the alleged rigging of the 2016 US Presidential elections. Meanwhile, spurred by George Floyd's death and the ensuing racial outcry, several large technology behemoths quit the facial recognition business, saying they were concerned about how the technology could be used for mass surveillance and racial profiling. Joy Buolamwini, a researcher at Massachusetts Institute of Technology, whose research on facial recognition bias[10] helped spur several organizations' re-examination of the technology, said in an email while testifying to the ban, 'Regardless of the accuracy of these systems, mass surveillance enabled by facial recognition can lead to chilling effects and the silencing of dissent.' Joy's research and work in this area can be seen in the widely watched Netflix documentary *Coded Bias*.

Bias in algorithms is dreadful, but we need to understand how it creeps in. Is it bias in the data fed into the models or is it the bias of the data scientist creating the model? It is humans who are biased and not AI. So, if for decades an insurance company has avoided giving loans to a certain group of people based on caste, religion, age group, or race, then the AI model will automatically exclude that group. The AI model would be trained using that data set which completely avoided a certain set of people.

This fear of bias should be addressed, as organizations are made up of people who are biased. End users will stop trusting organizations deploying AI models if the bias is not mitigated and declared in a transparent manner. IBM has published AI Fairness 360[11] which is a comprehensive open-source toolkit for handling bias in ML models. It has over seventy fairness metrics, ten bias mitigators, and extensive tutorials for industries like finance, human capital management, healthcare, and education. Organizations should encourage the use of these bias mitigators to provide confidence to internal employees and clients. Organizations should seed and cultivate an AI ethics organization that will have common policies written for all AI users.

4. *Fear of Ultimate Control over Humans*

'The singularity[12] is coming soon, and the world will be ruled by machines!'

This is the warning screamed out at readers in several blogs and articles, sending shivers down the spine of anyone who reads them. Singularity, as defined by Wikipedia, 'is a hypothetical point in time at which technological growth becomes uncontrollable and irreversible, resulting in unforeseeable changes to human civilization'. It is the vision of a future in which super-intelligent machines overtake humans.

And thanks to a steady stream of Hollywood movies, the doomsday vision due to AI has been embedded in our psyche. That AI will rule the world and humans will be enslaved is a fear spread by some AI researchers too. The AI takeover is, in fact, a hypothetical scenario in which AI will surpass human intelligence and be the dominant intelligence on earth, taking control over humans. This takeover includes a scenario when the entire human workforce will be replaced by AI and robots.

Stephen Hawking warned that advanced AI technologies 'could spell the end of the human race' because people would be unable to compete with them.[13] Elon Musk tweeted in 2014:[14] 'Hope we're not just the biological boot loader for digital superintelligence. Unfortunately, that is increasingly probable.' He also donated $10 million to the Future of Life Institute,[15] a leading AI safety research programme.

The fear of the unknown has always been a great motivator for humans. The sun was a mystery until Copernicus revealed its secrets and was ostracized for his findings. An airplane was considered a monster in its early days, and, more recently, mobile phones and the Internet were thought to spoil children until the COVID-19 pandemic struck and children in cities had no option but to attend their classes using mobile devices. A game changer for society is always viewed with doubt and fear due to its vast potential.

It's important for us to allay fears and bring in human-centred AI. As mentioned in the introduction, Germany has taken leadership in building the first ethical AI model used in the automotive industry. Rules, guidance, governance, and ethics councils can check these behaviours and reassure people that the world is a better place.

The fear of AI control is a well-defined problem intersecting AI and philosophy, and the only way to tackle it is to have an ethics council at each organization and ensure that AI models are tested for bias, intent, and trust. People feel safer and more empowered when they know that there is a governing council overseeing AI without vested interests. In 2019, several media newspapers reported that Google had dissolved its AI ethical advisory board within a few days of its formation as the members had too many ethical issues which they felt were out of their control.[16]

5. *Fear of Failure*

    Due to the apprehension that AI may not give the desired outcome, it is often simply not accepted or adopted in enterprises or sometimes not scaled. There are a set of people who discourage the use of AI as they believe from the outset that it will not meet stakeholder expectations or just not be able to meet the target. This is a fear of ignorance and can easily be addressed by training, learning, and giving a leadership focus to AI.

Ready to Change Organizations

An obstinate organization is one which is overly bureaucratic and not ready to take risks. Such an organization will never be able to implement AI as it takes time to show results and requires a lot of fine-tuning. Organizations which are agile, have a risk-taking culture, and celebrate failures are the ones which can implement AI much better. This is true especially for AI-led and AI-enabled organizations as they have existing structures. AI-born organizations are the newer lot where AI is fundamental to their existence and they might not have the same issues. However, as they grow, they need to be able to reorient their structures to make them more efficient and agile.

Failures in AI due to organizational culture are so detrimental that many organizations never recover from them and abandon AI completely. In such cases, if there had been an attempt to prepare the HR teams for the change, and explain what it will take for them to make this successful, the outcome could have been different.

To set up the right culture, the company leaders might have to make some changes to make AI scale. Let us discuss what kind of organization structure should be there for a better AI mindset.

Reorienting the Structure

A dilemma most leaders struggle with is whether they should create a central AI/data science/analytics organization or have AI experts embedded in each business unit to help the domain experts. Let us discuss the pros and cons and examples of each model.

In a centralized model, there is a central AI organization which sets up the governing methodologies and processes. This hub might also have a central group of data scientists who make models for the entire organization, along with a group of language experts and image and video data analysts. The idea is that such skills are rare, so the experts will provide services to different business units of the organization depending on requirements. If a marketing department needs AI to increase customer retention, it would work with this central department to help put in place an AI strategy and execute it.

Most organizations start with a centralized model, but as they grow, they realize the value of a decentralized hub and spoke model. A centralized model often fails as the responsibility of implementing AI often starts and finishes with the central department.

Hence, it is important to move to a hub and spoke model where business function heads have responsibilities and own the execution. All these heads should have defined AI leaders and undergo learnings on AI as they are key to the success of

AI. The hub takes the responsibility of AI governance, policies, ethics, and deep skills.

> *We do not have a centralized lab model of data scientists. We have several functional units such as search, recommendation, advertising, logistics, and all of them need data science models. Each functional unit has a mission, and they are trying to solve specific problems using data science. So, they have data scientists that report to the respective functional engineering leaders. In this manner they stay contained as a unit and bounded by common objectives. Now, these data scientists do not get to talk to each other and learn about common standards and practices. They might be actually solving the same kind of problem or wanting to use the right tools. Hence, we have evolved into a hybrid model where the senior-most data scientist in these functional units reports to me. My central organization is responsible for a bunch of functions which include hiring, employee evaluations and ratings, promotions, etc. Participation in external conferences, curation of internal conferences on data science topics, and even project reviews are done through this central hub. This helps to create a classic matrix organization which is the best of both worlds.*
> —Mayur Datar, chief data scientist, Flipkart

Max Life Insurance: Partnering with AI

The use of AI and big data is integral to insurance players today, for they are catering to an evolved, digitally savvy customer—one who has little time for personal interactions with insurance agents unless it's absolutely urgent, and wants to be shown products and services tailored to suit his preferences.

AI Works: Getting Its Due

Max Life Insurance,[17] India's largest non-bank private sector life insurer, covers health, pension, and annuity insurance schemes.

It offers child protection, retirement, savings, and growth plans to individuals and to groups. Headquartered in NCR, the company manages ₹90,407 crore of assets, with an assured sum of ₹1,087,987 crore and a paid claim percentage of 99.35 per cent (figures are as per the company's website).

So, when insurance companies began adopting AI predominantly, Max Life Insurance wasn't too far behind. The leading insurer was all too aware of India's rising maturity as an insurance market, which was being dominated by digitally aware customers.

Max Life had long nurtured a vision to be digitally forward. In 2010, the company set up a crucial business division called AI Works. Max Life felt the need to create this function and explore what it could do for insurance business. This operational unit directly rolled into the CEO and comprised some of the industry's most qualified analytics experts who were managing a slew of critical back end insurance processes with analytics.

For AI, 2010 was still early days the world over, and more so in India. Most business leaders didn't understand the value of analytics and were even less enthusiastic about investing in extensive capabilities to nurture this technology. But, by 2016, the market sentiment had changed. AI was no longer eliciting doubt but piquing the curiosity of C-level leaders. Regardless of the industry, every leader wanted to know how they could leverage the power of AI for their business.

And this is when AI Works truly had its moment of reckoning. This division largely dabbled with analytics until the mid-2010s, slowly fortifying Max Life Insurance's back end operational capabilities. Its sustained success bolstered confidence in AI: What else could this exciting technology do for the insurance business?

We interviewed Manu Lavanya, director and COO, to understand Max Life Insurance's AI journey, strategic vision, and, most importantly, the culture shift over the years. He said, 'In insurance, there is an immediate need to understand data across multiple dimensions that are not just restricted to back-end operations but the entire value chain—which includes customer acquisition, cohort identification, agent on-boarding, agent's success metrics, fraud detection, mortality prediction, and pretty much everything that's linked to growth. This was a huge breakthrough for business leaders, who were now keen on riding this wave.'

Until then, the autonomous business unit AI Works, which rolled into the CEO, was redirected to report directly to Manu, who had joined Max Life Insurance in January 2020. He was inspired to build value for AI Works within the organization and position it as the beating heart of all things AI for Max Life Insurance. The early days witnessed a persistent 'push' strategy, with team members saying: 'I can actually do something very exciting for you, which you cannot do on your own so please allow me to show you how.' But, over the past few years, this has graduated to a 'pull' strategy, as the demand for these niche problems-solving abilities with technologies like AI has started growing substantially. Today, AI Works takes the lead on a range of business use cases, including fraud detection, intent prediction and analysis, thirteenth-month persistence prediction, claims underwriting, payment renewals, and more.

EMPOWERING AGENTS, ONE ALGORITHM AT A TIME

While a push-to-pull strategy proved that the AI Works team was adding value to the insurance business in very strategic ways, let's look at how it actually enabled a very crucial stakeholder in the insurance ecosystem: the agent.

Who is an insurance agent? If you grew up in India in the late 1980s or early 1990s, an insurance agent would either pay you a home visit or call you on your landline to explain various insurance schemes and their benefits. Door-to-door sales were the bedrock of business growth in those days, and agents relied heavily on these personal interactions in the hope that the calls and visits would convert into a successful sale. Today, such interactions are nearly unimaginable. It is common to get hounded with calls and emails to purchase insurance, be it life or health. Employers these days have largely taken care of this by offering health insurance for employees and their families. The customer of today has drastically changed, so the agent must too. So, how does AI empower the agent?

The inflow of data aggregated and analysed by Max Life Insurance allows for hyper-personalization, customization, and even prediction of suitable insurance policies based on customer preference, all in a matter of minutes. A customer today would very much like to be wooed by a seller who knows him well, and this is where AI comes in.

'One of the most frustrating things an agent faces is rejection of a potential customer in underwriting, for myriad reasons like being medically unfit or financially unstable. This is after the agent has spent days, sometimes weeks, going after a customer, getting all the required documentation and approvals. They want the customer to be thoroughly vetted before they can close the sale. So, now, at the point of application, there are at least sixteen decision grids to assess customer eligibility, including their medical or financial condition, before they can be deemed fit for insurance,' says Manu.

This is possible with AI, which can assimilate reams of information and data points about a customer in a matter of seconds and present the same for further analysis by an agent, allowing them to decide if this sale is worth chasing or not. Similar applications of AI are currently being used to make renewals less reliant on humans and more machine-driven. Another interesting application is penny-drop verification to ensure sufficient funds are present in a customer's account to pay his insurance premium. This is especially useful for NRIs with Indian bank accounts who need immediate information on their account's fund status. AI enables predictions to identify which customers should be reached for penny-drop verification.

Need for an AI-First Culture

So, AI can do these wonderful things—it can predict what kind of insurance scheme is suited for a customer; it can initiate premium renewal automatically and complete the end-to-end transaction; it can help detect insurance fraud with incredible accuracy; it can also estimate your longevity looking at your image alone and accordingly suggest life insurance policies. But this is what we already know. Was getting this far easy?

Certainly not.

As mentioned earlier, setting up a separate function called AI Works certainly helped Max Life Insurance achieve its AI goals in a steadfast, dedicated manner. It also helped that the CEO at the time had a vision for the company's future, and fully endorsed investing in AI capabilities. But just getting the CEO's buy-in isn't sufficient. Key decision makers across the board had to be onboarded as well.

'There was huge resistance to change because everyone felt they could make better decisions than a bot. The dependency on heuristic learning was far higher than the belief in machine-based learning,' says Manu.

But the road was full of possibilities. The first order of business was changing the mindset across the value chain. Max Life Insurance launched a series of projects called Building the Intelligence Enterprise, which showcased the value of analytics to the organization. The express purpose of these projects was to create winners, use cases, studies, and show internal stakeholders the true value of AI and analytics.

There was an imperative need for creating awareness, building knowledge assets, and removing the proverbial black box that everyone believed AI functions in. In 2020, the organization conducted analytics training for all business leaders, which required them to learn concepts like random forest algorithms, descriptive verses, descriptive analytics, national variability, and so on. Additionally, it helped to strategically and specifically prove at least one heuristic model wrong.

'By doing this, you break the long-guarded belief that a heuristic-based learning model is the only way to go, and that AI really does deliver tangible results. It is critical to demonstrate this social experiment for a lasting impact. That's when belief in AI will grow,' says Manu.

All these strategies and steps required a team effort. Max Life Insurance worked with a range of partners, including consulting majors, start-ups, technology solution providers, policymakers, and others. While some aspects of strategy were outsourced, such as cloud and data infrastructure, other capabilities were retained in-house, such as data modelling and business change management.

Another key cultural change was brought in by mixing AI practitioners with business professionals, and vice versa, which made the existing talent pool versatile. So, today, an underwriting operations analyst will work on analytical modelling, while those in analytical modelling will be groomed in business operations and underwriting management. This cross-pollination of talent has been absolutely critical to Max Life Insurance's AI success. Its goal is that, in five years, one should not be able to differentiate between a data scientist and an insurance underwriter.

THE AI IMPACT, MEASURED

Bot-based servicing is at 21 per cent, with 75 per cent accuracy. This year, the goal is to take it to 30 per cent with 88 per cent accuracy. Collection rates touched 88 per cent, from 83 per cent, with the use of AI and ML in just one year.

AUGMENTING THE HUMAN TOUCH

When a personal tragedy befalls us, like an illness or the death of a loved one, words fail to convey condolences adequately. During such hard times, the way an insurance company treats bereavement and loss is crucial to their public image and standing. Machines are nowhere close to mastering this level of empathy, but there are many other tasks they can undertake with great efficiency and accuracy. While the human touch in this sector will remain a mainstay, AI can ease laborious processes to aid agents in what they do best: help another person in their hour of need.

6

AI and Users

Delighting the user is the singular outcome which an AI mission should focus on. Everything else, including people, technology, strategy, talent, and innovation are a means to the end goal of user satisfaction.

But, before one can delight the user, there needs to be a clear understanding of who the user is: not developers, not risk officers, not the CIO/CXOs who funded the AI initiatives and not the line of business leaders. End users are the group which is impacted by the AI the most.

Let's continue our example of location-based services in the context of cabs and food-delivery applications. Who are the end users there? The cab drivers or the delivery staff? This set of users is not the most technologically savvy or in some cases even (highly) educated. They simply need the capability to enter the destination in the app, find the optimal path, and then follow the step-by-step directions, including the traffic conditions. They do not care about the greatest and latest AI model powering the application, the scalable technology stack to make the app work seamlessly, or any other tools or processes which went into making the application! The other set of users are the customers who book cabs using these apps. For them, user satisfaction is measured if they are able to correctly track the vehicles, get a time estimate, and connect with the driver or delivery executive when needed. If the app is not able to satisfy these two sets of users, all the cutting-edge AI innovations are meaningless!

Similarly, let's look at crop yield prediction for farmers. Do you think farmers care about the number of hidden layers or the learning rate used during training for an app? All they are concerned with is an accurate prediction of the yield which can be used for planning purposes.

Very often, user needs force a relook at standard and established algorithms and systems. For example, recommendation algorithms have been around for decades and are the cornerstone of many online portals. However, Flipkart realized that, while buying clothes, customers want to get an idea of the quality of cloth used in their manufacture. The team inferred the quality of clothes from each seller based on feedback from other users and ratings to introduce a new metric called 'trust factor', which can be used to rank and recommend clothes. This is a great example that shows how established algorithms and technology may need to be improved to meet user demands.

It is a very important distinguishing factor to understand that the end user doesn't care about how an AI application was built but only *what* problem it solves for them.

However, it's also important to acknowledge that while the end user does not explicitly care about the AI back end indirectly she/he will be affected by it. If a location-based services application is not hosted on a fast, robust, and scalable infrastructure, then the drivers will face outages, slow responses, and other such problems which will certainly not delight them. Similarly, information about the number of layers is irrelevant, but the quality of prediction which directly correlates with the network architecture is important.

So, AI teams and AI users are two sides of the same coin, and their thinking needs to match for the successful adoption of AI. Non-technical user requirements have to be mapped to the technical AI goals, which the team can keep in mind while going through the AI life cycle. There needs to be a relentless focus on the end user's needs. The user also needs to mimic the broader market needs and, therefore, is increasingly intertwined with the business success. Think about the first time Apple decided to get rid of the physical keyboard in favour of the touch screen based on user feedback and innovation. In a few years, all other phones had got rid of physical keyboards too. The trend of removing the keyboard had a long-term impact. The companies which did not pay attention to the market demand ceased to exist.

Users versus Clients

It is extremely important to differentiate between users and clients for the AI team. The AI team's clients are the internal stakeholders who engage the AI team by providing them with the requirements, data, roadmap, infrastructure, etc. The clients will be responsible for adding the AI model into the products and then offering the same to the end customers.

In most cases, the AI team's first point of contact is someone in the client team as opposed to the end user. The client team (to the best of their abilities) will communicate the user requirements. However, it may not be able to capture all the nuances of what the client wants. Every minor slippage in translation of the user need by the client will be amplified in the resultant AI model. Therefore, it is essential for the AI team to be in touch with the end users. Not only does this interaction help the AI team understand user needs, it can also help the end user see different perspectives. Let us share a real-life AI development and deployment anecdote where the gap among the end user, client team, and technology team was glaring.

A big bank in India was facing huge waiting times (approximately 110 minutes per customer) at one of their physical branches. The bank used a token system and followed a 'first in, first out' or FIFO scheduling policy. The customer would come into the bank, get a token from the token machine, and then wait till her number was displayed on the panel.

The key problem was that the bank was not able to focus on high net worth individuals or the services which generate direct revenue. This led to huge customer dissatisfaction and loss of revenue for the bank. In fact, most customers came to the branch to withdraw small sums of money or get their statement of accounts. Based on inputs from the client team (mostly from sales and services), the AI team built a model to perform scheduling using a customer's net worth and the value of the service requested. The model performed very well on historical data and reduced the wait time of preferred customers by 80 per cent. The system was tested across multiple distributions and load settings and in all scenarios the results were excellent!

With the usual fanfare, the system was deployed in the branch. From a customer's standpoint, however, nothing changed. They took their tokens and waited for their number to be displayed on the panel. Within forty-five minutes of the bank opening, there was chaos—ugly scenes of customers shouting and a physical fight almost breaking out between the customers and the bank staff. The system was taken down, and the client and AI team were notified. So much for the sophisticated AI algorithm and thorough testing! So, what went wrong?

The teams went to the bank the next day to understand more. They talked to some customers and realized their error. In the earlier system, the customers were able to estimate their wait time by looking at the token numbers displayed on the panel and compare them with their own. For example, if the current token was 50 and the customer's token was 80, they knew that they had a longer wait. They would find a seat and wait. However, in the new non-FIFO system, they could not estimate this, and the ordering looked random to them. They all gathered around the display panel and started to get uneasy when token 50 was followed by 68 and not 51. The teams understood this and built a wait time estimation model and started showing expected wait times on the panel. With this, a sense of reasonability prevailed, and the customers were assuaged. They were able to see when they would be served and were satisfied.

This anecdote shows how the undesirable situation on the first day of deployment could have been avoided if the AI team had directly interacted and observed the customers by visiting the bank. They had instead relied on client teams who in turn changed the objective of this new scheduling to reduce wait times and totally discounted how it would impact the customers.[1]

Outcome versus Process

The focus of developing an AI roadmap should be on outcome and not on technology, sales, marketing, and so on. Remember, the outcome is the outcome for the user and not for the AI team. Outcome-driven thinking will evolve from the close collaboration of various teams (AI, clients, and users). Outcome means different things for each team:

- *Users*: As discussed earlier, the AI system needs to demonstrate value to the end user. This can be in the form of better decisions, faster decisions, getting more options with pros and cons, or automating something which the user cannot easily do. For example, AI-based stock trading software makes it easier for the user/trader to make an investment and trading decision by looking at insights on a single screen. The screen provides historical data, insights in terms of patterns, predictions, recent news/corporate action of the stock, etc. Without the software, the user would have to manage multiple windows, each hooked to different sources of information, and manually analyse the data. In real-time systems, like the stock market, digesting all the information and taking action in real time is a daunting exercise which only a small percentage of traders can do.
- *AI Team*: Outcomes for AI teams are more technical. The teams will care and be responsible for the accuracy, latency, robustness, and other such markers of the model.

In our stock trading app example, the AI team will focus on information integration from multiple sources: technical charts (time series), fundamental ratios (numbers), news (text), etc. Once integrated, the team will focus to build pattern-mining and prediction algorithms while keeping the millisecond response time in mind.
- *Client Team*: This team is interested in more customer acquisition and maintaining the differentiation in the market. It will be most knowledgeable about the different products in the market and also the most pressing user requirements.
- *CIO/Infrastructure Team*: The core platform on which the service is hosted is the main area of focus for this team. It will make sure that the platform has the most recent (and relevant) technology. This is the team which will ensure that storage, applications, and middleware are available. For example, in a trading app, there is a need for 'time series', 'text', and 'columnar' data storage and the associated processing libraries like Lucene, ARIMA, TensorFlow, etc. Uptime, scaling, fault tolerance, fallback, latency, etc. are the metrics of interest for this team.

As mentioned repeatedly, the teams need to work together towards this mission. However, it is important to understand the flow of information. The needs or requirements must flow from users to the technical teams. At this point, the requirements will be in business terms. The client and technical teams need to work with users to translate business requirements to technical requirements. For example, the user may say that the app should be fast with no delays. This needs to be quantified. What does fast mean? Should it be 10 milliseconds faster or 100 milliseconds faster? This translation will also result in documenting the non-functional requirements (NFRs), which are critical for applications in production.

Next, the technical teams need to work together to finalize the stack. This is always a give-and-take process since the AI team will always have the most recent stack, whereas, the infrastructure team will push back citing other efforts the same platform is supporting. In any case, this decision should not be based on the AI team's demand for the flashiest tech or the infrastructure team's resistance to on-board any new component. The choice really needs to pass a single and most crucial gate: Does the choice of components help in meeting user requirements? In between all these negotiations and translations, the offering and the business teams need to keep everything grounded by providing inputs and helping prioritizations. Since the team has a global and competition view, they will help to identify features as 'must-have' versus 'nice to have'. It will also be responsible for capturing the ROI for each feature, and that itself can help in prioritization.

There is no flowchart or cycle which can capture the exact sequence of these interactions. The bottom line is that teams need to work together.

User Journey for AI

Keeping the user as the central element in the AI mindset is very difficult in practice. How do we keep users engaged? How do we elicit requirements from users? How do we reproduce the requirements? These and other such questions often hinder user centrality.

There are multiple different ways to accomplish this. Let us look at some of them:

- *User Workshops*: Workshops are a great way to engage users to understand their requirements and priority of the problems where AI can help. Ideally, the client team, AI team, and users should come together for this exercise. The goal is not to build solutions but to understand the problems. During our discussions with the AutoAI design team,[2] it mentioned that many important and useful features in AutoAI have come through such workshops.

Many times, such workshops can be uncomfortable because the end users may not prioritize the hardest problem which the AI team wants to solve but rather bring out UX- and process-related requirements.

- *User Design Thinking*: Usually, a very hands-on way of working, this is another collaborative process where users and design teams come together to brainstorm on a problem. Participants are encouraged to speak up or use tools like post-its or murals to share an idea. The point is to gather as many ideas as possible without going too deep into any of them. Once the breadth of the ideas is there, then the team works to prune, prioritize, and select a few for deep dives. These ideas mostly shape the products. Running these sessions is an art, and the organization should hire or outsource their execution. If done right, they can be very engaging, hands-on, and full of energy. If done wrong, they can be extremely boring and a waste of time and effort. The choice of participants is crucial. To generate a wide range of ideas, it is important to get a diverse set of participants to get multiple perspectives on the same topic.
- *Sponsored Users*: Yet another way of engaging users is to work with trusted partners or customers. The core idea is to on-board a few users to the new AI services and let them try them out. These users should be personally motivated and committed to the outcome of the study. In fact, sponsored users are indeed those who understand and face the problem which is being solved by the AI system. Users who do not appreciate the problem will not be able to provide relevant feedback. As an example, if one has developed an AI system to tag and protect sensitive information before data is hosted on the cloud, then ideally financial industry clients are the best suited as sponsored users. These users should be active in providing feedback and making the service better. They should be open to collaboration and freely share their

experience in using the service. Sponsored users need to sign a non-disclosure agreement, so the IP confidentiality is preserved. Very often, sponsored users become the first paying customers of these services. The agreement and relationship with a sponsored user is managed by the client team or management; however, the AI team needs to constantly and directly interact with these users first-hand to understand the issues, feedback, and areas of improvement.

- *Beta Release*: Sponsored users are almost part of the extended team and provide (kind) feedback to system developers. The beta release is taking it one step ahead. This is the phase when all development, UI, and integration is done but there is a possibility that system bugs may exist. The beta release enables other users to use the system and report issues. Beta release users can also be chosen by the organization to limit the damage in case of bugs. However, users do expect the system to be complete at this stage.

Role of Users in Different Stages of AI

Let us look at the role that users play across the AI PoC to AI transformation stages:

1. *AI PoC*: While this is the test and trial stage for AI, user focus is important. However, correct expectations should be set on the objective of this phase, which is not to have a finished, ready-to-use system, but rather to educate the user on what is possible. Many times, users will overestimate what AI can do (this is partly the fault of the client team and AI team, who oversell AI). The PoC will go through a design workshop, including close collaboration with the AI team, lightweight system-building without full integration, mock-up screens, and manual interventions. Evaluating the PoC will need some vision and creativity from users. Many times, users get stuck on operational issues like where the

click button should be or the format of the reports, etc. In this phase, they should be told to look at the bigger picture, ignore the gaps, and extrapolate the experience. The focus should be on whether the AI system will help or not. It is important to choose the correct mix of users to engage with for this phase. Users with no imagination will bog the team down with unnecessary cosmetic details.

2. *AI Infusion*: This is the phase where users employ the system in production and generate value for themselves and the business. All users are equally important at this stage and no hand-picking should be allowed. Take the example of a map service; users with diverse educational backgrounds, socio-economic status, linguistics, etc.—all use the system. The service will only be successful if it caters to all of them. Users will continue to provide feedback for improvements. The prioritization, usefulness, and applicability of the feedback is done together by the technical and business teams. In this stage, users will not have patience for bugs or half-developed features. They will be demanding and brutal in rejecting the services. So, AI should only be rolled out when it is ready, and that too in gradual fashion. Some users may also need to go through training for adoption of the service. Remember, this is the phase of scaling, and scale will only come when all users are taken into consideration, and their requirements, knowledge, and expectations are taken care of.

3. *AI Transformation*: By the time organizations get to this stage, users have seen the benefits of AI and are fully on board, even enthusiastic about the opportunities AI can unlock! In the transformation stage, users become partners in AI development and co-creation. They are open to trying out new ideas. The best way to leverage users is to work on their complex problems (which the organization could not do in the first two phases). The difficult problems are risky in the sense that they may not be completely solved but the upside of engaging in this exercise is huge. So, the

organization needs to identify partners and users who share their belief and confidence in AI and go full steam ahead for the transformation stage.

HealthifyMe: Transforming Lives

HealthifyMe[3] is a Bengaluru-based health and nutrition start-up providing services such as calorie-tracking, one-on-one nutrition and fitness coaching, and AI-powered diets and workout plans. It is Asia's largest application, with around 15 million users on the platform and an in-house team of certified nutritionists, fitness trainers, doctors, and yoga coaches.

The company has adopted AI as their core competency to scale and deliver extremely high-quality service to users. Ria is their in-house-developed conversational AI agent which directly interacts with customers to provide guidance on smart diet plans. Before we go into the details of Ria's various components and the associated AI, let's look at the AI evolution at the company and how it impacts their users and their expert agents/nutritionists.

The company's AI journey can be divided into three stages. We add a Stage 0 to set the baseline.

Stage 0: This is the most rudimentary stage where the customer directly converses with the nutritionists to come up with a diet plan and get their queries answered. This model resembles the standard customer case/BPO/KPO model. Typically, these models work because of the availability of a large and relatively low-priced pool of agents. However, it is impossible to scale via this model since the agents (health experts in this case) are limited and costly. The number and availability of experts also have a negative impact on customers. Imagine a paying customer trying to reach the nutritionists and not getting through due to high demand.

Stage 1: To help the experts be more effective, the company decided to use AI to assist them. The AI model named Jarvis learnt from billions of previous conversations between agents and customers to learn patterns and build a recommendation model. From a customer viewpoint, nothing changed. The customer continued to engage with the agent who was now getting additional support, tips, and recommendations from AI models.

Stage 2: Things start to get interesting here from a customer's viewpoint. In this stage, the customer also starts to engage with the AI bot. The agent comes into the picture when the AI model cannot help the customer. This collaboration across AI and agents in a seamless fashion provides an unmatched experience. Now, users don't have to wait to be connected to the experts but can start to engage with Ria. Ria was launched in 2018 and in the first year it was able to handle around 39 per cent of overall user messages. With the feedback loop, retraining, and improvements over time, in 2019, this percentage grew to 60 per cent; that is, Ria was handling 60 per cent messages on its own. The important point to note is that the number of customers (and hence the messages) were also growing at a very fast pace. So, the 60 was on a much higher customer base.

Stage 3: This is the truly transformational stage. The company launched a 'Smart Plan' which had only two parties: Ria and the customer. Ria was able to answer 100 per cent of customer queries ranging from subjects like calories to recipe recommendation to diet plans. The human expert was removed from the equation entirely. Approximately, around 60 per cent of paying customers are on this Smart Plan. Ria allowed the company to scale beyond the number of available experts and hence the profits increased from 26 per cent in 2016 to around 75 per cent in 2019. Not only is Ria able to respond to all the queries, it can also do this in ten Indian languages.

How did HealthifyMe achieve the nirvana state of AI? One of the key accelerators was the investments made by the company in acquiring deep domain expertise in Indian food. As per

Tushar Vashisht, founder–CEO, HealthifyMe, there are three key variables for data for AI to succeed.

The first one is relevant domain data. The company has curated detailed nutrition and calorific values of a large number of Indian food ingredients. Moreover, it has also considered the different names each food item is known as in different parts of India. For example, a ubiquitous fruit like apple has more than ten varieties. The company built a deep knowledge base to understand these nuances.

The second variable is usable domain data. Not all data is usable or in a usable format. Correct annotations are essential for data to be used for learning purposes.

The final variable is self-sustaining data—how the data is gathered, generated, annotated, and managed. If data generation and annotation is a sponsored process, then, very soon, the process will be stifled due to monetary and effort requirements. It is important for this process to be organic. That's what HealthifyMe excelled at, by utilizing the past agent–customer conversations, validating AI recommendation with experts, training the AI with expert inputs. This circle of improving, leveraging, and using data enabled the company to become an AI-first company.

Apart from the data strategy and deep domain expertise, the relentless focus on user needs has also helped the company build solutions to the problems that matter. We have already discussed the multilingual aspects in terms of teaching AI different food names, and the fact that Ria can communicate in multiple languages. However, that is just one aspect. Let us look at a few more highly customized features on the app:

Food Diversity: No one wants to eat the same food every day. The smart plan has an in-built diversity component to cycle through different food choices.

Customization: Across India and Asia, people observe a lot of religious days which puts constraints on what can be eaten. The app has in-built learning algorithms to take care of such events which automatically suggest the 'right' meals for Ramadan and Navratri.

Ranking: Ranking of diets is interactive, based on user choices. Many times, a user may want to swap out an unavailable item in a recipe. Not only is this allowed but the calorie/nutrition value is recalculated based on such customization.

External Event Planning: During the COVID-19 pandemic, many users were requesting immunity-boosting plans. The AI system at HealthifyMe has enough customizable points that these requests are fulfilled without big changes to the core system.

The tech team at HealthifyMe consists of around 120 people who work in an agile fashion. The average time for a minimum viable product and model-building ranges from five days to two weeks. The teams are very cognizant of the fact that they should reuse what exists and only spend time on building new models or infusing domain knowledge in existing models. The HealthifyMe co-founder, Sachin Shenoy, shared an interesting incident when they had to scrap an internal model for image recognition in favour of the Google API. The developer team was not happy to let go of the home-grown model; however, the learning stayed with the company: to focus on rolling out new, high-quality features quickly by reusing existing assets.

7

Onwards, to an AI-Powered Future

We get asked the same million-dollar question by several business leaders: Which AI use case will bring us the maximum return on investment?

Yes, everyone wants more value from the technology deployed and does not want to waste time on experimentation or prototypes which do not scale. Many times, the intent to infuse AI in businesses is there but early failures deter leaders and prevent them from investing in AI. This is even more difficult when the failure is not due to technology but more due to the choice of use case which may be too early to gain acceptability. It is exceedingly difficult to make such leaders believe in AI again.

We talked to several start-ups to understand how they evaluated the AI market. The AI start-up ecosystem is the best measure to understand the adoption sentiment as it has all the dimensions we need. A typical AI-born start-up has a bunch of people who believe in AI technology and have an innovation idea. It has a strategy in place to study the market for business drivers and benefits for those for whom the use cases are intended. The AI patterns are well studied, and AI infusion methodology is applied through a build of prototypes, tests, and scale. There are a set of venture capitalists who will beat down the business model to understand the user base as they will give money only if it makes sense to invest. Investment decisions will be made after understanding the user types, culture readiness for adoptions, availability of talent, and the overall AI mindset readiness. Further investments are also all tied to the expansion of the user base. Indeed, the start-up system is the best cauldron to test the success of the AI mindset and can provide immense learning for established organizations.

Our discussions with start-up founders and venture capitalists led us to *pi* Ventures,[1] which is an early-stage fund focused on investing in disruptive ideas leveraging ML, AI, and IoT. We analysed their *pi* demand and supply resonance framework for start-up investing and adapted it for the adoption of use cases by organizations.

We back category leaders that leverage AI to differentiate themselves. Recent times have forced the world to go remote and pushed digital adoption, resulting in strong tailwinds that have expedited the adoption of AI even more. We believe that we are now at the second inflection point of modern-age AI and it will become pervasive across all industries, all regions and use cases. We intend to focus on the accelerating as well as emerging use cases of AI in our investment decisions.
—Manish Singhal, founding partner, *pi* Ventures

Here we explain the AI resonance framework based on the *pi* demand and supply resonance map,[2] which is the best example of technology adoption and investment decisions that we have studied till now. The *pi* demand and supply resonance map was first published as a blog by Manish Singhal in May 2021, and he says that it is based on his experience with over 1,700 start-ups, out of which 50 per cent were AI-born. This map is about technology trends and adoption patterns which serve as a great experiential tool, and we have modified it for building an AI adoption strategy called AI resonance framework. We have taken several examples from Manish's original blog as they hold true for AI adoption as well.

FIGURE 7.1: AI Resonance Framework

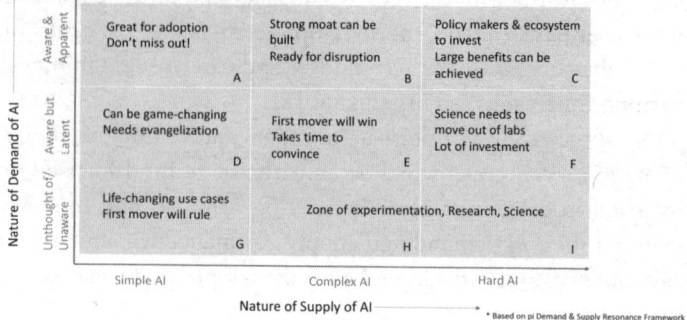

This framework is based on a simple fact: supply of AI and demand of use cases.

Demand is about the need for use cases by users in enterprises or even by end consumers. We broadly classify demand as apparent and needed (like the COVID-19 vaccine in 2021) or latent or unaware. According to the market demand at a given point in time, some use cases are more ready for adoption than others, and this is represented by the demand axis.

This demand can be met by a technology solution (represented by the supply axis) which can be simple to build and is available (incremental innovation), or complex AI or hard AI (leaning towards science).

AI research starts as hard AI but slowly moves towards being simple and easy to use. For example, consider the care of neural-network-based language models. The early language models in 2001 had limited ability to understand text and even less to generate text. They were used in academic and research settings to demonstrate small wins. Fast forward to 2021—we have GPT and GPT2 which can understand and generate complex and realistic text. The generated text is so real that it is difficult for an average reader to judge that it is AI. Moreover, due to advancements in cloud technology, hardware and API, these systems can be used by anyone now. This democratization, which took a few years, has now opened academic assets to the commercial world. The availability of technology moved leftwards on the X axis as the technology itself moved from being hard to simple and now it is no more in the research lab but in the hands of the users.

Explaining the framework in detail will require a book on its own. However, we will try to explain the key points of the framework and in the table below provide some examples of which technology maps to each cell.

TABLE 7.1: Technology Map for AI Resonance Framework

Block	Examples
A	Automation in enterprise workflows, precision agriculture
B	Exa-scale content curation and AI algorithms like search and recommendation
C	Trustworthy AI, automated data governance, policy framework
D	UX designs and innovation, AI-led drug discovery
E	Auto AI, Privacy-preserving AI
F	Large scale and multilingual language models
G	Federated learning on hybrid cloud
H	Secure computing (homomorphic computing)
I	Quantum AI

Use cases are born at the intersection of availability of technology and the needs of users. Some use cases are more ready for adoption than others. Let us understand the various blocks which are at the intersection of demand and supply in the graph as stated in Manish's blog.[3]

The demand for content recommendation on the internet was previously unthought of, though it has always been the easiest to manage from a technology perspective. We did not know we would need our internet search results to be ranked in order. But Google innovated and worked on this hitherto unseen demand, and applied recommendation algorithms to search results based on user behaviour. This was the start of an innovation which no competition has been able to beat until now.

Similarly, a simple clustering algorithm clubs together news items on Google News and is a point of contention for media houses across the globe as it beats their functioning. Similar recommendation algorithms are used by Netflix to recommend content to their users—also something no one had previously done. Block G is about that: simple AI mapped to previously unthought of demand. Today, recommendation systems are everywhere and are created using the easiest AI technologies. Pyxis One, an AI marketing infrastructure organization, is using similar recommendation algorithms to recommend content for sales and marketing. With the increase in demand, technology becomes more sophisticated, and people get brave enough to solve even harder problems.

So, which are the blocks for maximum return on investment?

Blocks A and B are about the use cases which are the most conducive for AI adoption. As the demand is apparent, it is quite easy to facilitate the uptake of these use cases. The culture for AI adoption is ripe and all business leaders should take advantage of this.

Block A is the best entry point for newcomers in AI. This is the reason we see most businesses starting their AI journey with chatbot use cases. Every business needs customer support, and chatbots are the best way to engage users and deploy AI. Meanwhile, those who build use cases around Block B are the winners as these organizations know how to build using complex AI and are tapping the demand in the market. This is exactly what BigBasket, Wysa, and Flipkart are doing. Being a first mover has given them enough advantage over the competition for the next few years and made them market disruptors. They have raced ahead of traditional organizations in their industry.

Block C caters to large societal problems where we need AI, but here the build of technology takes time. There is definitely an apparent demand in our society to save low birth weight babies or help detect cancer early or find a drug for treating COVID-19. But the AI needed to solve this is 'hard'. It needs several ecosystems to come together to solve an issue.

For instance, in the case of research on pancreatic cancer, hospitals need to provide data on thousands of patients; doctors or medical professionals need to annotate and label the data; and, of course, sophisticated ML algorithms need to get trained on this data and start giving predictions. These models will have to be run on highly compute-intensive computers and will need relearning with the help of doctors on the field and several iterations before they give even an 80 per cent accuracy. Another example is trustworthy AI. While technical folks have made a lot of progress in terms of novel algorithms, fair data sets, open-source toolkits, etc., the real and substantial impact will come once there is a regulatory framework around AI. This is outside the purview of pure technologists, and government bodies needed to lead this effort. The National Language Translation Mission,[4] announced in the Union Budget 2021–22, is an example of a policy framework which can change the speed of technology development. As per a report published by the *Economic Times* in February 2021,[5] the mission will create a 'voice-based internet' in Indian languages. The mission plans to use ML and speech recognition technologies for next-generation government apps that will be conversational in nature. This will be a major boost for AI for Indian languages, according to the report.

Block C needs huge investments and collaboration between the private and public sectors. The impact to society will be the most significant here.

While identifying and building use cases, do not leave out Blocks D and E as it takes a couple of years for demand to move from latent to apparent. These areas will face more initial hurdles in terms of evangelization but can help you create strong entry barriers for other players.

While we have mapped several technologies to the cells above, a few things need to be observed. First, the AI resonance framework is constantly in flux as technologies shift in their supply and demand parameters. Technology always becomes easier over time, as made clear by Moore's Law, where the number of transistors in an integrated circuit doubled every two years and, hence, the size of computers decreased from as large as a room to those that can fit in our hands. Consumer demand also keeps changing due to market forces.

INDIAai: India's AI Foundation

A cursory glance at global AI strategies provides some quick takeaways: AI is being developed at scale for economic growth, expanding digital skill sets for the future, and enhancing sustainability. However, India stands out for its commitment to social growth, inclusion, fairness, and explainability, as highlighted in Stanford University's Global AI Vibrancy Ranking 2020. AI in India is being utilized to empower Indians, address social inequalities, and nurture inclusion. This has been made possible as India is building a vibrant ecosystem, enabling different stakeholders to communicate and collaborate with one another, and allow an exchange of information. MeitY (the Ministry of Electronics and Information Technology), National E-Governance Division, and NASSCOM have come together with the sole purpose of creating this ecosystem and a knowledge repository for AI in India. With dedicated knowledge assets that cover the expansive AI ecosystem, in-depth feature stories on AI technologies, crucial national and international AI developments, interviews featuring AI leaders, and practitioners, INDIAai[5] is creating an AI-first ecosystem—the first of its kind in India, or anywhere else in the world for that matter. During our discussion with

Abhishek Singh, CEO, MyGov, and President, National E-Governance Division, MeitY, we discovered how the AI-first ecosystem is being built. He said, 'India has the inherent strength to be the next AI superpower with the right investments in building AI skills, research and developing population-scale AI solutions for social sectors like healthcare and agriculture that can be deployed across the world.'

INDIAai was launched on 30 May 2020, in a bid to foster the creation of a unified AI ecosystem and to bring together the AI community in India. Within a year of its launch, the portal has already established itself as a credible source of information and insights on happenings in AI in India— be it by industry, research, or government. There are detailed articles on visionary AI initiatives led by research institutions, not-for-profits, and enterprises, including IIT Kharagpur's AI solutions to augment India's legal system, Wadhwani AI's proprietary solution to tackle pests in cotton crops, Telangana's socially empowering AI mission, and Microsoft's ingenious use of helium balloon drones and TV spectrum to harness granular agricultural data. In addition, the portal showcases MEITy's work in spearheading the development of supercomputers at C-DAC and chatbots like MyGov Corona Helpdesk and MyGov Saathi for easy governance. In due course of time, INDIAai has embarked on its journey as a harbinger of research, with reports on AI standards, AI maturity index, and the Responsible AI Start-up Survey, to name a few. A particularly praiseworthy effort is the 21 Women in 21 Report, which highlights twenty-one women in AI. Not only is this reflective of the growing diversity in the AI landscape but it also echoes the sentiment that due representation breeds inclusion, benefiting everyone.

Data is sacrosanct to any AI endeavour, and India has reams of it. The biggest challenge is breaking down conventional silos and enabling seamless communication so data use is maximized. Recently, NASSCOM launched its report titled 'Digital India: Platformisation Play', which provides an in-depth insight into India's platformization approach to services like healthcare, transport, communication, governance, and agriculture, among others. Another highly ambitious mission which can be unique to India and cement its position as a leader in digital vernacular offerings is the National Language Translation Mission (NLTM). Announced in the Union Budget 2021–22, NLTM will aim to make available governance- and policy-related knowledge on the internet in major Indian languages. The success of these two national initiatives relies heavily on AI—they are expected to spur jobs, enable the growth of new skills, and create demand for products and services that have an indelible reliance on AI.

In the past few years, India has not shied away from expressing her AI ambitions and a keenness to achieve these goals with a cohesive strategy. Establishing a portal like INDIAai is a first and crucial step in that direction. Not only does it serve as a dependable information hub but it also reiterates the spirit of collaboration and cross-pollination of interests to further India's AI mission.

With 821 articles, 278 listed start-ups, 23 investment funds, 123 colleges, 89 case studies, 71 research reports, 538 national and international news items, 156 videos and 100-plus AI initiatives from government organizations, data sets, and AI standards, INDIAai is growing.

The AI Momentum

AI is more than a technology; like cloud computing, it's a mindset shift. As the technology becomes simpler and the demand for it increases, organizations will have to prepare themselves for a cultural change, upskill themselves, and continue to innovate with the right strategy. Users are going to demand increased value, and organizations will have to kickstart their AI flywheel and slowly make it build momentum.

COVID-19 accelerated demand by several years and made unaware or latent demand far more apparent.

Suddenly, we realized how widespread uncertainty is, and this taught us how our decisions and predictions cannot be merely based on historical data. The need for AI grew to help businesses plan for new exigencies. Airlines saw sudden cancellation requests, insurance companies had millions of records to process and upload, online grocery stores had multifold sales as soon as lockdowns were announced. None of the organizations would have been able to cope if they did not have automation in place along with AI algorithms.

AI is here to stay! In fact, technologies like cloud, quantum, and security will necessitate more innovations in AI, and enable AI to reach more people and have a much higher impact than we can imagine or predict. The future belongs to AI-led innovations, AI-taught workforces, AI-infused processes, AI-enhanced learning, and so on. AI ethics will increasingly play an important role in future organizations.

What we have seen so far is only a small preview, and the larger impact of AI is still to come. If an organization wants to be relevant in the future, then the time to invest in AI is now! New techniques are needed to handle the uncertain future and AI offers the best protection to leverage the changes around us. It is essential for traditional organizations to protect their future by investing now. New AI companies will be born as market demands catapult; these new organizations will continue to disrupt how we live. Businesses, in future, will have to do more with less; hence, investing in AI will provide them with exponential benefits.

8

AI Is Here to Stay

'We, the humans, created AI. Artificial intelligence is here to stay. It will define our lives; rather, it will be our lives.'

The first edition of this book, from which the above quote has been taken, was released in early September 2022, three months before ChatGPT stormed the world. In November 2022, we all woke up and saw that the entire digital world was on fire; Google called it 'code red', signalling a death knell to its search engine, and millions in India followed and contributed to OpenAI's userbase.

It's been three years since then, and who doesn't know about AI now? When we were writing the first edition of this book, we would debate how many would understand the full form of 'AI', some near and dear ones also pointing out that it would be confused with 'Air India', but we stuck to the term as we predicted it would become mainstream. Several readers asked us how we knew in 2020 and during the subsequent COVID years that AI would be the next wave. Frankly, we had not estimated this unprecedented growth, though we knew AI would become mainstream in enterprises and organizations. To quote ourselves from the first edition of this book, 'An idea whose time has come is unstoppable.' We had also mentioned the reason for our optimism in the market-readiness of AI: it stemmed from the leaps made in using lab science to produce COVID vaccines in record time. That phenomenon was the turning point, making everyone realize that science need not wait for years to be accessed by people, spurred by the population's demand for quick answers. Thus, humanity experienced a turning point in 2022, and so we mentioned in our book that the global AI race was on! Due to working in the Big Tech and conducting research for several years, we knew that deep research on AI had been going on, some breakthrough papers on AI had already been written and millions of dollars were already directed towards it. That the millions would become billions in a short span of time was unexpected. That AI would storm every household, with even ten-year-olds building AI businesses, and content generation would become useful—and even a pastime—for the entire society, was unknown even to us.

As our book was written in 2022, we have been asked by several people if it is still relevant and if they should buy it, because AI seems so different now.

First and foremost, any book written on AI is obsolete the moment it is published if we see it from the lens of data points and technology covered. In 1999, Vint Cerf, one of the founders of the internet, had said, 'They say a year in the Internet business is like a dog year—equivalent to seven years in a regular person's life.' At that time the internet was a tsunami, and we know that in our times, AI has become a tsunami in a much shorter span. Beyond North America, the internet took twenty-three years to reach 90 per cent users, while LLMs (large language models) took just three years to do the same. Every morning, we wake up to new technology releases—newer use cases are discovered, unique protocols created by the Big Tech to open up new datasets and startups formed to capitalize the new markets. What stays the same is the AI mindset which is occupying centre stage and that's what we have covered in our book. Hence, it is relevant even today and will be so for several years. The pioneering case studies covered by us showed the world that AI can be relevant and birth new business models, and today, these cases are shining examples of what AI can achieve. The IndiaAI Mission, which was only laying its foundation when we first wrote our book, is now a major force enabling India to compete in the global AI race. Viome, which was covered in our first edition, is a successful organization today; Niramai has reached more users globally and is inspiring several startups to build on AI. The foundations of AI were written in the first edition and have become large edifices which need to be studied, respected and replicated, all in the same breath. We talked about AI guardrails in our first edition and as society embraces AI even further, the need for these has amplified—organizations need a chief ethics officer (CEO) or at least an ethics committee in order to navigate the ethical and societal impacts of AI.

The five senses of the AI model, introduced and explored in our first edition, have been discussed in several forums. Whenever this model was presented, people loved it; we were happy to see what we wrote a few years ago has so much more relevance today. To quote from the first edition, 'As a foundation, the book is technology agnostic as we want to stress that AI is about a mindset.'

This new edition, with two new chapters, is about the new directions and possibilities which have opened up with AI's advancement, helping our readers to believe more in its power, build organizations with persona-based AI learning, focus on guardrails to prevent AI's misuse and create strategies which impact business. Let us understand how we need to reorient ourselves with the coming AI wave.

The AI Mindset

We talked about the fear of AI in our first edition. We also addressed bias, explainability and examples of AI going rogue, realizing the need to keep its reins in human hands. We are now making AI safety a new dimension of the AI mindset, due to its significance as AI adoption grows. We probably did not need road safety when cars had just been introduced and were used only by a few elites in the society. However, with time, car usage increased as they became affordable and so new highways were created for smoother rides. We then had to think about pedestrian safety, new rules to safeguard drivers, speed limits, and admittedly annoying but important speed bumps to break speed near populated areas. We employed human beings to monitor traffic signals and fine defaulters, arranged for extra deployments at busy signals, and even installed cameras when widespread human supervision was not feasible. And yet, we still have traffic jams, and in India, hundreds die in road accidents daily.

AI safety is needed for systems, software and generated content. Applications built for the common masses need safer guidelines while being developed. Safety is essential to improving AI's evolution. As new systems are being developed, it becomes more important to ensure explainability, apply bias filters and establish moderation guidelines, especially for citizen-facing applications.

AI and Strategy

If one chapter has stayed the same, it is the one on AI strategy. The concept of AI leaders and followers has become even more relevant with Generative AI (GenAI). The need for use case identification before you start implementing AI is key.

India has the largest potential of use cases, because we are still catching up with software evolution within our industries. As Agentic AI is getting infused in enterprise systems, new and faster agents need to be built.

Our traditional systems were reactive in nature, focusing on automating existing business processes. Digitization, however, introduced newer processes: you did not need the stamping of documents or credentialing, and so establishing and verifying identity became easier. With Agentic AI, we can build proactive systems which adapt with feedback, interact with external systems, perform multiple steps simultaneously and continue to learn with more operations. Till now, business analysis needed complex analytical skills—several trends had to be studied, presentations generated and graphs explaining thought processes built. These insights were worth a million dollars, and several follow-up meetings with relevant stakeholders also had to be scheduled, consuming a lot of time. However, now, gaining these insights has become easier through statistical and probabilistic methods; content creation in form of presentations is done on a daily basis through Claude, and OpenAI o3-mini is a go-to tool even for content writers. LLMs are being trained on volumes of data far beyond what a human brain can store, correlate and create, and this has made software development, a multi-step process, easier and swifter. 'Vibe coding', a term coined by the computer scientist Andrej Karpathy in February 2025, is a ground-breaking AI advancement, encouraging software development that emphasizes intuitive collaboration between humans and language models via natural language (NL) prompts.

Use cases have proliferated and will continue to do so. The business models of all large LLM providers are built so that they're widely adopted. Newer protocols are being introduced to enhance LLM usage as it is closely tied to the Big Tech's revenue models.

AI and Innovation

Innovation in AI has advanced from incremental improvements to the reimagining of businesses, governments and even society as a whole. Leading the charge, NVIDIA—we talked about their graphics processing unit (GPU) innovation in the previous edition—continues to push the envelope, not just with more powerful GPUs, but also by pioneering Agentic AI systems that can reason, plan and execute complex tasks autonomously. In infrastructure, new organizations like CoreWeave have emerged, which not only provide GPU infrastructure on a large scale but also support supercomputing and have signed a multi-billion-dollar contract with OpenAI.

We talked about generative adversarial networks (GANs) in our last edition, which are now central to the revolution in generating hyper-realistic photographs that help startups in media, entertainment, design, and also, sadly, allow the creation of deepfakes.

What's around the corner? Expect the rise of smart agent networks: autonomous orchestration of complex workflows, multimodal interfaces (voice, vision and text) and scalable infrastructure. Manus AI,[1] by the Chinese startup Monica.im, integrates reasoning and planning to execute complex, real-world tasks, progressing toward truly autonomous agents. Anysphere[2]—the maker of the AI-driven integrated development environment (IDE), Cursor—recently raised $900 million in Series C, soaring towards a $10 billion valuation. Its product generates 1 billion lines of code per day.

Multimodal research and innovations take AI closer to reality, as mentioned in our earlier edition, and we have now also seen Magma,[3] a multimodal foundation model, combining visual-spatial reasoning and agentic planning for UI navigation and robot manipulation and thus advancing embodied intelligence.

AI's breakthroughs and innovations in the next few years would span deep optimizations of models, algorithmic innovations, food safety, robotics, multimodal generation, drug discovery and deepfake detection. But the most relevant innovations would be applying AI to social transformations, where human issues of health, education and agriculture will be solved. India has twenty-two recognized languages. Bringing these to AI is one of the most relevant innovations as this touches the lives of all Indians, including them in this positive transformation.

AI4Bharat, a research lab at IIT Madras, was founded with a clear vision—to bridge gaps and make AI work for India's languages, cultures and people. The Nilekani Centre at

AI4Bharat was launched under the Wadhwani School of Data Science and AI. This is an open-source initiative dedicated to building high-quality datasets and AI models that enable speech recognition, machine translation and text-to-speech systems across all twenty-two scheduled Indian languages. The initiative is backed by strategic partners such as the Ministry of Electronics and Information Technology (MeitY) and the EkStep Foundation, and is aligned with India's broader goal of making AI accessible and inclusive. AI4Bharat is the official data management unit of Bhashini—a national initiative of MeitY, which has been implemented by the Digital India Corporation under the leadership of CEO Amitabh Nag. Unlike English, which has a vast pool of digitized text and speech available for training AI models, Indian languages suffer from a lack of structured, high-quality datasets. To overcome this, AI4Bharat has undertaken an extensive effort to collect, curate and annotate linguistic data at an unprecedented scale. This includes manual data collection from communities across the country as well as data mining from sources such as news archives, government documents and open-access platforms. Special emphasis has been placed on underrepresented languages such as Kashmiri, Bodo, Manipuri, Sindhi and Santali, ensuring that even communities with historically limited digital presence can benefit from AI-driven services. Beyond technology, AI4Bharat represents a new model for AI development—one that is open, collaborative and deeply rooted in public good. Unlike many AI initiatives that remain proprietary, AI4Bharat's datasets and models are freely available for startups, researchers and government agencies to build upon. The long-term impact of this work extends far beyond India. By successfully creating AI models for a linguistically diverse nation, AI4Bharat is pioneering a framework that can be adapted for other multilingual regions across the world, from Africa to Southeast Asia.

In the next few years, apart from smart agent networks, the autonomous orchestration of complex workflows, and multimodal (voice, vision, text) and scalable infrastructure, we will also witness AI-powered cybersecurity and biometric systems, quantum computing coupled with AI, and a continued focus on enhancing and empowering LLMs. The more we innovate to democratize AI (so that it can be used by billions), the more these innovations would matter to the masses. However, unfortunately, a few AI powerhouses will continue to hoard the AI compute.

AI and Talent

AI's impact on talent has disrupted all industries. While new AI-centric roles like chief AI strategist have appeared on LinkedIn, and more people have incorporated AI and GenAI into their existing roles, the fear of jobs vanishing due to AI looms large in people's minds. AI threatens to take over common junior tasks—for example, 50 per cent of the tasks performed by a market research analyst and 67 per cent of those performed by sales representatives can now be done through AI.[4] In white-collar fields like law and finance, AI may reduce the hiring of juniors, thus undermining training paths.[5] The career ladder has been disrupted, with companies preferring AI support over junior hires who were traditionally employed to sort lead generation data, answer customer queries via phone or email, generate content for ad campaigns, provide marketing support and take up several other such routine task-oriented jobs. Mid-level jobs too face extinction because anyone completing recurring tasks can be replaced by AI. This has unleashed a reskilling imperative—an anxiety around the relevance of traditional degrees is building up, with many professionals now pursuing online AI courses or integrating AI tools in their jobs to stay relevant. Every tech revolution brings this new challenge where the workforce needs to reskill, repurpose and reshuffle their roles, and those who do not keep up and pivot are left behind. If we could go back in time, it would be rather interesting to witness a mill worker feeling proud of their new job of producing cloth at a factory, while a local handloom worker witnessed their job become obsolete. In the present, the same mill worker sees their job vanishing due to the latest technological innovations. Similarly, the financial technology (fintech) industry grows due to automation, while a bank accountant sees their job vanishing; a call centre executive's job becomes redundant as AI-based voice bots take over.

The industry will shift and transform, and newer jobs will be created. We need to prepare and pivot in order to keep up.

The rise of influencers, content creation and the digital economy are all examples where the youth is professionally using the new skills they have acquired and building businesses based on these. In the future, creative and adaptive thinking roles will thrive, and bounded career models, an aftermath of industrialization, will give way to dynamic, multi-career paths.

For all those wanting to learn and understand AI, we should blend formal training with hands-on, real-world and ethical examples, including these in developing business use cases and letting the magic unfold!

Foundational awareness on AI is a must for executives and leaders should learn how to manage AI-human teams. They should incentivize curiosity, and encourage out-of-the-box thinking and ongoing role evolution. They should also embrace looped, flexible career paths instead of laddered, linear ones. India has a strategic advantage—with its deep technical talent base—to power AI innovation, especially through global capability centres (GCCs). Organizations like McDonald's, Bupa, Tesco and Best Buy are building AI engineering, analytics and product development capacity through Indian hubs.[6]

AI and Users

Delighting the user is the singular outcome that an AI mission should focus on. The agriculture sector illustrates both the potential and the challenges. Farmers, farmer producer organizations (FPOs), markets, government programmes and academia generate rich but disconnected datasets. If these datasets were discoverable and connected, they could directly improve decisions on what to sow, when to sell, how to access credit and which schemes to claim. OpenAgriNet (OAN) seeks to bring together advisory services, research institutions, markets and the government into a single, open and interoperable network, thus turning scattered information into consolidated, timely and trustworthy answers for farmers. The farmers do not care how AI was built or the fact they are using it—they want answers, in their regional languages, to very basic questions, for example, 'What is the market price I can get for my tur dal crop?' Project VISTAAR (Virtually Integrated System To Access Agricultural Resources)[7] aims to develop a unified, federated digital ecosystem for agriculture by integrating reliable, validated and up-to-date resources across platforms. It focuses on enhancing scalability, accessibility and inclusivity of digital solutions while enabling two-way communication in order to incorporate farmer feedback. Deploying AI-enabled chatbots at the ground level and subsequently integrating them with Agri Stack means these chatbots can be accessed in multiple languages, understand agricultural terms and are user-friendly for farmers who might not know how to even type in their own language. Hence, voice interfaces need to be developed to converse the same way farmers do with each other. This needs a reimagination after intense field testing and after understanding a farmer's user journey.

Towards an AI-Powered Future

AI for strategic autonomy is now the pursuit of nations across the world. In India, AI took us by surprise. We never heavily invested in our research and development (R&D), so we were not poised to invent the core technology. Our entrepreneurial streak was missing in deep tech, academic research in this area was not funded, and so we were miles away from creating an OpenAI or Perplexity.

AI was created and nurtured in the western world. So what does this mean for India? Where does it leave us? For our country, AI offers an unprecedented opportunity to skip traditional developmental pathways and leapfrog to a future which belongs to the people. AI in India is seen not as a mere technological advancement but a strategic tool for inclusive growth and access to opportunities that were not within our reach historically.

The growth of the internet left us with the largest pool of developers, the creation of new-age homegrown startups which we are so proud of and a software industry which generated millions of new jobs. India provides the scale. Each person in India's billion-plus population is seen as a data emitter and consumer, and is thus a gold mine. If Indians realize they want to change the game, are we in a position to bring about that change? Do we have any levers to change and if we do, what exactly are they?

AI usage by people in India and its applications to societal use cases are key areas which we can invest in, to further AI itself. People's social data points are the best food for AI to grow and serve humanity. Hence, identification of use cases for social benefit, improving them with guardrails and building AI which is usable by common people will benefit the planet. As the world has reaped the benefits of digital societies by creating open platforms, India should join hands with the Global South to create digital public goods (DPGs) and thus support and promote AI.

This means emphasizing on the creation of affordable AI, reducing its usage cost and lowering the entry barriers to it for social good. Today, the economics of AI adoption is lopsided across sectors, with higher costs for the social sector. This discourages organizations of this sector to bring forth the relevant use cases, keeping AI away from socioeconomic development and limiting it to the fewer hands that build siloed private architectures. AI, when used for social good, improves the economics for both private and public sectors. We need to ask a few questions to make AI work for us at a larger scale:

- What are the localization and regionalization needs for India? Can we look at evolutions of cultural datasets, tools and frameworks which benefit all? How can common data collection and curation, across twenty-two languages, help India?
- How can we bring down the cost of AI usage and adoption? Is there a shareable framework or tools repository, or any reference architectures and repeatable patterns which are open source and delivered as DPGs? Are there procurement models which reduce friction and decrease the time to market (TTM) of new use cases?
- What are the best examples of use cases in India, where the Lego blocks of AI have been broken down and applied to the most relevant use case at a large scale, thus benefitting millions of users across the sectors of healthcare, education, government service delivery, agriculture and climate?

Digital public infrastructures (DPIs) like Aadhar, UPI, DigiLocker and FASTag have been created in India during the last decade by learning how electricity, railways, roads, airways and highways bridge nations, people and the planet. A similar thinking should be applied to create societal AI systems so the entire planet can benefit and developing countries are not left behind. Currently, AI power is concentrated in a few hands who had the first mover advantage and the wherewithal to create the digital edifices. India should focus on identifying methodologies to create affordable access to computation resources, open datasets, open-source models, low-cost AI literacy programmes, policy support and community-led AI initiatives. Economic growth in regional and local societies will only happen when small businesses and entrepreneurs have access to the data and AI resources that can provide them market access and ease of business.

A case in point is Bhashini.[8] Launched in 2022 as part of the National Language Translation Mission (NLTM), Bhashini aims to eliminate language barriers in India's digital ecosystem by enabling real-time translation, speech recognition and text-to-speech services across all twenty-two scheduled Indian languages. Powered by advanced AI models developed in collaboration with AI4Bharat, Bhashini provides over 300 pre-trained language models through open application programming interfaces (APIs). These capabilities are being integrated into both government and private sector services, ensuring inclusive access to digital platforms. Citizens can now engage with government portals, helplines, grievance redressal mechanisms and financial services in their native languages, while private players in e-commerce, banking and customer service—such as Snapdeal and Federal Bank—are embedding Bhashini's multilingual voice and text solutions into their operations.[9]

The platform has already demonstrated impact at a large scale, delivering nearly six million inferences daily and also being used for the real-time translation of Prime Minister (PM) Narendra Modi's public address (into Tamil). Recent partnerships further extend Bhashini's reach: the Rajasthan government's Pehchan app uses Bhashini for multilingual registrations, and a June 2025 memorandum of understanding (MoU) with the Centre for Railway Information Systems (CRIS) brings multilingual AI solutions to railway passenger services.[10]

Bhashini's continued evolution is supported by open-source research at AI4Bharat, with a multi-year grant from Nandan Nilekani's EkStep Foundation to advance speech, translation and language-understanding models. These innovations are being integrated into India's national AI repository, AIKosh, reinforcing Bhashini as a foundational element of India's public digital infrastructure.

By bridging India's vast linguistic diversity, Bhashini is redefining digital inclusion. It empowers millions—be it farmers seeking advice, patients accessing healthcare or commuters navigating transport systems—to interact with technology in their own languages. As its capabilities expand, Bhashini is rapidly becoming a cornerstone of India's digital transformation.

India has created a national-level IndiaAI mission with a budget outlay of ₹10,371.92 crores, announced by the PM, with the vision of creating AI in India and making it work *for* India. The objective of the IndiaAI Mission is to propel innovation and build domestic capacities to India's tech sovereignty. It has a seven-pillar strategy focusing on democratizing computing access, improving data quality, developing indigenous AI capabilities, attracting top AI talent, enabling industry collaboration, providing startup risk capital, ensuring socially impactful AI projects and bolstering ethical AI. India wants to demonstrate to the world how this transformative technology can be used for social good and enhance its global competitiveness. In 2026, world leaders will gather in India for the first Global AI Summit to take place in the Global South. It will be held as a successor to the following important summits—the AI Safety Summit of 2023, organized in Milton Keynes, United Kingdom, which was followed by the AI Seoul Summit of 2024, held in Seoul, South Korea, after which came the AI Action Summit of 2025 (which was also co-chaired by India), held in Paris, France. The AI Seoul Summit stressed on AI safety and published the Frontier AI Safety Commitment which was signed by nineteen countries. This led to the launch of ten AI safety institutes by ten countries in the European Union (EU). The summit in Paris forged a coalition for environmentally sustainable AI with ninety-one partners. It also moved the needle with a Paris Declaration on maintaining human control in AI-enabled weapon systems, which was signed by twenty-six countries. These summits have produced significant outcomes where several countries came together for safe AI usage. India has the opportunity to shift focus from action to impact, while highlighting both the challenges and opportunities of making AI accessible to billions.

India is poised for growing with AI. Let the magic unfold!

9

Towards GenAI

So far, we have focused on AI and how enterprises can aspire to become AI-first enterprises. In this chapter, we discuss GenAI and Agentic AI, which have transformed the AI landscape and enabled enterprises to realize AI's benefits more rapidly and confidently. While most of the constructs we discussed so far hold true for GenAI, there are slight nuances which we will cover in this chapter.

GenAI refers to AI algorithms which are designed to create new content based on users' commands. This generative aspect differentiates GenAI from traditional machine learning (ML) systems. Typically, GenAI systems can be prompted to reply using natural language (NL) as opposed to the programming-based manner in which earlier AI systems interact. The scientific community has long tried to have human-like interactions with AI systems, but with limited success. However, the concept of transformer architecture, introduced in 2017 by Google researchers, changed the direction and momentum towards this goal. Sequential modelling allowed for large models to be trained on massive datasets. Since then, there are numerous large language models (LLMs) that have been released, like GPT (from OpenAI), Llama (from Meta), Claude (from Anthropic) and Granite (from IBM). Before we delve deeper into what it takes for enterprises to adopt LLMs, let us briefly understand why LLMs have gained so much prominence in such a short amount of time. Let us explore the technological factors that were instrumental in the rise of LLMs.

Availability of Specialized Hardware

Graphics processing units (GPUs), originally developed for rendering graphics, allowed for the parallelization of large matrix operations which are the cornerstone for training LLMs. Similarly, Google developed tensor processing units (TPUs) which were more suited for matrix operations. Recently, IBM announced the artificial intelligent unit (AIU) which is even more specialized for AI workloads. Such hardware, along with high-speed interconnects such as InfiniBand, allows for further parallelization. Now, instead of one GPU, models can be trained simultaneously on thousands—or even more—GPUs by breaking the training into smaller jobs. The availability of high bandwidth memory (HBM) found another puzzle piece by allowing faster data transfer from the storage to the processing unit, which allows the effective use of large datasets. The inference time also got drastically reduced due to better hardware. Finally, Software as a Service (SaaS), offered by all cloud service providers, enabled different stakeholders to access cloud computing without spending millions of dollars for procurement. This hardware innovation allowed for massive models with billons of parameters to be trained in just a few months.

Model Innovations

While transformer architecture provided an excellent base for training LLMs, there are a number of other innovations which expedited their further development. Optimized toolkits for training like TensorFlow and PyTorch introduced this evolution. Libraries like DeepSpeed and CUDA Deep Neutral Network (cuDNN) further added more efficiency for matrix operations. Advancement in deep parallelism techniques (pipeline, model and data) allowed thousands of GPUs to be in used in parallel for a common goal. Adaptive Moment Estimation (ADAM) and its variants allowed for updating weights to facilitate faster convergence. These techniques helped in building the base LLMs faster, but these were fairly generic. To customize the models, algorithmic advancements helped quite a bit. Fine-tuning the models helped in customising them for specific tasks. Instruction training allowed for fine-tuning with specific instruction datasets. Finally, reinforcement learning with human feedback (RLHF) allowed for human feedback to be accounted for and thus aligned LLMs with human preferences. Optimizations at the time of inference, including quantization—reducing the precision of numerical values and distillation by training a smaller model to mimic larger model—saved both money and time. These innovations, along with clever engineering, have allowed for models to be trained and used effectively.

Data Availability

Data is the fuel for LLMs. Without large, diverse and good-quality data, LLMs would not be as powerful as they are now. Presently, there is a plethora of digital data from websites, social media, code repositories, image sites, etc., available to be used as training data. Common Crawl is one of the most widely used training data repository. It covers various domains, diverse languages and is of a large size (8 petabytes [PB] and growing). Community-driven initiatives like ThePile,[1] GniessWeb[2] and Common Crawl[3] (mentioned earlier) focus on providing clean data for training. It is well-accepted that many enterprises will have their own data to be used for LLM training. To allow for that, there are efforts to build toolkits which will allow developers to clean their own data and use it. IBM's Data Prep Kit[4] is one of the most widely used toolkits.

Convergence of accessible hardware, software optimizations and the availability of large, diverse data drastically expedited the emergence of LLMS. These technical advances allowed for massive LLMs to be trained. However, any technology cannot gain such momentum without the users. Let us briefly look at what prepared LLMs for widespread usage in such a short amount of time.

Ease of Use

The NL interface, because of its ease of access, caught users' attention. Before this, most of the model innovations were limited to a technical audience. However, with the advent of LLMs, everyone is able to use these models. English has become a de-facto interaction language. The free availability of web interfaces like ChatGPT and Claude allows millions of users to experiment with LLMs using simple browsers on their laptops and mobile phones. These interactions have generated more training data, which has resulted in enhanced models and hence improved user experiences. And this in turn has resulted in more usage. This self-serving cycle has helped the models' development and widespread adoption.

An Open-Source Ecosystem

While web interfaces allowed for easy use, many companies (like OpenAI and Anthropic) also provided rich APIs so that developers could build new applications using LLMs without spending efforts on installation and maintenance. Companies like Meta and IBM went a step further and released Llama and Granite (respectively) as open-source models, thus providing unprecedented capabilities to developers, engineers and AI researchers who could then customize these models for their own unique needs. This low-entry barrier allowed for the massive uptake of LLMs in developer communities.

Business Productivity

No technology, even with a wide user base, will survive if it does not translate into business benefits. The benefits can be in the form of improved productivity or the establishment of new lines of business. AI copilots and AI assistants have made their way to serving customers and have thus improved business. AI is projected to enhance human productivity and unlock an astounding $16 trillion in value by the year 2030.[5] This potential economic benefit is encouraging enterprises to pilot LLMs in a variety of use cases, from code generation to customer service, and provide quick feedback to the developer community for further improvements.

The confluence of financial benefits, ease of building new applications and end users' convenient usage has helped in the quick adoption of LLMs in a variety of new, exciting ways.

Common Use Cases for GenAI

In this section, we look at some of the common use cases which have been embraced by multiple organizations. The goal is not to provide a comprehensive list, but rather, the most frequent applications of LLMs and how these benefit enterprises.

Software Development

GenAI has transformed all aspects of software development and management. Enterprises have found a great use of LLMs in code generation and completion, test case generation, code porting from one language to another, code explanation and documentation generation. The NL interfaces allow relatively new developers to write and maintain complex codes. The popular systems in this domain are Microsoft Copilot, IBM watsonx Code Assistant and Cursor. Recent studies have shown that developers are witnessing 50 per cent performance improvements using these models as they reduce the time spent on repetitive tasks like creating boilerplate codes, documentation, etc. The curve for learning new coding languages has become significantly faster. Integrated environments also help users to complete all tasks on the same UI and not shift between IDE, documentation, web search, etc. Vibe coding (popularized by computer scientist Andrej Karpathy in 2025) is the perfect example of human-machine collaboration in this domain. However, there are a few areas that require caution. The generated code might be wrong or inefficient. In projects where the code base is large and complex, error debugging, uniform coding standard and a lack of structure might pose issues in the long run. Security vulnerabilities may also crop up in the generated codes. Generating codes without due diligence might be detrimental for businesses.

Analytic Systems

These systems allow non-technical users to ask business intelligence (BI) queries in English and get the answers directly, in the form of tables, charts or dashboards. The most common example of this is the NL to structured query language (SQL) generation. As with code generation, it allows non-technical users, executives, sellers, etc., to get required information without it getting routed through data engineers. Today, many commercial offerings like IBM Watson, Tableau GPT and Microsoft Excel support such features. It is a technically challenging problem to map a user's NL query to precise columns, generate SQLs which are grounded with actual schema to make them executable and also ensure the resultant SQLs are performant. Most out-of-the-box systems do not understand the domain-specific details provided by users in their NLs. So it is imperative to impart domain knowledge to such systems.

Text Capabilities

Generating text is one of the core capabilities of LLMs. This has found great use in enterprises, in various use cases ranging from authoring documents, writing emails, summarizing large documents, generating meeting notes and action items, etc. It is evident that such capability saves a lot of time and makes content creation relatively easy. However, hallucinations are the most common issues that crop up while using LLMs. Many times, the produced text looks correct and reads well but contains facts where are either wrong or were not present in original documents provided to the LLM. Grounding the text generation with domain documents could help alleviate this problem to an extent. A deep, human review of the generated text is required before it is used.

Search Capabilities

Since LLMs can understand language in a semantic sense, it makes them a perfect choice of semantic searching across enterprise documents, chats and other knowledge bases. Compared to traditional keyword-based searches, the LLM-powered retrieval-augmented generation (RAG) provides higher-quality answers while accommodating for the nuances of NL utterances. LLMs that are trained on publicly available data may not do well while dealing with unseen enterprise data. Grounding is a popular technique used to handle this issue, where an LLM is provided with indexed enterprise data and uses *only this* data to augment and generate responses. RAG is a very active area of research, with a focus on improving accuracy and performance while managing hallucinations.

Conversational AI

We have already discussed some aspects of conversational AI earlier, however, it is important to reiterate that LLMs have transformed the AI assistant or chatbot technology. The use of AI assistants for customer service, fulfilling customer requests and for front-end automation is widely accepted. Unlike human agents working in multiple shifts, the AI assistant can work twenty-four seven, leverage all previous interactions and provide a better customer experience. However, its accuracy remains an issue. The AI assistant can get stuck in loops, sometimes providing unhelpful or repetitive answers, adding to a customer's frustration. Sensitive information handling and leakage is another issue which needs to be tackled. A human-in-the-loop (HITL) approach might work the best here, where AI performs a task till it is fully confident and hands over complex, nuanced cases (requiring a personalized touch) to human experts. Nonetheless, despite some of their shortcomings, largescale AI assistants have been deployed across diverse industries.

Multimodal AI

Recently, there has been a proliferation of non-text LLMs. GPT-4o, IBM Granite Vision, Claude Sonnet, Llama Vision and GROK Imagine are some prominent examples of LLMs which can understand and/or generate multimodal content. These allow users to ask natural questions based on a set of images. For example, one can upload their CT scan image and ask for the diagnosis or upload a picture of a plate of food and ask for the calorie count. The other application of multimodal AI is generating content from NL. One can explain a certain, required image through plain text and the GenAI model can then generate it. However, deepfakes pose a big problem to image generation as they challenge the credibility of digital media and can naturally be misused. Additionally, training and inferencing in multimodal models is more complex and compute-intensive (than that required for text-only models).

In short, LLMs are playing increasing prominent roles across different industries due to their ability to enhance productivity, reduce errors, increase interactions via conversations, democratize access to otherwise non-used data (like enterprise knowledge bases) and deliver measure impact. However, hallucinations, understanding domain knowledge, regulatory and compliance concerns and a lack of standardization pose challenges which the AI community is currently tackling.

Let us now deep-dive into data-related challenges for an LLM's lifecycle.

Training Time: Training an LLM requires large amounts of data, usually found through crawling the web or obtained via third-party providers. It is imperative that one only uses data that is compliant. It is also important to have agreements in place, and maintain data and metadata provenance (like the name of the author, the timestamp, the license under which the data has been obtained, etc.) This information will be handy in case of regulatory audits. Even authorized data can be of poor quality due to markup, code scripts, profanity and overall low-quality text. And so we need to make sure that high-quality text is used for training.

Duplicate data is another dimension which causes data quality degradation. A lot of duplicate or near-duplicate data (different versions of the same page) gives an illusion of abundant data, but this only has marginal utility and ends up consuming excessive resources. Additionally, the model may begin seeing this duplicate text as high-importance text due to its recurrence. Publicly available data will also contain sensitive personal information (SPI) or personally identifiable information (PII) data. This kind of data needs to be removed before the model is trained.

Finally, English-language data often dwarfs data in other languages, which results into English-only LLMs that have limited usage for local scenarios and restricted cross-lingual generalization abilities.

Enterprises seeking to train an LLM should have legal agreements in place for data procurement. They should also establish a tight data-quality management mechanism to ensure high-quality data is procured, and lastly, should closely work with local partners to access cross-lingual data.

Customization Time: As discussed earlier, a base model often does not perform all tasks well. So customization through fine-tuning—including parameter-efficient fine-tuning (PEFT)—and instruction tuning are often applied to it. Getting quality annotated data free from annotator biases is an extremely challenging and costly affair, to be done extremely carefully.

A base model's performance on generic tasks can also deteriorate due to catastrophic forgetting—a phenomenon where a model learns a narrow domain via new examples, but, in the process, forgets some of the generalized knowledge it previously held. Replay buffer is a common technique used to handle this problem, where the model is shown samples of past data to ensure that earlier knowledge is preserved.

Finally, in many domains, the availability of new data is very limited, which results in suboptimal fine-tuning. In such cases, synthetic data generation might help to mitigate data paucity.

LLM Evaluation: Evaluating LLMs can be bit tricky. Since LLMs get trained on large amounts of data, it is very possible that the training set has already been through the training pipeline, which renders the evaluation useless. Therefore, it is important to have a holdout dataset which is not 'seen' by the LLMs. Similarly, input data drift should be identified to trigger fine-tuning in case the user's way of using the LLM has changed.

Inference Time: During the time of inference, it is important to have proper guardrails so that inappropriate questions can be diverted and remain unanswered. Similarly, adversarial samples should be detected and removed. In many cases, users input SPI/PII data in their requests or questions. Utmost care should be taken to safely store questions with such personal information.

To summarize, data is the most critical aspect of LLM, directly impacting the quality of outcomes and user experience. Additionally, data quality management is an ongoing mechanism and not a one-time activity.

Surprisingly, apart from having good-quality data, the order in which it is used also has a significant impact on model training. For this, researchers have used multiple strategies like random shuffling, curriculum learning (simpler to complex examples), etc., and it is an active area of research.

Enterprises also need highly scalable and fault-tolerant computing infrastructure with thousands of GPUs that are connected via high-speed interconnects. Due to such large computational resources, the energy requirement is also high. As per some estimates, GPT-4 was trained on 20,000 A100 GPUs for three months, consuming 50 million kilowatt-hour! As discussed earlier, enterprises need to adopt a software stack which can efficiently use the large compute pool.

Model size plays an important role in training. While large models perform better than smaller ones, at some point, the law of diminishing returns comes into play—the incremental improvement is not proportional to an increase in the model size and the costs incurred due to this increase. The size of the model is also influenced by how the enterprises want to use it. Many enterprises would want to host the model on private clouds to be sure about data protection. Hosting very large models may pose problems due to large storage, memory and computational needs. Thus, the model size should be determined on the basis of the available compute resources in the private cloud.

In short, model training is an extremely complex process where small changes can make significant differences. Model training is, in fact, a mixture of art and science.

And now we come to the last piece of the puzzle—inference. Once the model has been trained, it is hosted and made available to several end users, serving millions of requests each day. Therefore, the inference needs to consume minimal resources and provide answers with low latency. This can be realized through a combination of techniques. Quantization helps in reducing computational requirements by converting higher-precision decimal weights to lower-precision ones. This reduces the model size. Distillation is another technique which aims to teach a smaller model by transferring knowledge from a large model. Leveraging specialized inference engines like vLLM and TensorRT is another alternative. Llm-d is a visionary project by Red Hat and other organizations,[6] which provides a variety of techniques—including vLLM, KV Caching, high-performance APIs, Kubernetes clusters, etc.—to empower LLMs at an organizational scale.

Apart from computational efficiency, inference engines also need to take care of handling inappropriate questions that involve hate speech, self-harm, violence, etc. Users revealing private information while interacting with LLMs (via prompts or NL utterances) also need to be handled carefully. In most cases, these issues are solved through the application of guardrails on the LLM's inputs and outputs. IBM's Granite Guardian is a widely accepted guardrail mechanism.

Context length poses yet another challenge. It is usually not possible to fit all the required information in a certain command or request. For example, a user may want to ask questions on red books (official or canonical collections of data, regulations or writings) and product manuals. However, it would be impossible to fit all red books in a single prompt, and without proper information, the LLM would not be able to effectively answer the user's questions. RAG is one well-established way of handling this problem, where the appropriate section of the data (red books, in this case) can be retrieved and passed as context. The model can then answer questions through those parts of the red books. We have already discussed the need for providing base models with domain-specific knowledge so that they become useful for leveraging proprietary and private enterprise knowledge.

To summarize, inferencing may look simpler than training, but, in reality, it is equally challenging since it is required to be affordable, have low latency, guard against unfavourable user behaviour and also manage context limitations. Gartner has estimated that, by 2028, as the market matures, more than 80 per cent of data centre workload accelerators will be specifically deployed for inference rather than training.[7]

Generalized LLMs vs Focused SLMs

As already established earlier, generalized LLMs like GPT, Llama, etc., are extremely powerful and can help users in variety of tasks and use cases. However, they are very expensive to train, manage and serve. This led to the following question: Does every use case and each enterprise need such large models to solve their problems? And its answer—no—led to the emergence of focused SLMs. Typically, SLMs are characterized as models with less than 10B parameters. They don't have broad capabilities like LLMs, but are optimized for domain, speed and storage. To create an SLM, one starts with an LLM, distills it to create a smaller (10B) model and then fine-tunes this SLM with data from domains like finance, healthcare, etc. SLMs can be hosted on private clouds, high-end laptops and edge devices. They perform well in a particular domain, but do not showcase generalization property. Some prominent SLMs are CodeMistral-7B, BioMistral-7B and FinGPT.

The research in this area is evolving towards a hybrid architecture using both SLMs and LLMs, where LLMs are used for generalized reasoning while domain-specific tasks are handled by SLMs. Another way to split the work is letting SLMs handle simple queries while the complex ones can be routed to LLMs. Just like APIs and SaaS solutions democratize the access to LLMs, SLMs will allow users to host the model in their infrastructure for well-defined and focused use cases.

Mapping GenAI to the Proposed AI Mindset Framework

In Chapter 1, we proposed the AI mindset framework with multiple dimensions. Now, let us try to understand what it takes for an enterprise to take on the LLM journey.

Strategy: Defining the LLM strategy is not too different from defining AI strategy. Organizations need to crisply define the use cases where LLMs can help and extrapolate the potential benefits. Because LLMs are often poised as a magic bullet which can solve all use cases, enterprises need to carefully evaluate *where* LLMs are actually required. There could be problems which are still best solved by traditional AI models. In fact, organizations should resist the urge to simply replace the traditional AI model with LLM models. They should look for opportunities where LLMs' power gets harnessed effectively, leading to the creation of new lines of business (LOBs). The organizations should also look at data which has remained unused due to the limitations of AI models. For example, IBM's Docling converts PDFs and PPTs to JavaScript Object Notations (JSONs) and markdown files which can then be easily consumed by LLMs. This allows for large amounts of enterprise knowledge to be used for different use cases, which was not possible earlier—a perfect use of LLMs! The organization should also think of the primary consumers of LLMs—these models could be used internally, by employees, to boost productivity and solve use cases for customers, or they could be used externally to acquire new businesses.

Technology: As discussed previously, an organization should consider providing its employees authorized access to enterprise data so that the out-of-the-box base model can be fine-tuned. It should also provide access to commercial LLM APIs or the infrastructure to host open-source models. Similarly, during the inference, cost will easily increase once everyone starts to use the models. This can be an expensive undertaking, so the right model decision and technology stack choices, based on the relevant use cases, should be made. It is also favourable to invest in building a strong test harness which can help benchmark different settings, models and training paradigms faster and systematically.

Talent: It is crystal clear that talent is needed to successfully work with LLMs. In fact, many studies have shown that talent is more important than even having access to LLMs. A study by Deloitte[8] notes that the lack of talent is the biggest barrier to AI adoption. Similarly, a study conducted by McKinsey[9] shows that 46 per cent present-day leaders identify skill gaps in their workforces as a significant barrier to AI adoption. Without the right talent and skills, an organization may actually lose money by executing proof of concepts (PoCs) which cannot be scaled and thus create zero quantifiable value. To use GenAI, we need to hire diverse talent profiles, including data engineers (to manage data quality), AI researchers/engineers (to make LLMs work for the use cases), systems engineers (to support applications from the infrastructural and software stack viewpoints) and compliance officers (to ensure every aspect is following regulatory guidelines and is auditable). In addition, domain experts are needed to work closely with engineers for fine-tuning and testing the quality of the outcomes.

Culture: The discussion on culture in Chapter 5 holds true for GenAI as well. The important addition is that the GenAI ecosystem is changing at a rapid pace. Therefore, an organization should be flexible to learn new things, update its components and experiment timely. There is a new model released every few months, which claims to be better than all the others; new benchmarks are set, and new middleware components—like the Model Context Protocol (MCP) and Agent Communication Protocol (ACP), etc.—are released. If an organization is not flexible and proactive in working with newer components, it will be tough to maintain the differentiation

Innovation: Chapter 2 outlines relevant facets of innovation. In the world of GenAI, most of the innovation takes place in the open-source community. Industry leaders like IBM and Meta have released Granite and Llama as open-source software (OSS) models. OSS not only provides a level playing field for all participants (especially the ones who do not have infrastructure to train their own models), it also brings the community together to use it, provide feedback and subsequently improve it. Considering GenAI is still in its early stages, OSS provides a sense of trust and auditability, which in turn increases GenAI's adoption. In fact, OpenAI, which has kept GPT as proprietary model for so long, has recently provided two open-source GPT variants. This shows the growing realization of the open-source movement's importance in GenAI's growth.

So far, we have discussed GenAI models which seek to bring a high degree of automation to tasks like coding, summarization, content creation, etc. However, to build truly autonomous systems, we need to do more. Agentic AI is one such venture. AI agents represent autonomous systems which can observe the environment, reason and make decisions, work towards accomplishing goals and even correct themselves. The core components of an AI agents are as follows:

Perception: This module is responsible for ingesting and preparing data for analysis. The inputs can come in multiple formats, including sensor data, logs, user utterances, images, audios, etc. They can also be characterized as human-generated (NL utterances) or machine-generated (sensors). The module understands, processes and represents these inputs in usable formats. As discussed earlier, data quality directly influences the quality of AI systems. Perception is responsible for high-quality data.

Planning: One core property which differentiates AI agents from other AI systems is their capability to plan the sequence of action before execution. A larger goal is often accomplished by breaking it into smaller, atomic tasks and then sequencing these smaller tasks. The planning module is the brain behind the agentic system. In absence of an intelligent planning module, the agentic system will produce suboptimal outcomes.

Action: Once the plan is in place, the action module executes it. For this, the module may leverage external tools or APIs. The tool-calling functionality allows AI agents to interact with external tools and APIs, which makes them incredibly powerful. Using these external tools, the AI agents augment their knowledge and also access updated information. For example, a user may ask: 'What is the weather in New Delhi?' Now LLMs are fundamentally trained on static data and have no way to answer this question. However, with tool calling, LLMs can invoke external weather API to get this information. The AI agents can be provided with a set of tools which they can use during planning and execution. The MCP, developed by Anthropic (an AI safety and research company), is emerging as a standard way for LLMs to access and use external tools. It brings a standardization for developers to expose the tools in a consistent format (via MCP servers) that AI agents can then discover and use. It also reduces the need for custom integrations.

Memory: While AI agents work to accomplish various tasks, it is important for them to retain the knowledge they have gained from various interactions. Memory does that. Primarily, there are two types of memory, the first one being short-term memory, which keeps the current conversation and goal in the context window. This helps the AI agent in maintaining coherence and a conversational flow. For complex tasks which require multi-step reasoning, short-term memory helps in spreading information across subtasks. However, the short-term memory is limited by the LLM's context length, resulting in context overflow. It will forget information once the context length limit is reached. This is when the second type of memory—long-term memory— comes into play, using persistent data storage to store the knowledge across different interactions. Long-term memory allows LLMs to customize and personalize interactions for users.

Communication: Communication allows AI agents to collaborate with humans or even other AI agents. The collaboration can be for information exchange, to ask for help in complex scenarios and to ultimately work towards the common goal. One common use of communication is to bring human beings in the loop for their validation and approvals. For example, an AI agent trying to achieve database performance optimization may recommend creating partitions and an index. However, such state-changing operations should first be approved by data engineers. Communication allows for such human-machine interactions before and during the execution stage.

Refection: AI agents can self-evaluate their actions, discover errors or suboptimality, and self-correct accordingly. This is a crucial component, allowing them to learn from past experiences and achieve improved performance. Apart from learning from mistakes, reflection also allows AI systems to adapt to changing environments. Additionally, reflection is used to critique generated plans and correct them. These reflections are stored in the AI agents' long-term memory, allowing them to recall earlier lessons, avoid making the same mistakes and hence improve their decision-making.

There are a number of frameworks that can help developers build, manage, test and deploy AI agents. All of the core modules described above are provided to developers for them to build a robust agent. LangChain, CrewAI and IBM's BeeAI are some of the popular frameworks. These allow agentic systems to develop swiftly.

Our goal was not to deep dive into GenAI or Agentic AI, rather point to the readers the rapidly evolving nature of GenAI ecosystems. We encourage readers to study these concepts in detail and implement AI systems for their use cases to better understand these concepts and also gain hands-on experience.

GenAI is one of the most transformative capabilities that we may encounter in our lifetimes. It has transformed AI from merely *doing* what has been asked, to *thinking* how to do it and even *creating*. And this is just the beginning of the AI revolution. With more and more investments being poured into this area, we will witness fast progress on all fronts, be it LLMs, Agentic AI, artificial general intelligence (AGI) or the diverse use cases which are presently being developed. With such rapid innovation, it is important for organizations to adopt newer technologies with more agility. At the same time, they must be conscious of the cost implications of adopting LLMs and use these models judiciously.

NOTES

INTRODUCTION
1. NIST, 'NIST AI System Discovers New Material' [Online]. Available at: https://www.nist.gov/news-events/news/2020/11/nist-ai-system-discovers-new-material.
2. Nature, 'On-the-Fly Closed-Loop Materials Discovery via Bayesian Active Learning' [Online]. Available at: https://www.nature.com/articles/s41467-020-19597-w.
3. Wikipedia, 'Turing Test' [Online]. Available at: https://en.wikipedia.org/wiki/Turing_test.
4. IBM, 'A Computer Called Watson' [Online]. Available at: https://www.ibm.com/ibm/history/ibm100/us/en/icons/watson/.
5. 'AlphaGo Zero' [Online]. Available at: https://www.deepmind.com/blog/alphago-zero-starting-from-scratch.
6. 'IBM Project Debater' [Online]. Available at: https://research.ibm.com/interactive/project-debater/.
7. 'Crew Assistant CIMON Completes Forst Tasks in Space' [Online]. Available at: https://www.airbus.com/en/newsroom/press-releases/2018-11-crew-assistant-cimon-successfully-completes-first-tasks-in-space.
8. Healthifyme, Available at: 'https://www.healthifyme.com/in/' [Online].
9. Wysa, 'Wysa' [Online]. Available at: https://www.wysa.io/.
11. E. Yodlee, 'Yodlee' [Online]. Available at: https://www.yodlee.com/oceania.
12. 'Blue Sky Analytics' [Online]. Available at: https://blueskyhq.io/.
13. 'Zuri Blue Sky Analytics' [Online]. Available at: https://zuri.blueskyhq.io/.
14. N. Bostrom, *Superintelligence: Paths, Dangers, Strategies*, Oxford University Press, 2014.
15. M. Neilson. [Online]. Available at: https://michaelnielsen.org/.
16. V.C. Müller and N. Bostrom, 'Future Progress in Artificial Intelligence: A Survey of Expert Opinion', in Vincent C. Müller (ed), *Fundamental*

Issues of Artificial Intelligence, 553-571, Springer, 2016 [Online]. Available at: https://philpapers.org/rec/MLLFPI.
17 'AI@50 Survey' [Online]. Available at: https://aiimpacts.org/ai50-survey/.
18 https://250.dartmouth.edu/highlights/artificial-intelligence-ai-coined-dartmouth
19 'Trolley Problem' [Online]. Available at: https://en.wikipedia.org/wiki/Trolley_problem.
20 R M.C.L. Alexander Kriebitz, 'The German Act on Autonomous Driving: Why Ethics Still Matters' [Online]. Available at: https://link.springer.com/article/10.1007/s13347-022-00526-2.
21 IDC Whitepaper, 'Are We Ready for a People-First Automation Mindset?' [Online]. Available at: https://cdn.idc.com/cms/ccFile/d88f77cea902aa09c617/IDC_whitepaper_-_A_Robot_for_Every_Worker-_Are_We_Ready_for_a_People-First_Automation_Mindset.pdf.
22 'TensorFlow Webpage' [Online]. Available at: https://www.tensorflow.org/.
23 'Yardi School of Artificial Intelligence (ScAI), IIT Delhi' [Online]. Available at: https://scai.iitd.ac.in/; 'School of AI and Data Science, IIT Jodhpur' [Online]. Available at: https://aide.iitj.ac.in/.
24 'Central Board of Secondary Education Launches AI Curriculum' [Online]. Available at: https://cbseacademic.nic.in/ai.html.
25 'Artificial Intelligence Could Be a $14 Trillion Boon' [Online]. Available at: https://fortune.com/2019/10/09/artificial-intelligence-14-trillion-boon-only-if-overcome-one-thing/.
26 E. Schmidt and J. Rosenberg, *How Google Works*, Grand Central Publishing, 2014.
27 Wikipedia, 'I know it when I see it' [Online]. Available at: https://en.wikipedia.org/wiki/I_know_it_when_I_see_it.
28 IBM Newsroom, 'CBSE Collaborates with IBM To Integrate AI Curriculum in 200 Schools across India,' [Online]. Available at: https://in.newsroom.ibm.com/2020-07-16-CBSE-IBM-AI-Curriculum.
29 'Introduction to Generative adversarial networks' [Online]. Available at: https://developers.google.com/machine-learning/gan.
30 'Better Language Models and Their Implications' [Online]. Available at: https://openai.com/blog/better-language-models/.
31 'Reinforcement Learning 101' [Online]. Available at: https://towardsdatascience.com/reinforcement-learning-101-e24b50e1d292.
32 'A Rare Peek into IBM's True North Neuromorphic Chip' [Online]. Available at: https://www.nextplatform.com/2018/09/27/a-rare-peek-into-ibms-true-north-neuromorphic-chip/.

33 'L'Oréal's Modiface Brings AI-powered Virtual Makeup' [Online]. Available at: https://www.loreal.com/en/articles/science-and-technology/l-oreal-modiface-brings-ai-powered-virtual-makeup-try-ons-to-amazon/.
34 'AlterEgo' [Online]. Available at: https://www.media.mit.edu/projects/alterego/overview/.
35 'RDF Triple Stores vs Labeled Property Graphs: What's the Difference?' [Online]. Available at: https://neo4j.com/blog/rdf-triple-store-vs-labeled-property-graph-difference/.

CHAPTER 1 AI STRATEGY

1 Indiaai, 'Corporate Innovation - Axis Bank' [Online]. Available at: https://indiaai.gov.in/company/axis-bank.
2 Locus, 'Homepage' [Online]. Available at: https://locus.sh/.
3 INDIAai, 'INDIAai - 21 women in '21' [Online]. Available at: https://indiaai.gov.in/research-reports/indiaai-21-women-in-21.
4 Wysa, 'Wysa' [Online]. Available at: https://www.wysa.io/.
5 R. Nozick, 'NEWCOMB'S PROBLEM AND TWO PRINCIPLES OF CHOICE' [Online]. Available at: https://web.archive.org/web/20190331225650/http://faculty.arts.ubc.ca/rjohns/nozick_newcomb.pd
6 W. Newcomb, 'Newcomb's Paradox- Wikipedia' [Online]. Available at: https://en.wikipedia.org/wiki/Newcomb%27s_paradox.
7 Wikipedia, 'Expected utility hypothesis' [Online]. Available at: https://en.wikipedia.org/wiki/Expected_utility_hypothesis.
8 Wikipedia, 'Strategic Dominance' [Online]. Available at: https://en.wikipedia.org/wiki/Strategic_dominance.
9 S. Government, 'National Artificial Intelligence Strategy' [Online]. Available at: https://www.smartnation.gov.sg/files/publications/national-ai-strategy.pdf.
10 J. Collins, *Good to Great*, India: Harper Collins, 2001.
11 J. Collins, 'The Flywheel Effect', Oct 2001. [Online]. Available at: https://www.jimcollins.com/concepts/the-flywheel.html.
12 J. Collins, 'The Flywheel Effect', Oct 2001. [Online]. Available at: https://www.jimcollins.com/concepts/the-flywheel.html.
13 Locus, 'Homepage' [Online]. Available at: https://locus.sh/.
14 S. Kapoor, 'How to Choose the Right Pattern to Infuse AI into Your Business' [Online]. Available at: https://www.thehindubusinessline.com/opinion/how-to-choose-the-right-ai-model-for-your-business/article30025328.ece.

15. N. Aayog, 'National Strategy For Artificial Intelligence' [Online]. Available at: https://indiaai.gov.in/documents/pdf/NationalStrategy-for-AI-Discussion-Paper.pdf.
16. INDIAai, 'RAISE India Summit,' [Online]. Available at: https://raise2020.indiaai.gov.in/.
17. Nature, 'The Race to the Top among the World's Leaders in Artificial Intelligence', December 2020. [Online]. Available at : https://www.nature.com/articles/d41586-020-03409-8.
18. Qualcomm, 'Qualcomm ventures,' [Online]. Available at: http://www.qualcommventures.com/.
19. I. Hyderabad, 'Department of Artificial Intelligence' [Online]. Available at: https://ai.iith.ac.in/news-and-events/all-news/nvidia-establishes-india-first-nv-ai-centre-at-iit-hyderabad.html.
20. N. Kashinath, 'Applied Singularity Meetup' [Online]. Available at: https://www.meetup.com/AppliedSingularity/?_cookie-check=NsizLSEQHmHrVYGp.
21. e. a. Shalini Kapoor, 'AI Maturity Framework for Enterprise Applications,' [Online]. Available at: https://www.ibm.com/downloads/cas/OB8M18WR.
22. J. Collins, 'The Flywheel Effect' Oct 2001. [Online]. Available at: https://www.jimcollins.com/concepts/the-flywheel.html.

CHAPTER 2 AI AND INNOVATION
1. 'Phrasee' [Online]. Available at: https://phrasee.co/futureaihub/ebay-embraces-ai/.
2. Available at: https://www.ibm.com/watson/stories/humana.
3. 'The Self-Driving Car Timeline—Predictions from the Top 11 Global Automakers' [Online]. Available at: https://emerj.com/ai-adoption-timelines/self-driving-car-timeline-themselves-top-11-automakers/.
4. '18 Impressive Applications of Generative Adversarial Networks (GANs)' [Online]. Available at: https://machinelearningmastery.com/impressive-applications-of-generative-adversarial-networks/.
5. Sigtuple [Online]. Available at: https://sigtuple.com/products/.
6. 'OWKIN' [Online]. Available at: https://owkin.com/.
7. Qiang Yang, et al., Federated Learning, Morgan and Claypool, 2019.
8. Available at: https://en.wikipedia.org/wiki/GPT-3.
9. Available at: https://onezero.medium.com/for-some-reason-im-covered-in-blood-gpt-3-contains-disturbing-bias-against-muslims-693d275552bf)
10. 'VIOME' [Online]. Available at: https://www.viome.com/.

CHAPTER 3 AI AND TECHNOLOGY

1. 'Amazon Mechanical Turk' [Online]. Available at: https://www.mturk.com/.
2. 'Jgraph' [Online]. Available at: https://github.com/jgraph.
3. Available at: https://titan.thinkaurelius.com/.
4. Available at: https://neo4j.com/.
5. 'Learn How to Set up a CI/CD Pipeline from Scratch' [Online]. Available at: https://dzone.com/articles/learn-how-to-setup-a-cicd-pipeline-from-scratch/.
6. 'Unfied Payment Interface' [Online]. Available at: https://www.npci.org.in/what-we-do/upi/product-overview/.
7. 'General Data Protection Regulation' [Online]. Available at: https://gdpr-info.eu/.
8. 'AutoAI' [Online]. Available at: https://www.ibm.com/in-en/cloud/watson-studio/autoai/.
9. 'AutoML' [Online]. Available at: https://cloud.google.com/automl/.
10. 'What Is Generalization in Machine Learning?' [Online]. Available at: https://deepai.space/what-is-generalization-in-machine-learning/.
11. 'AI Explainability 360' [Online]. Available at: https://aix360.mybluemix.net/.
12. Available at: https://en.wikipedia.org/wiki/Tay_(bot)/.
13. K. Eykholt, et al., 'Robust Physical-World Attacks on Deep Learning Models' 2018. [Online]. Available at: https://arxiv.org/abs/1707.08945/.
14. Available at: https://developer.dnb.com/.
15. 'What Is Metadata and Why Is It As Important As the Data Itself?'[Online]. Available at: https://www.opendatasoft.com/en/blog/what-is-metadata-and-why-is-it-important-data/.
16. Rakesh Agrawal and Ramakrishnan Srikant, 'Fast Algorithms forMining Association Rules in Large Databases,' in Very Large Database Conference, 1994.
17. 'Catalog External Assets for a 360° Data Lineage' [Online]. Available at: https://towardsdatascience.com/catalog-external-assets-for-a-360-data-lineage-448c8f6bf2b2/.
18. N. Gupta, et al., 'Data Quality Toolkit: Automatic Assessment of Data Quality and Remediation for Machine Learning Datasets' [Online]. Available at: https://arxiv.org/abs/2108.05935/.
19. 'Cleaning Big Data: Most Time-Consuming, Least Enjoyable Data Science Task, Survey Says' [Online]. Available at: https://www.forbes.com/sites/gilpress/2016/03/23/data-preparation-most-time-consuming-least-enjoyable-data-science-task-survey-says/?sh=4b-be29246f63/.

20. '5 Outer Detection Techniques That Every "Data Enthusiast" Must Know' [Online]. Available at: https://towardsdatascience.com/5-outlier-detection-methods-that-every-data-enthusiast-must-know-f917bf439210/.
21. J. Huang, 'O2U-Net: A Simple Noisy Label Detection Approach for Deep Neural Networks' in IEEE/CVF International Conference on Computer Vision (ICCV), 2019.
22. 'Data Protection Rule in Watson Knowledge Catalog' [Online]. Available at: https://medium.com/ibm-data-ai/data-protection-ruledpr-in-watson-knowledge-catalog-8a19c3bc0959/.
23. 'General Data Protection Regulation' [Online]. Available at: https://gdpr-info.eu/.
24. 'IBM Research AI Testing' [Online]. Available at: https://research.ibm.com/teams/ai-testing/; 'Testing AI Platforms, Machine Learning-Based Validation, and Robotic Process Automation to Enhance QA efficiencies' [Online]. Available at: https://www.infosys.com/services/validation-solutions/service-offerings/machine-learning-qa.html/.
25. 'Simple Guide to Confusion Matrix Terminology' [Online]. Available at: https://www.dataschool.io/simple-guide-to-confusion-matrix-terminology/.
26. 'AI FactSheets' [Online]. Available at: https://aifs360.mybluemix.net/.
27. 'Google Model Cards' [Online]. Available at: https://modelcards.withgoogle.com/about/.
28. 'Why AI investments Fail to Deliver' [Online]. Available at: https://www.infoworld.com/article/3639028/why-ai-investments-fail-tode-liver.html/.
29. 'IBM Adversarial Robustness 360' [Online]. Available at: https://art360.mybluemix.net/.
30. 'IBM Watson OpenScale' [Online]. Available at: https://www.ibm.com/in-en/cloud/watson-openscale/model-risk-management/.
31. K.R. Varshney, Trustworthy Machine Learning, Chappaqua, New York, USA, Independently Published, 2022.
32. J. Buolamwini and T. Gebru, 'Gender Shades: Intersectional Accuracy Disparities in Commercial Gender Classification,' in FAT, 2018.
33. A. D'Amour, 'Fairness Is Not Static: Deeper Understanding of Long Term Fairness via Simulation studies,' in FAT, 2020.
34. 'AI Fairness 360' [Online]. Available at: https://aif360.mybluemix.net/.
35. 'AI Explainability 360' [Online]. Available at: https://aix360.mybluemix.net/.

36 M.T. Ribeiro, S. Singh and C. Guestrin, '"Why Should I Trust You?": Explaining the Predictions of Any Classifier' [Online]. Available at: https://arxiv.org/abs/1602.04938/.
37 S. Lundberg and Su-In Lee, 'A Unified Approach to Interpreting Model Predictions' [Online]. Available at: https://arxiv.org/abs/1705.07874/.
38 Available at: https://www.licenses.ai/open-source-license)
39 'Niramai—A Novel Breast Cancer Screening Solution' [Online]. Available at: https://www.niramai.com/.

CHAPTER 4 AI AND TALENT

1 Kuki, 'Kuki' [Online]. Available at: https://www.kuki.ai/.
2 Wikipedia, 'Loebner prize' [Online]. Available at: https://en.wikipedia.org/wiki/Loebner_Prize.
3 Kaggle, [Online]. Available at: https://www.kaggle.com/.
4 CoLab, 'Welcome to Colaboratory' [Online]. Available at: https://colab.research.google.com/?utm_source=scs-index.
5 Udemy, 'Udemy' [Online]. Available at: https://www.udemy.com/.
6 Gartner, 'TalentNeuron' [Online]. Available at: https://www.gartner.com/en/human-resources/research/talentneuron.
7 Glassdoor, 'Glassdoor' [Online]. Available at: https://www.glassdoor.co.in/index.htm.
8 Available at: https://visit.figure-eight.com/People-Powered-Data-Enrichment_T
9 S. Mehra, 'Yes, Non-Techies Too Can Work in AI. Here's How!' [Online]. Available at: https://indiaai.gov.in/article/yes-non-techies-too-can-work-in-ai-here-s-how.
10 Nicolaus Henke, Jordan Levine and Paul McInerney, 'Analytics Translator: The New Must-Have Role' [Online]. Available at: https://www.mckinsey.com/business-functions/quantumblack/our-insights/analytics-translator.
11 Yodlee [Online]. Available at: https://www.yodlee.com/oceania.

CHAPTER 5 AI AND CULTURE

1 E. Farrow, 'Mindset Matters: How Mindset Affects the Ability of Staff to Anticipate and Adapt to Artificial Intelligence (AI) Future Scenarios in Organisational Settings' [Online]. Available at: https://rdcu.be/cOqIm.
2 C.S. Dweck, Mindset: Changing the Way You Think to Fulfil Your Potential. Constable & Robinson, 2012.
3 E. Farrow, 'Mindset Matters: How Mindset Affects the Ability of Staff to Anticipate and Adapt to Artificial Intelligence (AI) Future Scenarios

in Organisational Settings' [Online]. Available at: https://rdcu.be/cOqIm.
4. Tim Fountaine, Brian McCarthy, and Tamim Saleh, 'Building the AI-Powered Organization', Harvard Business Review [Online]. Available at: https://hbr.org/2019/07/building-the-ai-powered-organization.
5. Invest India [Online]. Available at: https://www.investindia.gov.in/.
6. Invest India, 'BFSI- Fintech & Financial Services' [Online]. Available at: https://www.investindia.gov.in/sector/bfsi-fintech-financial-services.
7. 'Slowly but Steadily, Computers Are Changing the Indian Way of Life and Work', *India Today*, 31 December 1987. [Online]. Available at: https://www.indiatoday.in/magazine/cover-story/story/19871231-slowly-but-steadily-computers-are-changing-the-indian-way-of-life-and-work-799649-1987-12-31.
8. IBM, 'AI Explainability 360', [Online]. Available at: https://aix360.mybluemix.net/.
9. IBM Research, 'AI FactSheets 360' [Online]. Available at: https://aifs360.mybluemix.net/?_ga=2.84668633.1717739901.1653632110-667372379.1653632110.
10. J. Buolamwini, 'Facial Recognition Software Is Biased towards White Men, Researcher Finds', The Verge, 11 February 2018. [Online]. Available at: https://www.media.mit.edu/articles/facial-recognition-software-isbiased-towards-white-men-researcher-finds/.
11. IBM, 'AI Fairness 360' [Online]. Available at: https://aif360.mybluemix.net/.
12. Wikipedia, 'Technological Singularity' [Online]. Available at: https://en.wikipedia.org/wiki/Technological_singularity.
13. R. Cellan-Jones, 'Stephen Hawking Warns Artificial Intelligence Could End Mankind', BBC, 2 December 2014 [Online]. Available at: https://www.bbc.com/news/technology-30290540
14. Elon Musk, 'Twitter', 2014. [Online]. Available at: https://twitter.com/elonmusk/status/496012177103663104?lang=en.
15. Future of Life Institute [Online]. Available at: https://futureoflife.org/.
16. Vox, 'Google's Brand-New AI Ethics Board Is Already Falling Apart', 3 April 2019. [Online]. Available at: https://www.vox.com/future-perfect/2019/4/3/18292526/google-ai-ethics-board-letter-acquisti-kay-coles-james.
17. Max Life Insurance [Online]. Available at: https://www.maxlifeinsurance.com/.

CHAPTER 6 AI AND USERS

1. Interested readers can find more details here: S. Mehta, 'A System for Providing Differentiated QoS in Retail Banking,' in IJCAI, 2011.
2. AutoAI, Available at: https://www.ibm.com/in-en/cloud/watson-studio/autoai.
3. Healthifyme [Online]. Available at: https://www.healthifyme.com/in/.

CHAPTER 7 ONWARDS, TO AN AI-POWERED FUTURE

1. M. Singhal, 'pi Ventures' [Online]. Available at: https://www.piventures.in/.
2. M. Singhal, 'DeepTech Investing: Points of Inflection' [Online]. Available at: https://www.piventures.in/blog/deeptech-investing-points-of-inflection.
3. M. Singhal, 'DeepTech Investing: Points of Inflection' [Online]. Available at: https://www.piventures.in/blog/deeptech-investing-points-of-inflection.
4. MEITY, 'NLTM' [Online]. Available at: https://www.meity.gov.in/national-language-translation-mission.
5. S. Agarwal, 'AI, ML to Drive Budget 2021's National Language Translation Mission' [Online]. Available at: https://economictimes.indiatimes.com/tech/technology/ai-ml-todrive-budget-2021-national-language-translation-mission/articleshow/80674800.cms?utm_source=contentofinterest&utm_medium=text&utm_campaign=cppst.
6. MEITY, 'Homepage' [Online]. Available at: https://indiaai.gov.in/.

CHAPTER 8 AI IS HERE TO STAY

1. M. Shen, et al., 'From Mind to Machine: The Rise of Manus AI as a Fully Autonomous Digital Agent' [Online]. Available at: https://arxiv.org/abs/2505.02024?utm_source=chatgpt.com.
2. Wikipedia, 'Anysphere (Company)' [Online]. Available at: https://en.wikipedia.org/wiki/Anysphere_%28company%29?utm_source=-chatgpt.com.
3. J. Yang, et al., 'Magma: A Foundation Model for Multimodal AI Agents' [Online]. Available at: https://arxiv.org/abs/2502.13130?utm_source=chatgpt.com.
4. World Economic Forum, 'How AI Is Reshaping the Career Ladder, and Other Trends in Jobs and Skills on Labour Day', 30 April 2025 [Online]. Available at: https://www.weforum.org/stories/2025/04/ai-jobs-international-workers-day/?utm_source=chatgpt.com.

5. 'A White-Collar World Without Juniors?', *Financial Times*, 25 March 2025 [Online]. Available at: https://www.ft.com/content/8e730692-fd9c-45b1-84dc-7ea16429c5c6.
6. 'Multinationals Turn to India's Back Offices for AI Engineers', *Financial Times*, 21 July 2025 [Online]. Available at: https://www.ft.com/content/a46ee948-07c0-4083-9610-1d85d7e15cc7?utm_source=chatgpt.com.
7. Ministry of Agriculture & Farmers Welfare, 'Project VISTAAR', PIB, 4 February 2025 [Online]. Available at: https://www.pib.gov.in/PressReleasePage.aspx?PRID=2099755.
8. Ministry of Electronics & IT, 'Government of India Expands AI-Driven Skilling', PIB, 19 March 2025 [Online]. Available at: https://www.pib.gov.in/PressReleasePage.aspx?PRID=2113095&utm_source=chatgpt.com.
9. ET Government, 'Snapdeal Collaborates with Bhashini to Boost Language Translation Efforts for Digital Inclusion', 12 June 2024 [Online]. Available at: https://government.economictimes.indiatimes.com/news/technology/snapdeal-collaborates-with-bhashini-to-boost-language-translation-efforts-for-digital-inclusion/110925326; The Banking and Finance Post Magazine, 'Federal Bank Join Hands with Bhashini to Boost Chatbot Feddy with Vernacular Language Support', 1 October 2024 [Online]. Available at: https://bfsi.eletsonline.com/federal-bank-join-hands-with-bhashini-to-boost-chatbot-feddy-with-vernacular-language-support/.
10. 'Language No Longer a Barrier at Railways: BHASHINI and CRIS Sign MoU; Will Offer Multilingual AI Solutions', *The Times of India*, 9 June 2025 [Online]. Available at: https://timesofindia.indiatimes.com/business/india-business/language-no-longer-a-barrier-at-railways-bhashini-and-cris-sign-mou-will-offer-multilingual-ai-solutions/articleshow/121731345.cms.

CHAPTER 9 TOWARDS GenAI

1. 'The Pile' [Online]. Available at: https://pile.eleuther.ai/.
2. IBM, 'Introducing the GneissWeb Dataset' [Online]. Available at: https://research.ibm.com/blog/gneissweb-for-granite-training.
3. 'CommonCrawl' [Online]. Available at: https://commoncrawl.org/.
4. IBM, 'Data Prep Kit' [Online]. Available at: https://github.com/data-prep-kit/data-prep-kit.
5. A. Krishna, 'How Governments and Companies Should Advance Trusted AI', IBM Newsroom, 13 September 2023 [Online]. Available at: https://newsroom.ibm.com/How-governments-and-companies-should-advance-trusted-AI.

6. Red Hat, 'Red Hat Launches the llm-d Community, Powering Distributed Gen AI Inference at Scale' [Online]. Available at: https://www.redhat.com/en/about/press-releases/red-hat-launches-llm-d-community-powering-distributed-gen-ai-inference-scale.
7. Gartner, 'Gartner Predicts by 2028, 80% of GenAI Business Apps Will Be Developed on Existing Data Management Platforms', 2 June 2025 [Online]. Available at: https://www.gartner.com/en/newsroom/press-releases/2025-06-02-gartner-predicts-by-2028-80-percent-of-genai-business-apps-will-be-developed-on-existing-data-management-platforms.
8. Deloitte, 'New Deloitte Survey Finds Expectations for Gen AI Remain High, but Many Are Feeling Pressure to Quickly Realise Value While Managing Risks' [Online]. Available at: https://www.deloitte.com/in/en/about/press-room/gen-ai-survey.html.
9. McKinsey & Company, 'Superagency in the Workplace: Empowering People to Unlock AI's Full Potential' [Online]. Available at: https://www.mckinsey.com.br/capabilities/mckinsey-digital/our-insights/superagency-in-the-workplace-empowering-people-to-unlock-ais-full-potential-at-work?utm_source=chatgpt.com.

ACKNOWLEDGEMENTS

Bringing any dream to reality requires perseverance and dedication. As COVID-19 threw a gauntlet at us by forcing us to move to remote work, we finally got the time to dedicate ourselves to fulfilling our dream of writing a book on AI. We reached out to industry icons in the field of AI and learnt from their experiences, successes, and failures. Our collaborations across industries dispelled several myths and uncovered truths and innovations that were happening in India and across the globe. We were delighted to meet practitioners across the industry who have applied the simplest of innovations in large-scale projects and are reaping the benefits

This book will be incomplete if we do not recognize the industry leaders with whom we conducted our interviews that helped us refine and concretize the AI mindset framework with real success stories. We would like to sincerely thank a few people whose ideas shaped the book: Mani Subramanian, Abhishek Singh, Mayur Datar, Pramod Singh, Arnab Kumar, Professor Jay Lee, Devendra Sharnagat, Shanti Ekambaram, Manu Lavanya, Guruduth Banavar, Tushar Vashisht, Sachin Shenoy, Professor S. Raghunath, Geetha Manjunath, Raghav Gupta, Parul Gupta, Jo Aggarwal, Nishith Rastogi, Mehul Kapadia, Swati Jain, Amita Agarwal, Shilpi Jain, Smitha Suryanarayanan, and Usha Rengaraju.

Endorsement from the industry is key to the success of the AI concepts which are covered in the book. We would like to thank all the leaders who agreed to review the book and provided their advice and comments. Sincere gratitude to Amitabh Kant, Abhishek Singh, Girish Wagh, Pramath Raj Sinha, C.P. Gurnani, Vivek Agarwal, Shanti Ekambaram, Ritu Arora, Hitesh Oberoi,

Raghav Gupta, Nitendra Rajput, Professor Rajendra Srivastava, T.N. Hari, Pankaj Rai, Ruchir Puri, Pankaj Jalote, Shivani Rai Gupta, Sriram Raghavan, Varun Nagaraj, Atul Jalan, Himanshu Nautiyal, Muthukumari S., and Pranshu Patni for their support to this book.

We would like to thank Manish Singhal for his invaluable advice on AI adoption and connecting us with several AI start-ups. Manish's frameworks are visionary and have been adapted for AI in our book. Pankaj Rai, aka 'Walking LinkedIn', connected us with several leaders mentioned above and this gave us a solid understanding of India's AI landscape.

We would like to express our deep gratitude to Dr Sumit D. Chowdhury for introducing us to the Bloomsbury team and guiding us through our writing journey. Others who explained the travails of an author's journey to us include Anuranjita Kumar, Brinda S. Narayan, Amitabh Satyam, A.B. Vijay Kumar, and T.N. Hari. Writing is a discovery process and Shalini would like to thank her teachers Harry Youtt and Judith Prager at UCLA Extension Writers' programme for teaching her the art of creative non-fiction. Shalini would also like to thank Amrita Chowdhury for introducing her to Rashmi Bansal, whose workshop provided fresh insights into non-fiction writing.

We would like to thank Gaurav Sharma and Gargi Dasgupta for their valuable feedback.

We are grateful to Anusha Ravishankar for introducing us to Ayushi Saxena. This book would not have the structure and flow if not for the valuable inputs and sharp editing by Ayushi, who kept us honest and relevant. We would like to thank Sindhuja Balaji, who helped us shape a few case studies while she was in between jobs. We are full of immense gratitude towards Samarpan Agarwal, a young design student, who understood exactly what our book was about and conceptualized the cover design image for it. We owe sincere gratitude to Jinnica Sarda for transcribing the interviews for us.

ACKNOWLEDGEMENTS

We are hugely indebted to Praveen Tiwari and Nitin Valecha at Bloomsbury India, who believed in us, patiently explained the publishing process to us, and helped us in this maiden journey. Others in the editorial team provided the clarity we needed and supported us through several rounds of copy-edits and proof corrections.

Shalini would like to thank her parents for enabling her to dream, her husband, Rajeev, and children, Keshav and Rohan, for providing untiring support and *un*artificial intelligence to make this dream happen.

Sameep would like to thank his parents for always being the guiding beacons, and his wife, Ankita, and son, Parth, for their unconditional support, love, and sacrifice. They put up with many last-minute cancellations of vacation and weekend plans without too many complaints.

Lastly, we would like to thank our friends, colleagues, and well-wishers, who have been eagerly waiting for the release of this book. This book has been written completely with natural intelligence and brain power and we thank our belief in humanity for that!

INDEX

5G 68

AAAI Conference on Artificial
  Intelligence 86
Access control 56, 123, 135, 136, 154
Accuracy 47, 67, 105, 108, 121, 124, 126,
  140, 142, 143, 148, 150, 151, 157, 158,
  164, 194, 205, 213, 214, 215, 220, 235,
  261, 262
ACM SIGKDD International
  Conference on Knowledge Discovery
  and Data Mining 86
Acquisition 26, 27, 30, 76, 94, 112, 123,
  127, 128, 129, 142, 153, 154, 156, 211,
  221
Agriculture 67, 185, 233, 237, 238, 245,
  248, 249, 251
Agentic AI 243, 244, 255, 270, 272, 273
AI@50 conference 9
AI applications 31, 57, 70, 131, 150, 183
AI adoption 11, 15, 16, 18, 20, 25, 28,
  29, 30, 31, 38, 40, 41, 44, 46, 68, 76,
  112, 117, 172, 174, 187, 217, 225, 230,
  231, 232, 233, 234, 243, 248, 250, 251,
  252, 259, 269, 270, 271, 287
AI-born organizations 41, 42, 43, 44,
  48, 52, 70, 96, 183, 184, 201, 207, 230,
  231
AI journey 15, 17, 18, 19, 22, 23, 25, 26,
  27, 28, 32, 33, 34, 35, 37, 38, 48, 54,
  59, 63, 69, 71, 75, 96, 113, 114, 120,
  127, 136, 144, 159, 169, 172, 176, 177,
  180, 182, 184, 191, 194, 196, 210, 222,
  226, 234, 237
  learning 28, 177, 182
  phases of 25, 27
  stages of 18, 114
AI-led companies 40, 43, 44, 46, 47, 48,
  70, 76, 96, 106, 164, 183, 201, 207,
  233, 239
Algorithm 3, 4, 6, 10, 14, 15, 20, 21, 35,
  42, 53, 55, 57, 58, 64, 67, 70, 78, 81,
  82, 83, 85, 90, 91, 92, 95, 97, 99, 103,
  105, 108, 109, 110, 111, 122, 126, 131,
  133, 137, 139, 149, 152, 158, 161, 163,
  164, 170, 185, 186, 187, 188, 192, 193,
  203, 205, 211, 213, 217, 219, 221, 228,
  233, 234, 235, 239, 255
  innovative-domain infused 78, 110
  learning 97, 122, 158, 228
  recommendation 21, 217, 233, 234
AlphaGo 5, 6, 75, 93
Amazon 43, 82, 84, 94, 101, 112, 194,
  204
Amazon Web Services Time Stream 101
Analytics 11, 23, 29, 30, 40, 60, 75, 76,
  77, 79, 89, 95, 106, 115, 120, 122, 131,
  136, 153, 154, 159, 169, 171, 174, 176,
  178, 179, 184, 185, 186, 187, 189, 192,
  193, 194, 195, 200, 208, 210, 213, 248
  data 76, 186, 187, 193
  fraud 77, 79
  in-house 77, 95
  team 23, 77, 89, 95
APIs 96, 116, 117, 118, 125, 126, 129,
  137, 138, 139, 147, 148, 151, 155, 156,
  158, 194, 229, 232, 252, 258, 266, 267,
  268, 271
Apple 81, 92, 93, 94, 217
Applications 13, 30, 31, 55, 57, 60, 65,
  69, 70, 75, 78, 81, 83, 85, 90, 91, 100,
  108, 109, 113, 116, 117, 131, 132, 133,
  134, 135, 137, 138, 143, 145, 146, 147,
  150, 151, 153, 158, 159, 160, 163, 165,

173, 175, 176, 183, 204, 212, 216, 217, 221, 226, 243, 250, 258, 259, 269
  downstream 113, 132, 138
Architects 61, 62, 78, 115, 117, 179, 182
Architecture 27, 31, 97, 112, 116, 118, 119, 125, 137, 141, 144, 165, 179, 184, 186, 187, 217, 251, 255, 256, 267
Artificial intelligence (AI)
  adoption of 11, 15, 46, 51, 112, 210, 217, 231, 242, 250, 251, 269, 270
  benefits of 19, 35, 48, 73, 169, 225
  concepts of 13, 24, 41, 168, 196
  confidence in 49, 210, 226
  fears of 8, 10, 23, 24, 35, 175, 201, 207
  governance 19, 47, 127, 150, 184, 209
  implementation of 15, 39, 66, 68, 69, 184, 200, 208
  infusing 51, 84, 115, 176
  initiatives 19, 40, 116, 144, 182, 216, 237, 238
  investments 4, 19, 38, 46, 47, 51, 52, 58, 68, 75, 213, 230, 239
  language of 168, 169, 194
  learning 4, 68, 108, 167, 171, 177, 242
  mission 35, 184, 189, 216, 237, 238, 241
  need for 43, 54, 182, 189, 239
  power of 4, 7, 8, 27, 76, 79, 210
  promises of 6, 8, 153, 195
  researchers 79, 111, 122, 189, 206, 258, 269
  scaling 21, 47, 115
  scientists 113, 121, 124, 138, 160
  solutions 39, 194, 195, 196, 237, 252
  success or failure of 16, 17, 58, 70, 115, 167, 172, 173, 214
  tasks 83, 120, 130, 134
  technologies 15, 47, 48, 173, 206, 234, 236
  usage of 59, 69, 173, 250, 251, 254
  value of 27, 59, 96, 114, 213
Auditability 116, 125, 138, 153, 270
Audits 32, 78, 124, 125, 130, 135, 153, 154, 155, 156, 263
  trails 124, 125, 153, 154, 263

Automation 11, 26, 29, 38, 55, 68, 84, 113, 116, 178, 239, 248, 262, 270
Awareness 41, 68, 204, 213, 248
AWS Sagemaker 119, 151, 159

Bandwidth 41, 95, 256
Banking 29, 76, 77, 78, 79, 80, 173, 201, 252
Behaviour 2, 5, 7, 13, 44, 45, 48, 57, 62, 69, 78, 148, 157, 160, 183, 186, 187, 197, 207, 234, 267
Bias(es) 6, 10, 11, 15, 58, 70, 71, 72, 121, 130, 134, 140, 154, 157, 158, 159, 170, 187, 188, 204, 205, 207, 242, 243, 264
  annotator 264
  data 134, 157, 158
  group 158, 159
  individual 158, 159
BigBasket 7, 33, 39, 40, 53, 94, 115, 119, 152, 153, 169, 186, 234
Big data 80, 97, 184, 209
Blogs 58, 87, 129, 187, 188, 205, 231, 233
Brand 41, 43, 81, 110, 176
Breast cancer 7, 163, 164, 166
Bug triaging 181
Build vs buy question 60
Business
  AI 241, 259
  drivers 51, 52, 54, 59, 70, 72, 184, 230
  goals 122, 140, 141
  outcomes 16, 71, 100, 121
  owners 54, 61, 112
  problems 58, 140, 171, 185
  requirements 121, 143, 196, 221
  use cases 76, 77, 78, 211
  users 61, 69, 91, 114, 141, 143, 149, 150, 160, 162, 203
Business intelligence (BI) 78, 120, 134, 178, 186, 260
Business process 11, 47, 54, 61, 80, 84, 130, 132, 139, 143, 243
Buzzwords 22, 36, 190

Capability 1, 6, 10, 40, 42, 70, 80, 82, 83, 107, 115, 116, 139, 151, 153, 184, 195, 210, 213, 214, 216, 270

INDEX

Car 9, 13, 26, 29, 55, 77, 81, 82, 93, 100, 126, 173, 203, 242
Chatbot 11, 29, 64, 72, 96, 103, 104, 106, 112, 172, 173, 188, 192, 199, 234, 237, 249, 262
China 67
Choices 22, 34, 44, 45, 101, 141, 144, 203, 228, 229, 268
Classification 108, 121, 142
Cleaning 113, 120, 134, 156, 186
Clients 7, 17, 19, 28, 48, 54, 57, 69, 153, 170, 173, 194, 196, 199, 200, 202, 205, 218, 220, 223
Closed-Loop Autonomous System for Materials Exploration and Optimization (CAMEO) 3
Cloud 22, 30, 31, 40, 68, 77, 78, 82, 84, 97, 99, 111, 115, 119, 136, 145, 146, 151, 165, 171, 214, 223, 232, 233, 238, 239, 256, 265, 267
  hybrid 136, 151, 233
  private 265, 267
  technology 30, 145, 165, 232
Coding 12, 78, 146, 244, 260, 270
Collaboration 31, 41, 49, 65, 66, 79, 96, 111, 113, 181, 200, 220, 223, 224, 227, 235, 238, 244, 253, 260, 272
Communication 2, 16, 41, 99, 113, 176, 185, 196, 238, 249, 269, 272
Company 7, 11, 12, 22, 26, 30, 34, 38, 40, 43, 46, 47, 52, 57, 68, 73, 80, 81, 82, 84, 86, 87, 88, 89, 90, 91, 93, 94, 95, 96, 97, 108, 109, 110, 111, 112, 115, 117, 128, 129, 135, 155, 183, 192, 193, 194, 195, 196, 201, 204, 205, 208, 210, 213, 214, 218, 226, 227, 228, 229, 239, 271
  AI-enabled 38, 40, 43
Competition 28, 38, 39, 47, 67, 82, 96, 172, 173, 222, 234
Competitive advantage 34, 46, 53
Complexity 6, 27, 101, 103, 136, 141, 178
Compliance 39, 78, 122, 123, 126, 152, 154, 263, 269
Computer 5, 15, 20, 75, 79, 108, 109, 168, 244, 260
  vision 7, 75, 79
Computing 14, 20, 95, 108, 156, 233, 238, 247, 253, 256, 265
Conference on Neural Information Processing Systems 86
Consent 123, 126, 129, 152
Constraints and pitfalls 51, 53, 58, 63, 98, 121, 150, 160, 162, 228
Consultants 11, 69, 175, 189, 192
Costs 2, 5, 6, 7, 22, 30, 32, 33, 42, 53, 54, 56, 60, 62, 71, 72, 74, 85, 88, 94, 101, 111, 114, 117, 118, 119, 128, 129, 145, 148, 156, 165, 171, 173, 179, 183, 189, 250, 265
COVID-19 3, 7, 206, 229, 232, 235, 239, 240
Credit 14, 31, 32, 77, 78, 98, 118, 123, 154, 157, 160, 161, 168, 249
  agent 14, 160, 161
  approval 154, 157, 160
  risk 31, 32, 78
Credit/debit card 77, 98, 118, 123, 168
Cultural change 23, 24, 31, 69, 171, 198, 201, 214, 239
Culture 15, 19, 23, 24, 25, 29, 30, 31, 33, 34, 35, 36, 40, 41, 50, 69, 73, 75, 86, 87, 88, 92, 95, 173, 184, 197, 198, 200, 201, 207, 208, 210, 213, 230, 234, 269
  innovation 35, 41, 86, 87, 95
  of innovation 35, 87, 95
Customer experience 5, 7, 11, 53, 54, 79, 105, 262
  better 7, 11, 53
Customer relationship management (CRM) 77, 117, 131
Customer(s) 6, 7, 25, 27, 38, 40, 53, 57, 58, 72, 77, 80, 81, 91, 92, 93, 96, 102, 106, 107, 112, 114, 117, 131, 138, 155, 159, 169, 175, 186, 194, 196, 210, 212, 216, 217, 218, 219, 220, 223, 224, 226, 227, 247, 252, 259, 262, 268
  acquisition 26, 27, 30, 211, 221
  experience 5, 7, 11, 53, 54, 79, 105, 262
  satisfaction 41, 117, 186
  service 252, 259, 262
Customization 104, 212, 228, 229, 264
CXOs 11, 35, 87, 106, 113, 216
Cybersecurity 79, 181, 247

Dartmouth AI conference 9
Data
  access 33, 129, 135, 139
  acquisition 127, 128, 142, 153, 156
  analysis 151, 178, 185
  analysts 75, 77, 89, 208
  analytics 76, 186, 187, 193
  architects 61, 62, 78, 117, 179, 186
  availability of 98, 107, 120, 257
  collecting 72, 132, 170
  collection 66, 82, 113, 120, 163, 246, 251
  deletion 120, 129, 136, 139, 140
  engineers 60, 76, 77, 179, 186, 187, 189, 260, 272
  enterprise 77, 116, 128, 132, 261, 268
  governance 78, 123, 233
  high-quality 84, 123, 138, 246, 253, 264, 270
  historical 6, 8, 90, 121, 219, 220, 239
  lake 32, 77, 78, 131
  life cycle 127, 128, 186
  lineage 123, 130, 140
  management 71, 72, 120, 128, 138, 186, 246
  missing 132, 134, 154
  needs 120, 128, 138, 141, 151, 263
  new 98, 122, 127, 141, 182
  old 122, 132, 140, 204
  payload 122, 126, 151, 152
  quality 58, 70, 73, 130, 131, 132, 134, 139, 253, 263, 264
  recency 132
  right 28, 58, 112, 136
  science 75, 125, 142, 146, 175, 178, 179, 182, 186, 187, 190, 192, 193, 195, 196, 208, 209, 246
  scientists 4, 15, 16, 17, 23, 32, 36, 48, 60, 61, 62, 74, 77, 117, 123, 131, 139, 141, 144, 145, 150, 151, 152, 157, 175, 179, 181, 182, 184, 185, 186, 187, 189, 190, 191, 193, 195, 196, 200, 205, 208, 209, 214
  sets 28, 62, 66, 84, 97, 120, 127, 130, 132, 134, 135, 136, 138, 139, 154, 181, 186, 192, 194, 204, 205, 235, 238, 241, 246, 249, 251, 255, 256, 257, 264
  sources 32, 101, 119, 138, 173
  steward(s) 78, 113, 121, 131, 142
  store 22, 77, 138
  tracking 28, 30, 59, 79, 88, 99, 108, 120, 140, 163, 185, 202, 217, 220
  types 100, 101, 130, 136, 203
Database(s) 90, 91, 101, 136, 137, 141, 186, 187, 272
'Deep Blue', IBM's computer 5, 10, 93
Deep learning 7, 75, 79, 83, 185, 192
Detection 70, 78, 83, 121, 126, 149, 152, 157, 158, 159, 165, 166, 200, 211, 245
Developers 17, 77, 83, 118, 125, 145, 146, 147, 149, 216, 224, 250, 257, 258, 259, 271, 272
Devices 98, 99, 206, 267
DevOps 111, 113, 146, 147, 187
Diet plans 7, 64, 226, 227
Digital transformation 16, 48, 77, 184, 191, 253
Digital public infrastructures (DPIs) 251
Diseases 1, 2, 7, 10, 11, 83, 109, 110, 163, 164, 166, 200, 235
DNA 2, 95, 110, 194
Documentation 143, 144, 212, 259, 260
Domain knowledge 79, 104, 111, 200, 229, 260, 263
Dominant strategy principle 46, 47, 48
Drug 1, 2, 3, 108, 233, 235, 245
  discovery 2, 3, 108, 233, 245
Due diligence 27, 54, 81, 92, 136, 145, 260

Economy 13, 183, 190, 248
Ecosystems 49, 51, 52, 65, 66, 67, 68, 69, 71, 72, 73, 78, 87, 211, 230, 232, 236, 237, 249, 252, 258, 269, 272
Education 66, 67, 91, 134, 143, 150, 205, 245, 251
Effectiveness 40, 81, 152
Efficiency(ies) 3, 4, 5, 6, 31, 39, 41, 53, 81, 98, 139, 156, 169, 174, 178, 215, 256, 266
  operational 39, 139, 156
Email(s) 81, 104, 105, 113, 139, 174, 205, 212, 261
Empathy 41, 42, 62, 64, 198, 215
Employees 10, 17, 22, 28, 31, 34, 38, 40, 41, 49, 56, 57, 73, 76, 78, 79, 86, 87,

88, 89, 92, 94, 103, 104, 130, 135, 136, 168, 169, 170, 171, 172, 174, 175, 176, 177, 181, 182, 183, 185, 192, 197, 198, 200, 201, 205, 209, 212, 268
Encryption 99, 109, 126
Engineering 16, 22, 40, 75, 79, 97, 111, 117, 143, 144, 178, 179, 183, 186, 187, 191, 195, 209, 248, 257
 data 40, 75, 117, 186
 software 143, 144, 187
Engines, recommendation 29, 43, 78, 193
Enterprises 5, 11, 12, 13, 15, 16, 18, 19, 21, 22, 24, 25, 26, 27, 30, 31, 32, 33, 34, 38, 44, 46, 47, 48, 49, 54, 63, 66, 67, 70, 72, 73, 77, 80, 82, 84, 86, 92, 93, 96, 97, 99, 102, 103, 104, 105, 107, 109, 114, 115, 116, 118, 119, 123, 127, 128, 129, 130, 131, 132, 134, 136, 139, 140, 141, 144, 145, 153, 161, 163, 188, 189, 207, 232, 233, 237, 240, 243, 255, 259, 261, 263, 265, 266, 267, 268
 data 77, 116, 128, 132, 261, 268
 data warehouse 77, 80, 93
Error(s) 3, 9, 38, 90, 99, 102, 103, 108, 116, 122, 133, 134, 143, 146, 155, 173, 194, 219, 260, 263, 272
Excel sheets 106, 181
Execution 27, 30, 101, 102, 208, 223
 plan 27, 101, 102, 270, 271, 272
Expectations 16, 40, 91, 92, 121, 125, 184, 189, 194, 196, 207, 224, 225
Expected utility 45, 46, 47, 48
Experts 10, 14, 17, 23, 49, 59, 60, 66, 68, 69, 71, 78, 103, 107, 176, 181, 183, 188, 189, 190, 191, 208, 210, 226, 227, 228, 262, 269
 AI 23, 176, 183, 208
 domain 17, 189, 208, 269
 NLP 60, 188, 191
Explainability 71, 124, 125, 160, 161, 203, 236, 242, 243

Face/Facial recognition 1, 20, 135, 142, 143, 147, 148, 158, 204, 205
Failure(s) 16, 17, 37, 41, 47, 48, 55, 56, 57, 58, 64, 69, 74, 75, 168, 171, 172, 189, 191, 200, 207, 230
Fault tolerance 115, 137, 221

Fear 4, 5, 8, 9, 10, 22, 23, 24, 35, 38, 64, 95, 175, 197, 200, 201, 202, 203, 204, 205, 206, 207, 242, 247
Feasibility 27, 88, 90, 91, 166
Feedback 32, 52, 79, 90, 92, 122, 126, 148, 149, 155, 159, 170, 200, 217, 218, 223, 224, 225, 227, 243, 249, 257, 259, 270
 loop 52, 122, 126, 159, 227
Field service 53, 58, 68
Filter/Filtering 14, 78, 84, 85, 91
Finance 14, 43, 77, 79, 178, 185, 205, 247, 267
Fintech 7, 79, 178, 193, 194, 201, 202, 248
Flipkart 7, 40, 53, 73, 74, 112, 117, 209, 217, 234
Flywheel 19, 39, 40, 49, 50, 51, 52, 73, 77, 78, 184, 198, 239
 strategy 19, 39, 49, 50, 51, 52, 73, 78, 184
Focus vs AI journey 33
Food delivery 82, 117, 216
Forecasting 5, 67, 90, 153, 168
Frameworks 6, 11, 19, 70, 115, 186, 196
France 67, 253
Fraud 7, 57, 77, 78, 79, 202, 211, 213
 detection 57, 78, 211

Game 5, 6, 20, 39, 44, 45, 46, 69, 81, 87, 92, 195, 206, 232, 250
Game theory 44, 45, 46
Gender 121, 124, 157, 159, 160, 163, 199
Generative pre-training (GPT) 20, 105, 106, 112, 232, 240, 255, 258, 260, 262, 265, 267, 270
Germany 9, 206
Github 113, 146, 147
Global AI Vibrancy Ranking 2020 236
Global Data Protection Regulation (GDPR) 123, 139
Google 14, 24, 43, 81, 93, 111, 112, 113, 144, 159, 165, 181, 207, 229, 233, 234, 240, 255, 256
Governance 19, 32, 47, 71, 78, 98, 113, 116, 119, 123, 124, 125, 126, 127, 129, 138, 139, 147, 150, 151, 153, 154, 156, 159, 160, 161, 184, 206, 209, 233, 236, 237, 238

Government(s) of India 48, 49, 65, 66, 202
GPUs 83, 112, 115, 244, 256, 265
Graphs 22, 78, 90, 116, 118, 136, 137, 141, 189, 233, 244
Grocery 33, 117, 169, 239
Group discussions 41, 113, 187
Guidance 182, 206, 226

Hackathon 41, 68, 75, 181
Hardware 12, 27, 30, 91, 115, 116, 232, 256, 257
Health/Healthcare 2, 7, 13, 24, 42, 67, 79, 81, 83, 106, 109, 125, 163, 173, 175, 181, 203, 205, 209, 212, 226, 237, 238, 245, 251, 267
  mental 7, 42, 106
HealthifyMe 7, 53, 64, 226, 227, 228, 229
Highest expected utility 45
Highest paid person's opinion (HIPPO) 40
High-risk zones 8
Hindu Business Line, The 54
Hire(s)/Hiring 4, 11, 22, 23, 30, 31, 40, 76, 82, 86, 95, 125, 134, 143, 149, 157, 175, 181, 182, 183, 184, 187, 191, 209, 223
Hosting 12, 111, 145, 165, 265
Human
  error 9, 38
  intelligence 9, 56, 206
Human resource (HR) 16, 31, 77, 89, 103, 104, 140, 143, 172, 174, 183, 208

IBM 5, 6, 20, 75, 81, 82, 86, 88, 92, 93, 94, 107, 108, 109, 144, 149, 151, 155, 159, 161, 203, 204, 205, 255, 256, 257, 258, 259, 260, 262, 266, 268, 270, 272
Identification 30, 130, 194, 211, 243, 250
Images 7, 12, 13, 14, 20, 73, 74, 79, 83, 84, 87, 100, 101, 112, 120, 126, 128, 136, 147, 148, 163, 164, 165, 169, 181, 187, 191, 193, 208, 213, 214, 229, 262, 270
  analysis 7, 84, 169
  recognition 13, 83, 100, 112, 229

Inclusion 67, 70, 90, 95, 104, 165, 236, 237, 253
Index 111, 136, 137, 138, 237
India 7, 38, 48, 49, 65, 66, 67, 98, 103, 136, 137, 152, 178, 190, 192, 195, 201, 202, 209, 210, 211, 218, 228, 236, 237, 238, 240, 241, 243, 245, 246, 248, 249, 250, 251, 252, 253, 254
INDIAai.gov.in 38, 40, 187, 236, 237, 238
Indian fintech market 202
Indian Institute of Science (IISc), Bangalore 68, 79
Indian Institutes of Information Technology 68
Indian Institutes of Technology 68
Indian languages 107, 227, 235, 238, 246, 252
Industry 4, 17, 18, 20, 23, 27, 28, 31, 33, 35, 39, 42, 43, 47, 62, 66, 68, 71, 73, 80, 82, 87, 95, 106, 115, 148, 173, 176, 178, 180, 185, 189, 201, 202, 203, 204, 206, 210, 223, 234, 237, 248, 250, 253, 270
Industry–academia partnership 68
Information 68, 86, 104, 116, 123, 124, 128, 129, 130, 186, 223, 236, 252, 262, 263, 264
  personal 123, 124, 129, 130, 263, 264
  sensitive 123, 128, 223, 262, 263
Information architecture (IA) 112, 119, 141
Information technology (IT) 43, 56, 65, 66, 77, 80, 91, 97, 103, 105, 145, 147, 178, 182, 183
Infrastructure 12, 30, 66, 67, 71, 72, 82, 95, 97, 119, 120, 153, 156, 184, 214, 217, 218, 222, 234, 244, 245, 247, 253, 265, 267, 268, 270
Infusion 18, 21, 25, 29, 30, 31, 32, 33, 34, 50, 51, 54, 55, 56, 75, 91, 115, 117, 118, 119, 140, 184, 225, 230
Initiatives 19, 36, 40, 74, 88, 116, 144, 178, 182, 216, 237, 238, 246, 251, 257
Innovation(s) 2, 4, 8, 13, 14, 16, 17, 19, 20, 21, 22, 28, 31, 33, 34, 35, 36, 38, 41, 53, 65, 66, 68, 75, 80, 81, 82, 83, 84, 85, 86, 87, 88, 90, 91, 92, 93, 94, 95, 96, 97, 100, 101, 105, 109, 111,

119, 164, 165, 166, 184, 199, 216, 218, 230, 232, 233, 234, 239, 244, 245, 247, 248, 252, 253, 256, 257, 258, 269, 273
culture 35, 41, 86, 87, 95
feasibility 86, 88, 166
forms of 86, 93, 94
Insurance 7, 45, 46, 47, 81, 173, 189, 199, 205, 209, 210, 211, 212, 213, 214, 239
companies 7, 210, 239
policy 45, 46, 47, 199, 212, 213
Integrated development environments (IDEs) 22
Integration 32, 90, 94, 121, 132, 143, 146, 221, 224
Intellectual property (IP) 66, 82, 86, 94, 224
Intelligence 1, 8, 9, 11, 37, 56, 64, 67, 78, 102, 120, 149, 178, 206, 240, 245, 260, 273
Interactions 14, 21, 40, 48, 57, 59, 209, 211, 212, 218, 222, 255, 258, 262, 263, 271, 272
International Conference on Machine Learning 86
International Data Corporation report 10
Internet of Things (IoT) 7, 68, 132, 231
Interventions 6, 41, 42, 78, 147, 149, 171, 188, 224
Inter- vs intra-enterprise innovations 93
Invention 10, 13, 14
Investments 4, 11, 19, 21, 25, 26, 27, 28, 30, 33, 34, 47, 58, 66, 67, 68, 75, 77, 80, 81, 82, 88, 91, 92, 95, 96, 112, 113, 114, 115, 117, 131, 146, 175, 201, 202, 220, 227, 230, 231, 232, 234, 235, 237, 238, 273
funds 66, 67, 238
Investment vs RoI 34
IPhones 92, 93, 94

Japan 67
Job description (JD) 84, 85, 184
Jobs 10, 22, 43, 83, 89, 175, 183, 192, 197, 199, 201, 202, 238, 247, 248, 250, 256
JP Morgan Chase (JPMC) 109

Key performance indicators (KPIs) 27, 90, 119, 140, 143, 152, 153

Kotak Mahindra Bank 75, 76, 77, 78, 79
Kubernetes 16, 95, 145, 165, 266

Language(s)
AI 168, 169, 194
coding 78, 260
models 241, 244, 252, 255
natural 26, 81, 89, 100, 106, 131, 244, 255
Latency 125, 140, 220, 221, 265, 266
Lavanya, Manu 210, 211, 212, 213, 214
Leadership 16, 23, 24, 37, 40, 50, 73, 88, 89, 172, 174, 178, 184, 195, 200, 206, 207, 246
Learning and development (L&D) 176, 182
Learn/Learning 4, 6, 7, 11, 17, 20, 28, 31, 36, 52, 58, 64, 65, 66, 67, 68, 71, 75, 79, 86, 91, 93, 96, 97, 98, 99, 100, 101, 105, 108, 109, 121, 122, 123, 124, 126, 136, 140, 145, 147, 148, 149, 154, 156, 157, 158, 167, 168, 170, 171, 173, 175, 176, 177, 178, 179, 180, 181, 182, 183, 185, 192, 198, 199, 207, 208, 213, 214, 217, 228, 229, 231, 233, 239, 242, 255, 257, 260, 264
AI 17, 31, 98, 123, 136, 150, 167, 176, 181, 182, 242
algorithms 97, 122, 158, 228
experiential 167, 170, 171
journey 28, 177, 182
model 121, 140, 145, 147
paths 31, 175, 177, 180
phase 121, 122, 124, 145, 171
Life cycle 60, 68, 79, 112, 116, 119, 120, 127, 128, 148, 153, 154, 159, 186, 189, 217
Lineage 123, 130, 139, 140, 154, 155, 156
Line(s) of business (LoB[s]) 17, 128, 216, 259, 268
LinkedIn 87, 89, 183, 247
Loan 57, 63, 121, 158, 159, 160, 161, 168, 188, 205
approval 159, 160, 161
Location 34, 82, 97, 124, 131, 136, 137, 157, 158, 160, 163, 165, 216, 217
Locus 39, 53, 54, 58
Logistics 54, 59, 74, 209

Machine learning (ML)
    models 11, 12, 14, 29, 40, 53, 57, 64, 66, 67, 74, 75, 76, 77, 78, 79, 83, 117, 183, 184, 185, 186, 187, 189, 190, 192, 205, 214, 231, 235, 255
    Operations (ML Ops) 77, 78, 111, 187
Machines 1, 5, 7, 64, 101, 105, 200, 205, 206
Maintenance 24, 30, 32, 55, 101, 112, 186, 200, 258
Management Development Institute, Gurgaon 181
Marketing 16, 23, 43, 117, 157, 183, 208, 220, 234, 247
Marketplace 8, 66, 183, 199
Markets 2, 3, 4, 5, 10, 15, 21, 31, 38, 39, 42, 43, 46, 47, 53, 58, 80, 81, 82, 83, 84, 86, 93, 107, 157, 172, 179, 181, 183, 185, 190, 191, 196, 199, 202, 210, 217, 218, 220, 221, 230, 232, 234, 236, 239, 241, 249
    leaders 15, 47, 80, 82, 84, 86, 93, 107
    shares 39, 46, 83
Massively open online courses (MOOC) 180
Matching 85, 91, 102, 132, 133
Maturity 19, 65, 69, 70, 71, 72, 210, 237
    framework 69, 70, 72
Max Life Insurance 7, 53, 209, 210, 211, 212, 213, 214
MeitY (Ministry of Electronics and Information Technology) 66, 236, 237, 246
Messages 7, 20, 81, 114, 174, 227
Metadata 127, 130, 131, 134, 138, 139, 144, 154, 155, 187, 263
Methodology(ies) 2, 4, 7, 11, 15, 21, 34, 40, 46, 51, 54, 58, 59, 64, 91, 109, 119, 126, 130, 142, 144, 146, 147, 172, 176, 179, 200, 208, 230, 251
Metric(s) 19, 29, 41, 119, 121, 125, 126, 130, 132, 138, 140, 141, 143, 151, 153, 157, 162, 205, 211, 221
    quality 121, 130, 138
Microsoft 84, 86, 94, 126, 149, 178, 237, 259, 260
Mindset 15, 16, 17, 18, 19, 21, 23, 24, 25, 27, 29, 31, 33, 34, 35, 36, 37, 38, 40, 47, 48, 69, 73, 90, 171, 178, 184, 185, 186, 197, 198, 199, 203, 208, 213, 222, 231, 238, 241, 242, 268
    change 23, 40, 198
    framework 15, 18, 19, 27, 268
    growth 31, 197, 198, 203
Modelling 40, 116, 120, 121, 132, 139, 141, 187, 214, 255
Model(s)
    AI 12, 25, 42, 56, 62, 63, 98, 114, 116, 123, 124, 142, 143, 152, 153, 155, 157, 162, 163, 169, 170, 172, 194, 203, 204, 205, 206, 216, 218, 226, 227, 242, 246, 252, 262, 268, 272
    biased 54, 59, 157
    fair 124, 158, 159
    learning 121, 140, 145, 147
    local 97, 98, 99
    needs 15, 121, 143, 151, 162
Monitoring 22, 71, 91, 151, 152, 170
Multi cloud 97, 99, 136
Multiple sources 132, 133, 221

NASSCOM 66, 236, 238
National AI strategy 19, 49, 65
Natural Language Generation (NLG) 100, 105, 106, 107
Natural language processing (NLP) 26, 27, 57, 60, 72, 78, 79, 92, 106, 107, 188, 189, 191
    expert(s) 60, 188, 191
    model(s) 26, 27, 57, 60, 72, 78, 79, 92, 106, 107, 188, 189, 191
Natural language understanding (NLU) 81, 89, 92, 100, 103, 104, 105, 107
Netflix 7, 34, 43, 82, 84, 193, 205, 234
Network 6, 30, 67, 83, 193, 196, 217, 232, 249
    neural 6, 20, 100, 157, 196, 256
Niramai Health Analytix 163, 164, 165, 242
NITI Aayog 48, 65, 66, 107
Normalization 107, 120, 132, 154
Nutrition 7, 53, 64, 161, 162, 204, 226, 228, 229
NVIDIA technologies 68, 83, 192

Offerings 17, 32, 42, 66, 78, 80, 86, 93, 111, 149, 151, 176, 180, 194, 212, 218, 222, 238, 260
Online learning 180, 182, 192
Open source 22, 30, 60, 111, 119, 145, 146, 149, 159, 161, 203, 205, 235, 246, 251, 252, 258, 268, 270
   toolkits 159, 161, 205, 235
Optimization 3, 39, 53, 54, 58, 71, 95, 108, 151, 178, 203
Optimizing 121, 122, 131, 168
Options 9, 44, 45, 61, 109, 116, 117, 122, 142, 161, 180, 185, 220
Organization
   AI-enabled 23, 38, 42, 43, 44, 46, 47, 48, 70, 72, 183, 201, 207
   AI-led 40, 43, 44, 47, 48, 70, 76, 201, 207
   kinds of 37, 38, 43, 208
   large 68, 80, 181
   traditional 38, 43, 47, 53, 234, 239
   type of 37, 38, 43
Outcome(s) 11, 15, 16, 41, 45, 46, 51, 52, 63, 69, 70, 71, 76, 77, 100, 121, 124, 125, 130, 142, 149, 157, 169, 174, 198, 207, 208, 216, 220, 223, 248, 254, 264, 269, 271
   business 16, 71, 100, 121
Outcome vs process 220
Outsource 60, 94, 128, 171, 191, 223

Partnership(s) 23, 68, 71, 79, 94, 170, 196, 199, 200, 252
Patterns 30, 51, 54, 55, 56, 57, 58, 59, 75, 93, 110, 117, 118, 119, 121, 133, 144, 158, 159, 160, 185, 186, 194, 220, 221, 227, 230, 231, 251
Payload data 122, 126, 151, 152
Performance 11, 27, 31, 83, 93, 115, 124, 125, 126, 137, 142, 149, 150, 151, 152, 153, 157, 259, 261, 264, 266, 272
Pipeline 22, 95, 116, 143, 146, 147, 154, 155, 186, 256, 264
   AI 97, 155
   CI/CD 116, 147
Planning 25, 27, 39, 53, 54, 58, 59, 109, 217, 229, 245, 270, 271
   route 54, 58, 59, 109
Platform as a service (PaaS) 30, 115

Platform(s) 7, 30, 53, 66, 74, 76, 77, 78, 82, 85, 86, 88, 91, 111, 112, 114, 115, 116, 117, 118, 119, 145, 180, 192, 193, 194, 221, 222, 226, 246, 249, 250, 252
Policy(ies) 19, 32, 45, 123, 126, 128, 129, 134, 135, 136, 138, 154, 184, 199, 209, 212, 213, 232, 251
   access control 123, 136, 154
Predicting 132, 168, 172, 189
Predictions 4, 5, 44, 45, 63, 90, 98, 109, 110, 121, 132, 137, 139, 154, 160, 168, 181, 187, 211, 212, 216, 217, 220, 221, 235, 239
Prioritization 222, 225
Privacy 8, 47, 89, 98, 99, 135, 163, 174, 233
Process 1, 2, 3, 4, 5, 11, 15, 20, 22, 25, 29, 30, 31, 32, 33, 34, 38, 41, 46, 47, 53, 54, 55, 56, 58, 59, 60, 61, 64, 72, 79, 80, 81, 84, 85, 86, 87, 88, 90, 91, 92, 102, 108, 110, 116, 119, 122, 123, 128, 129, 130, 131, 132, 135, 139, 140, 141, 143, 144, 146, 147, 154, 165, 193, 195, 204, 208, 210, 215, 216, 221, 223, 228, 239, 244
   AI-enabled 29, 59, 60
   existing 29, 32, 56
Productivity 3, 7, 85, 116, 170, 174, 259, 262, 268
Product(s) 4, 7, 16, 17, 20, 24, 31, 33, 36, 39, 45, 73, 74, 77, 78, 79, 80, 81, 83, 92, 93, 101, 131, 159, 161, 169, 170, 176, 186, 190, 191, 193, 195, 204, 209, 218, 221, 223, 229, 238, 245, 248, 266
Professionals 42, 68, 175, 192, 193, 214, 235, 247
Programming 22, 85, 97, 116, 185, 186, 192, 252
Projects 4, 11, 19, 22, 24, 28, 49, 52, 58, 60, 62, 75, 119, 144, 171, 172, 176, 181, 182, 183, 184, 191, 192, 193, 196, 213, 253, 260
Proof of concept (PoC) 18, 20, 25, 26, 27, 28, 29, 31, 33, 34, 35, 58, 61, 75, 77, 91, 95, 113, 114, 115, 119, 145, 169, 184, 224, 269
Prototypes 25, 37, 47, 49, 50, 52, 54, 61, 62, 176, 191, 230

Python 40, 114, 181, 192

Quality 7, 22, 58, 70, 73, 74, 77, 81, 84, 89, 93, 105, 120, 121, 123, 125, 127, 130, 131, 132, 134, 138, 139, 141, 143, 149, 169, 178, 191, 195, 217, 226, 229, 246, 253, 257, 261, 263, 264, 265, 269, 270
   assessment 120, 131, 132, 134
   metrics 121, 130, 138
Quantum computers 108, 109
Query(ies) 11, 14, 89, 101, 102, 103, 104, 105, 120, 125, 131, 136, 137, 138, 155, 182, 226, 227, 247, 260, 267

RAISE India Summit 2020 66, 67
Ranking 85, 229, 236
Readiness 22, 24, 70, 230, 231, 240
Reasoning 100, 160, 188, 245, 267
Re-engineering 22, 178, 183, 191
Regulations 82, 123, 126, 129, 138, 139, 157, 204, 266
Reinforcement 6, 20, 79, 93, 122, 144, 257
   learning 6, 20, 79, 93, 257
Religion(s) 121, 157, 158, 163, 205
Research and development (R&D) 12, 2266, 67, 80, 95, 96, 101, 111, 116, 136, 141, 146, 149, 249
   tools 12, 22, 116
Researchers 2, 3, 49, 68, 79, 84, 97, 106, 108, 109, 111, 122, 163, 206, 246, 255, 258, 265, 269
Resistance 24, 94, 213, 222
Reskilling 22, 30, 34, 175, 182, 183, 192, 193, 203, 247
Resonance framework 231, 232, 236
Resource Description Framework (RDF) 22, 101, 116, 118, 137
Resources 13, 31, 39, 59, 97, 99, 116, 141, 189, 249, 251, 252, 263, 265
Response time 153, 174, 221
Résumés 84, 85, 134, 140, 141, 143, 149, 157, 190, 196
Retraining 142, 148, 151, 152, 159, 227
Return on investment (RoI) 11, 21, 27, 30, 32, 34, 36, 47, 59, 62, 91, 92, 100, 114, 119, 140, 145, 149, 156, 175, 230, 234

Revenue 12, 32, 41, 76, 81, 82, 86, 118, 135, 156, 219, 244
Rewards 20, 84, 88, 92
Ria 7, 64, 226, 227, 228
Risks 8, 25, 31, 32, 45, 77, 78, 79, 84, 88, 92, 116, 155, 157, 163, 171, 200, 207, 216, 253
   credit 31, 32, 78
Risk vs reward 84, 92
RNA 2, 109, 110, 111
Roadmap 17, 18, 30, 48, 115, 183, 184, 186, 199, 218, 220
Robustness 40, 47, 125, 149, 151, 162, 220
Route 24, 25, 39, 53, 54, 58, 59, 109, 117
   optimization 39, 53, 108
   planning 54, 58, 59, 109
Rules 6, 63, 64, 104, 123, 160, 161, 162, 188, 243

Sales 16, 27, 47, 82, 89, 98, 101, 106, 117, 131, 152, 183, 194, 195, 196, 211, 219, 220, 234, 239
   representatives 247
   team 27, 194, 195
Scalability 27, 30, 95, 119, 150, 151, 162, 249
Scale 12, 13, 20, 27, 28, 30, 32, 33, 34, 42, 49, 61, 70, 71, 72, 74, 78, 83, 100, 111, 115, 165, 182, 184, 187, 189, 202, 208, 225, 226, 227, 230, 233, 236, 237, 245, 246, 250, 251, 252, 266
Scaling 21, 31, 47, 72, 115, 221, 225
Score 14, 70, 71, 72, 160, 161, 162, 203
Security 8, 13, 27, 31, 47, 79, 116, 128, 138, 139, 147, 152, 239, 260
Selection 28, 84, 120, 152, 185, 198
Self-driving cars 13, 81, 93, 100, 126
Sensitive personal information (SPI) 123, 124, 130, 154, 263, 264
Sensors 7, 56, 63, 98, 113, 128, 270
Sentiment 6, 93, 114, 210, 230, 237
Servers 98, 99, 146, 271
Services 12, 22, 30, 31, 42, 53, 57, 58, 68, 77, 80, 81, 82, 83, 84, 86, 91, 92, 93, 96, 97, 111, 129, 137, 147, 148, 152, 155, 173, 193, 196, 204, 208, 209, 216, 217, 218, 219, 221, 223, 224, 225, 226, 238, 246, 249, 252

Sharing and distribution 4, 41, 98, 99, 123, 136, 138
Singapore 48, 49, 67
Singh, Pramod 194, 195, 196
Skilling 13, 15, 23, 31, 66
Skill(s) 4, 12, 16, 19, 22, 23, 28, 29, 30, 40, 53, 58, 59, 60, 71, 72, 76, 79, 85, 113, 147, 149, 164, 167, 170, 175, 177, 182, 183, 184, 185, 186, 187, 188, 190, 191, 195, 198, 208, 209, 236, 237, 238, 244, 248, 269
   compass 175, 182, 183, 190
   right 19, 59, 60, 147, 191, 269
   sets 40, 53, 58
Social media 26, 87, 93, 114, 129, 257
Software 12, 22, 27, 30, 54, 63, 64, 75, 91, 115, 116, 141, 143, 144, 150, 163, 187, 189, 192, 195, 201, 204, 220, 243, 244, 250, 256, 257, 259, 265, 269, 270
Software as a service (SaaS) 30, 43, 256, 267
Speech recognition 12, 79, 235, 246, 252
Stack 21, 22, 30, 31, 35, 111, 112, 114, 115, 117, 118, 166, 216, 221, 222, 249, 265, 268, 269
Stakeholders 15, 27, 35, 49, 59, 61, 62, 63, 65, 66, 68, 90, 91, 92, 114, 115, 141, 153, 164, 165, 166, 184, 187, 189, 207, 211, 213, 218, 236, 244, 256
Start-ups 7, 30, 39, 42, 66, 67, 68, 106, 163, 181, 190, 214, 226, 230, 231, 238, 241, 242, 245, 246, 250
Storage 95, 101, 113, 119, 126, 128, 129, 136, 140, 154, 162, 168, 186, 221, 256, 265, 267, 271
Storytelling 62, 63, 184, 185
Strategy(ies) 10, 18, 19, 28, 30, 31, 32, 33, 34, 35, 36, 37, 38, 39, 41, 43, 44, 45, 46, 47, 48, 49, 50, 51, 52, 65, 73, 75, 76, 78, 93, 94, 106, 107, 119, 158, 171, 175, 176, 183, 184, 191, 198, 208, 211, 214, 216, 228, 230, 231, 232, 236, 238, 239, 243, 253, 265, 268
   flywheel 19, 39, 49, 50, 51, 52, 73, 78, 184
Subramanian, Mani 115, 119, 153, 169
Success(es) 11, 16, 17, 18, 20, 25, 29, 30, 31, 40, 41, 58, 64, 69, 70, 71, 74, 76, 78, 114, 115, 120, 164, 167, 168, 169, 171, 172, 173, 195, 208, 210, 211, 214, 217, 231, 238, 255
Superintelligence 8, 9, 10, 206
Sustainability 192, 204, 236

Tagging 129, 130, 131, 154
Talent 12, 19, 22, 28, 30, 31, 32, 33, 34, 35, 36, 55, 60, 66, 71, 79, 81, 87, 92, 94, 95, 116, 120, 167, 175, 181, 182, 183, 194, 214, 216, 231, 247, 248, 269
   AI 19, 22, 60, 116, 175, 182, 253
   pool 79, 94, 214
   right 12, 92, 95, 269
Tasks 83, 120, 130, 134, 137
   AI 83, 120, 130, 134
Tay bot 7, 43, 96, 103, 104, 105, 126, 149, 173, 174, 213, 227
Teams 32, 40, 47, 76, 77, 90, 94, 114, 121, 128, 133, 139, 140, 141, 142, 145, 146, 147, 187, 190, 218, 219, 220, 221, 222, 223, 224, 248
   support 115, 195, 196
Techniques 42, 69, 71, 72, 74, 93, 107, 140, 141, 158, 161, 163, 178, 185, 194, 203, 239, 256, 257, 265, 266
TensorFlow 12, 40, 221, 256
Test cases 125, 144, 150, 162
Testing 106, 116, 125, 141, 142, 143, 144, 146, 149, 150, 154, 162, 178, 186, 187, 219, 249, 269
   black-box 125, 150
   model 141, 142
   usability 186, 187
   white-box 125, 142, 149
Texts 12, 14, 20, 26, 42, 57, 81, 85, 93, 100, 103, 105, 106, 107, 114, 128, 136, 137, 149, 173, 188, 221, 232
The Five Senses of AI 167, 168, 242
Thinking 28, 30, 59, 79, 88, 99, 108, 120, 163, 185, 202, 217, 220, 223, 248, 251, 273
Tool and technology 241, 242, 246, 248, 259, 253, 258, 259, 262, 268
   AI 15, 47, 48, 173, 206, 234, 236
   right 21, 60, 61, 114, 116, 146, 199, 209
   stack 21, 22, 31, 35, 111, 112, 114, 118, 166, 216
   trends 41, 81, 96, 97, 231

INDEX

Touch 7, 18, 165, 167, 181, 198, 214, 215, 218, 262
Tracking 39, 82, 113, 140, 153, 226
Traffic 24, 29, 68, 100, 109, 126, 216, 243
Training 3, 15, 20, 32, 83, 97, 98, 99, 107, 112, 114, 122, 124, 125, 131, 141, 142, 147, 148, 152, 159, 163, 168, 170, 175, 179, 180, 182, 186, 192, 207, 213, 217, 225, 228, 246, 247, 248, 256, 257, 258, 262, 263, 264, 265, 266, 267, 269
    data 83, 97, 107, 114, 122, 124, 131, 142, 147, 148, 152
Transformation 16, 17, 18, 21, 25, 32, 33, 34, 41, 48, 50, 67, 74, 75, 76, 77, 91, 113, 117, 119, 154, 176, 181, 184, 186, 191, 198, 199, 201, 224, 225, 226
    AI 34, 41, 50, 75, 117, 119, 184, 191, 199, 224, 245
    digital 16, 48, 77, 184, 191, 253
Trust and fairness 11, 31, 41, 47, 73, 82, 112, 121, 124, 125, 126, 127, 150, 151, 153, 156, 157, 158, 159, 160, 162, 169, 187, 195, 200, 203, 204, 205, 207, 217, 236, 270
Twitter 7, 87, 126

Uber 28, 43, 82, 84
Udemy's 2020 Workplace Learnings Trend Report 182, 183
UI 39, 114, 224, 245, 260
Uncertainty 4, 8, 100, 239
USA 3, 14, 67, 98, 109, 179, 193, 204
USA's Food and Drug Association (FDA) 3
Use cases 8, 9, 19, 20, 22, 28, 31, 37, 43, 51, 54, 58, 59, 61, 64, 65, 69, 70, 72, 76, 77, 78, 83, 122, 124, 143, 152, 154, 168, 169, 173, 178, 180, 182, 186, 211, 213, 230, 231, 232, 233, 234, 235
    AI 37, 178, 241, 243, 244, 248, 250, 251, 259, 261, 267, 268, 269, 272, 273
    business 76, 77, 78, 211
User(s) 241, 242, 248, 249, 251, 255, 258, 259, 260, 262, 264, 265, 266, 267, 270, 271
    business 61, 69, 91, 114, 141, 143, 149, 150, 160, 162, 203
    end 95, 117, 118, 159, 160, 188, 216, 217, 218, 220, 223
    inputs and scale 34, 42, 152
    query 101, 102, 103
Users vs clients 218
Utility 45, 46, 47, 48, 152, 160, 263

Vaccine 1, 3, 232, 240
Validation 142, 149, 150, 195
Value generation 25, 26, 131
Vendors 7, 28, 30, 33, 60, 61, 82, 178, 191, 199
Videos 20, 57, 82, 100, 120, 128, 136, 208, 238
Viome Life Sciences 30, 53, 109, 110, 111, 119, 164, 242

Wellness 2, 109, 189, 193, 194
Where AI 3, 23, 50, 51, 54, 59, 70, 195, 207, 212, 222, 262
Why AI 51, 52, 53, 59, 70, 195
Worker(s) 16, 24, 69, 137, 248
Workforce 22, 66, 125, 175, 181, 183, 206, 247, 269
Workshops 9, 59, 61, 68, 69, 186, 222, 223, 224
    design 59, 61, 224

ABOUT THE AUTHORS

Shalini Kapoor is a widely regarded technologist with twenty-five years of experience in incubating and innovating cutting-edge technologies in AI and the Internet of Things. She has fifteen patents and has been honoured as an IBM Fellow and as Emerging Woman Leader of India by CII.

Sameep Mehta is a leader in the area of AI with over fifty patents and over eighty publications. He finished his PhD from the Ohio State University in 2006. This book is the outcome of his vast experience in incubating AI research agenda, performing research, and making the technology available to customers.